MW00710119

Poisonous
Plants
of South Africa

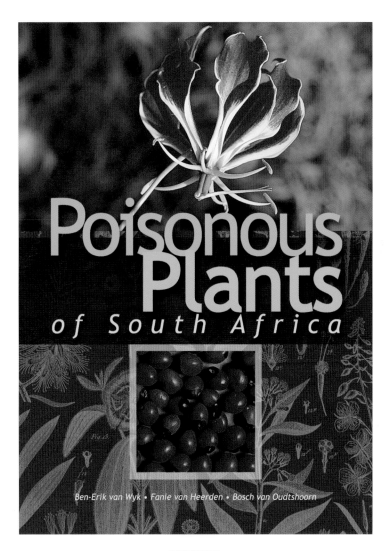

Poisonous
Plants
of South Africa

Ben-Erik van Wyk • Fanie van Heerden • Bosch van Oudtshoorn

BRIZA

Published by

BRIZA PUBLICATIONS
CK 90/11690/23

PO Box 11050
Queenswood 0121
Pretoria
South Africa
www.briza.co.za

First edition, first impression, 2002
First edition, second impression, 2014

ISBN 1875093 303   (10-digit ISBN)

ISBN 978 1 875093 304   (13-digit ISBN)

Disclaimer
Although care has been taken to be as accurate as possible, neither the authors nor the
publisher make any expressed or implied representation as to the accuracy of the
information contained in this book and cannot be held legally responsible or accept liability
for any errors or omissions. Some plants are highly toxic and may cause injury or death.
The authors or publisher can also not be held responsible for claims arising from the
mistaken identity of plants. In cases of suspected poisoning, immediately consult a medical
professional or qualified veterinarian.

Managing editor: Reneé Ferreira
Proofreader: David Pearson
Cover design: Andrew Breebaart, De Luxe Design
Distribution maps: CartoCom, Pretoria
Typesetting: Melinda Stark, Lebone Publishing Services
Reproduction: Unifoto, Cape Town
Printed and bound by Tien Wah Press (Pte.) Ltd, Singapore

Cover photographs:

Top front – *Gloriosa superba*

Bottom front – Seeds of *Abrus precatorius*

Spine – *Boophane disticha*

Back cover – *Adenium multiflorum*

Contents

Acknowledgements

The authors wish to thank the following institutions and persons:

- The National Botanical Institute, for use of the herbarium and library. The friendly assistance of the librarians and herbarium staff is much appreciated. The use of some slides from the NBI collection (see list below) is also gratefully acknowledged.
- Persons and institutions who contributed slides, or provided support or encouragement: Robert Archer, Philip Desmet, Florapix Library, Peter Goldblatt, Pitta Joffe, Kolie Louw, Natalie Low, John Manning, Jan Myburgh, NBI collection, Gideon Smith, Mike Stewart, Hotze en Kobus van Heerden, Ernst van Jaarsveld, Frits van Oudtshoorn, Braam van Wyk, Eben van Wyk, Piet van Wyk, Robyn van Zyl, Lisa Vidulich, Alvaro Viljoen, Anne Lise Vlok, Ron Wright, Pieter Winter and Pieter Zietsman.
- Rand Afrikaans University, for institutional support to BEvW and FRvH over many years.
- Briza Publications and the production team, especially Reneé Ferreira, David Pearson and Melinda Stark.

PHOTOGRAPHIC CONTRIBUTIONS

All photographs were taken by Ben-Erik van Wyk, except for those listed below. These are arranged alphabetically from top to bottom and from left to right, according to photographer and page number. **Robert Archer**: 153a, 161e; **Philip Desmet**: 215d; **Florapix Library**: 230; **Peter Goldblatt**: 153d; **Pitta Joffe**: 101c, 123ab, 201ab; **John Manning**: 51c, 153bc, 161ab, 187d, 213ac, 215b; **NBI collection**: 81d, 95c, 201c, 209c; **Fanie van Heerden**: 11a, 25b, 91ac, 121c, 125a; **Frits van Oudtshoorn**: 41ac, 197d, 199bcde; **Braam van Wyk**: 161d, 197ab; **Eben van Wyk**: 149abd; **Piet van Wyk**: 107abcd, 113abc, 167b, 179bc, 203b, 207ab; **Anne Lise Vlok**: 213de; **Ron Wright**: 246; **Pieter Zietsman**: 175b.

Introduction

Poisonous plants grow in almost every garden in South Africa and form an important part of our indigenous flora. Since they grow everywhere, it is not practical to eradicate them all – it is far better to learn to identify them and to teach our children about them. **This book is a photographic guide to the most commonly occurring poisonous plants in South Africa.** It will hopefully contribute to a better awareness of the dangers of these plants amongst the general public and help health care professionals (traditional healers, nurses, pharmacists and doctors) to quickly identify poisonous plants in an emergency situation. The only way to prevent accidental poisoning is to learn more about these harmful but often very attractive plants. Infants are especially at risk, and should be kept away from danger until they are old enough to identify and recognise poisonous plants.

Plants, unlike animals, cannot run away when threatened, so they have devised cunning chemical defence systems to deter plant-eating animals and to sometimes even kill them. The harmful substances can either cause superficial irritation or discomfort through contact with the skin, or serious poisoning when ingested in sufficient quantities. Because herbivores (and stock animals) have to eat large amounts of plant material every day, severe poisoning and deaths are quite common. Most human fatalities occur when poisonous plants are mistaken for food plants. Examples are wild tobacco leaves (*Nicotiana glauca*) that are sometimes mistaken for traditional spinach or *marog*, and purging nut seeds (*Jatropha curcas*) that are mistaken for edible nuts. Infants driven by their curiosity may nibble on poisonous plants but they rarely eat sufficient amounts to cause anything more than temporary discomfort or distress. Poisoning through traditional medicine is relatively rare (less common than for orthodox medicine) and usually occurs when herbal medicine is used outside the safeguards of the traditional knowledge system. Like orthodox medicine, medicinal plants have to be biologically active in order to be effective, so that there is always a danger of poisoning through overdose.

According to statistics of the Poison Unit of the Johannesburg General Hospital, plants are responsible for about 6,5% of all poisoning cases (about 500 cases and enquiries per year). The top 10 culprits in the Johannesburg municipal area are syringa berries (*Melia azedarach*), elephant's ear leaves (*Alocasia macrorrhiza* and *Colocasia esculenta*), oleander leaves (*Nerium oleander*), arum lily leaves (*Zantedeschia aethiopica*), delicious monster leaves (*Monstera deliciosa*), thorn apple seeds or *malpitte* (*Datura* species), crab's eyes or lucky bean seeds (*Abrus precatorius*), dumb cane leaves (*Dieffenbachia* species), Jerusalem cherry fruits (*Solanum pseudocapsicum*) and poinsettia latex (*Euphorbia pulcherrima*). For other parts of the country, the following plants can be added to the list: wild tobacco leaves (*Nicotiana glauca*), castor oil seeds (*Ricinus communis*), purging nut seeds (*Jatropha curcas*), tung nut seeds (*Aleurites fordii*), cycad seeds (*Encephalartos* species), wild granadilla (*Adenia digitata*), wild cucumber fruits (*Cucumis* species) and *gifappel* (*Solanum* species).

The introductory chapters give a brief overview of the subject, including general discussions of human and animal poisoning in South Africa, the chemical compounds responsible for poisoning and ways in which the plants and their compounds are studied by scientists. In the main part of the book, the poisonous plants are arranged in two main sections. In the first, nearly 100 genera of indigenous and naturalised exotics are presented. Maps are provided as an additional means of identifying the plants. In the second section, about 50 of the most common poisonous garden plants are briefly described and illustrated. Finally, lists of poisonous plants are provided as a quick reference to farmers, gardeners, parents, students, health care professionals and anyone else interested in the poisonous plants of South Africa.

Human poisoning in South Africa

The true incidence of poisoning in South Africa is not well documented. Reports are fragmented and refer to certain regions of the country or to a particular large hospital or poison centre. The most recent publication by Du Plooy and others (2001) is an important contribution to our knowledge of human poisoning in South Africa. It is of great interest to note that the reported incidence of plant poisoning (excluding traditional medicines) in one major academic centre in South Africa is identical to that reported in the United States, namely 5–6% of all acute poisoning.

Having monitored and documented all admissions to a University Hospital for acute poisoning over many years, the findings of Du Plooy and fellow researchers regarding the five-year period 1996 to 2000 were as follows: They categorised all acute poisoning cases into five groups: paraffin, pesticides, medicines, plants and traditional medicines. The total number of admissions, with the percentage of the grand total, for these five groups were:

	Number of cases	Percentage of total
Paraffin	1 083	52,4%
Pesticides	645	31,2%
Orthodox medicines	133	6,4%
Plants	108	5,2%
Traditional medicines	98	4,7%
Total	2 067	

Food poisoning, alcohol intoxication and animal bites and stings were excluded from the analysis.

Although these figures still raise concern, especially regarding paraffin and pesticide poisoning, they at least put plant and traditional medicine poisoning into perspective by demonstrating the relative low incidence of both these in practical real-life terms (*i.e.* only about 5% of hospital admissions for acute poisoning for each).

By far, the largest number of acute poisonings occur in the age group 1–5 years, which is not surprising considering that pre-school children are highly prone and vulnerable to plant poisoning. Children should be taught never to eat plants, unless provided to them as food by their parents or someone absolutely trustworthy. Sadly, even adults are sometimes poisoned by confusing a toxic plant with something they thought was edible. Because toxic plants are abundant in gardens and the veld, it should be left only to experienced botanists and other experts on edible plants to distinguish between plants that are safe to eat or poisonous.

Symptoms of human poisoning may vary and depend on the type of plant and quantity ingested. The following may occur:
- Nausea and vomiting
- Stomach pains or cramps
- Local irritation, with burning, itching or local pain. This could involve the mouth, skin or eyes
- Diarrhoea
- Difficult breathing
- Disturbed vision
- Delirium or hallucinations
- Convulsions
- Loss of consciousness
- Palpitations or quick and irregular pulse or heartbeat

Some examples of plants known to have caused fatal human poisoning are illustrated here.

References
1. **Du Plooy, W.J., Jobson, M.R., Osuch, E., Mathibe, L. & Tsipa, P. 2001.** Mortality from traditional-medicine poisoning: a new perspective from analysing admissions and deaths at Ga-Rankuwa Hospital. *S. Afr. J. Sci.* 97: 70.
2. **Venter, C.P. & Joubert, P.H., 1988.** Aspects of Poisoning with Traditional Medicines in Southern Africa. *Biomedical and Environmental Sciences* 1: 388–391.
3. **Hardman, J.G., Gilman, A.G. & Limbird, L.E. 1996.** *Goodman & Gilman's The Pharmacological Basis of Therapeutics,* 9th edition. McGraw-Hill, New York.
4. **Lawrence, R.A. 1997.** Poisonous Plants: When they are a threat to children. *Pediatr. Rev.* 18: 162-168.

Nerium oleander – oleander

Aleurites fordii – tung nut

Jatropha curcas – purging nut

Callilepis laureola – impila

Datura stramonium – thorn apple

Nicotiana glauca – wild tobacco

Animal poisoning in South Africa

Farm animals and game often depend entirely on wild plants for their daily food intake. Both grazers and browsers may nibble on poisonous plants but few species are sufficiently toxic to cause harm in small mouthfuls. Under normal circumstances there are rarely any problems, because the bulk of the daily intake of plant material is non-toxic. Furthermore, small amounts of toxins can be broken down or rendered harmless by microorganisms in the rumen. For this reason, monogastric animals (pigs, ostriches, chickens, etc.) are often more sensitive than ruminants (cattle, sheep, goats, etc.). However, when drought and other factors (such as veld fires) cause temporary or permanent shortages of suitable grazing, hungry animals may be forced to eat poisonous plants that they would normally avoid. Poisoning may also occur when animals are moved from one area to another (or even from one camp to another) so that they come into contact with toxic plants that they have not yet learnt to avoid.

The direct costs of plant poisonings and mycotoxicoses to the livestock industry in South Africa have been conservatively estimated to be more than R100 million per year[1]. The annual cattle losses were estimated at nearly 38 000 head and small stock losses nearly 265 000 head[1]. The real impact is much more severe, because poisonous plants also reduce the growth, productivity and reproductive health of animals[1]. Furthermore, the cost of not utilising poisonous pastures and the loss in land value when pastures become infested with toxic plants, also have to be considered[1].

An excellent review of livestock poisoning is available, in which maps are provided to show the main areas of the different types of plant poisonings[1]. In this publication, the main criteria for diagnosing the type of poisoning are also presented[1]. It is estimated that only six main types of poisoning are responsible for 60% of all stock losses in South Africa[1]. For cattle, these are cardiac glycosides (33%), seneciosis (10%), *gifblaar* poisoning (8%), *gousiekte* (4%), *Lantana* poisoning (3%) and diplodiosis (2%). In small stock (sheep and goats), the six leading killers are *geeldikkop* and *dikoor* (28%), *vermeersiekte* (13%), cardiac

glycosides (10%), seneciosis (5%), *gousiekte* (2%) and diplodiosis (2%). At the end of this book (see p. 263), each of the most important types of livestock poisonings is briefly discussed and a list is given of plants that are known to be the main culprits in South Africa. Clinical signs of poisoning are briefly dealt with under each of the poisonous plant species, but for more exact and detailed information, the references[1-3] given below should be consulted.

In the home and garden, domestic animals and pets may be poisoned when they ingest poisonous plants. Animals differ widely in their sensitivity to various poisons so that it is hard to predict the amount of toxic plant material that will cause problems. Birds (parrots, canaries, etc.) are considered to be more susceptible than other animals.

The main type of livestock poisoning are listed below (see page 263 for a list of plants).

Main types of livestock poisoning
Cardiac glycoside poisoning
    Acute poisoning (also known as *tulp* poisoning, *slangkop* poisoning)
    Chronic poisoning (*krimpsiekte*)
Liver poisoning
    without photosensitivity
        seneciosis (*jaagsiekte, stywesiekte*)
    with photosensitivity
        lantana poisoning
Gifblaar poisoning
Gousiekte
Geeldikkop and *dikoor*
Vermeersiekte
Diplodiosis
Nervous disorders
    vaalsiekte, kaalsiekte, lakseersiekte,
    albiziosis, cynanchosis,
    stootsiekte, pushing disease,
    phalaris staggers, *maldronksiekte*
Gastrointestinal disorders
Kidney, bladder and reproductive system
    oxalate poisoning
Hydrogen cyanide poisoning (prussic acid poisoning, *geilsiekte, blousuurvergiftiging*)

References
1. **Kellerman, T.S., Naudé, T.W. & Fourie, N. 1996.** The distribution, diagnoses and estimated economic impact of plant poisonings and mycotoxicoses in South Africa. *Onderstepoort J. Vet. Res.* 63: 65-90.
2. **Kellerman, T.S. & Coetzer, J.A.W. 1985.** Hepatogenous photosensitivity diseases in South Africa. *Onderstepoort J. Vet. Res.* 52: 157-173.
3. **Kellerman, T.S., Coetzer, J.A.W. & Naudé, T.W. 1988.** *Plant Poisonings and Mycotoxicoses of Livestock in Southern Africa.* Oxford University Press, Cape Town.

Chrysocoma ciliata (*bitterbos*) causes *kaalsiekte* and *lakseersiekte* in small stock

Nguni cattle

First aid treatment

Emergency treatment of poisoning by unskilled persons should be handled with great care and caution. Supportive therapy (see below), as in other medical emergencies, is the most important aspect of handling a case of plant poisoning. The saying 'treat the patient, not the poison' remains the most basic rule. It is critically important to get the poisoned person to the nearest hospital with emergency facilities as soon as possible. Stay calm and think logically and systematically.

The purpose of induction of vomiting is to prevent further absorption of the poison from the stomach. However, although many textbooks on poisoning or first aid state that vomiting should be induced, it should be remembered that in the case of plant poisoning, vomiting should not be tried as a first aid measure, because of the danger of inhaling (aspiration) plant material into the lungs during the process. Also, vomiting frequently occurs spontaneously in any case, due to the irritation caused by ingestion of toxic plants.

Fortunately, because of the bad and unpleasant taste of poisonous plants and the accompanying pronounced irritation of the inside of the mouth and throat, most people will not eat enough plant material to develop serious signs of poisoning.

Activated charcoal (*geaktiveerde houtskool*) (*Carbo Medicinalis*) is the most effective adsorbent, the most universally applicable and thus the most recommended universal antidote. It should not be confused with ordinary (inactive) charcoal or even burnt toast, both of which are ineffective for this purpose.

Activated charcoal is a deep black, very fine, odourless and flavourless powder, capable of adsorbing (binding) various substances, including toxins, poisons and medicines, because of its large surface area and porosity. These dangerous substances are thus inactivated. Activated charcoal is available from most pharmacies and administering it to a person with plant poisoning could be an important first aid action. The recommended dose is 50 g to 100 g in 100 ml water for adults and 25 g to 30 g in 50 ml water for children. If successful intake and retention of this mixture has taken place, chances are good that most of the toxic or poisonous ingredients from the plant will be bound and inactivated in the gut and excreted harmlessly from the body via the faeces (stool).

It is very important to keep parts of the plant(s) involved for further identification – leaves on a stem, flowers and fruit if possible. These must be taken together with the poisoned person to the emergency section of a hospital where quick identification of the plant will expedite correct and optimal treatment.

It is also of vital importance to have the telephone number of the poison centre in your area at hand, or use the national **Netcare Poison Centre number 0800 333 444**, in order to obtain emergency information in suspected cases of poisoning by plants. The **general emergency number 082-9311** can also be used.

Supporting the vital basic life functions of an individual with plant (or any other) poisoning is the most essential component of successful treatment, starting at the point of first aid and continuing right through in hospital. This entails active support by people trained in first aid (or hospital personnel), of the patient's respiratory and cardiovascular systems (breathing and heart functions), to keep the patient alive. It may even involve CPR (cardio-pulmonary resuscitation) or artificial ventilation in hospital.

Gastric lavage (*maagspoeling*) may be indicated in certain cases, but this depends on a medical doctor's discretion. This procedure must only be performed in a hospital or emergency room by trained medical staff. It entails 'washing out' of the stomach contents by means of a thick tube that is placed into the patient's stomach and through which a certain volume of water is administered and then sucked out immediately afterwards. The process is repeated several times until only clear liquid is sucked out, meaning that all harmful material that had been in the stomach has been removed. It is usually of no use to do gastric lavage if more than four hours have elapsed since intake of the poisonous plant, because by then most of the ingested material will have passed into the intestines. Usually, activated charcoal is placed into the stomach through the tube after completing the washing out procedure.

There are no known specific antidotes available. As mentioned before, identification of the particular plant involved will assist substantially in treating the patient with appropriate medicines to counteract the effects of the poison or toxin. For example, administrations of the drug physostigmine may be necessary in severe cases of *Datura* (thorn apple) poisoning, where it may be life saving. Drug treatment, however, must only be undertaken by experienced medical professionals.

Where the skin or eyes are affected by plant poisons (e.g. *Euphorbia* sap / juice or poison ivy), the following first aid steps should be taken as urgently as possible:

1. Skin: wash and rinse affected parts thoroughly with soap and water.
2. Eyes: repeatedly wash and rinse with copious amounts of clean water only.

References

1. **Conradie, W.S. & Greeff, O.B.W. 1994.** *Advanced First Aid Manual for SA First Aid League.* Medpharm Publications, Irene.
2. **Hardman, J.G., Gilman, A.G. & Limbird, L.E. 1996.** *Goodman & Gilman's The Pharmacological Basis of Therapeutics,* 9th edition. McGraw-Hill, New York.
3. **Sommers, De K. 1982.** *Die Behandeling van Akute Vergiftiging.* Butterworth, Durban.
4. **Merck 1997.** *The Merck Manual of Diagnosis and Therapy,* 16th edition. Merck, Rahway, New York.

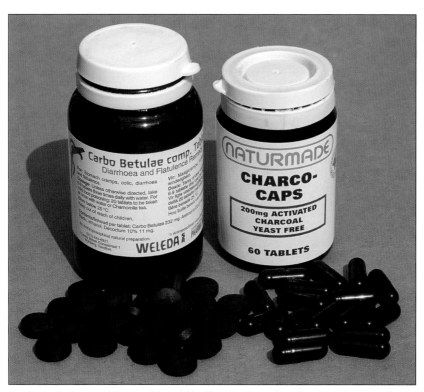

Activated charcoal is capable of binding toxins, thereby inactivating them

Methods of testing for toxicity in humans

There is no absolute or specific test that will accurately predict toxicity of any particular plant or chemical (including pharmaceutical) substance for humans.

Tests are usually done in several animal species (so-called *in vivo* experiments) and laboratory models (*in vitro* experiments). Amongst other things, the LD_{50} toxicity test can be performed. This means determining the lethal dose for 50% of a certain group of animals. This is a crude test that has become controversial, not only because of humanitarian and ethical concerns, but also because it is not clearly predictive of safety in humans. Despite differences between species, however, carefully researched animal studies still provide valuable information regarding toxic effects of new chemical entities in humans, including potential beneficial (therapeutic) effects. The oral, dermal and inhalation LD_{50} results may differ greatly. For example, a substance may be harmless when ingested but quite toxic when absorbed through the skin or lungs.

Measurement of blood and tissue levels of the substance under investigation also provides important scientific information regarding its absorption, distribution and excretion from the body. Again, extrapolation from animals to humans is not absolute. Therefore at least two (usually more) species are studied. The route of administration (e.g. oral or by injection) should be the same as the proposed one for humans.

Further specialised tests are conducted on animals to evaluate special forms of toxicity, e.g. carcinogenicity (the potential to induce cancer), mutagenicity (the potential to induce cellular damage and / or changes) and teratogenicity (the potential to damage the foetus, or offspring). Where the substance is intended for local superficial application to the human body, e.g. the skin, the eye or the mucous membranes like the mouth, special tests are always first performed for an extended period of time on similar animal organs or body parts.

In principle, all these animal tests and studies can and should also be used when evaluating the safety and toxicity of new or unknown substances of plant origin.

Laboratory models or *in vitro* studies usually make use of human cells that are grown in suspension cultures. A solution with suspended live cells is transferred to each of a large number of small wells or hollows in a test plate (see photograph of a typical 96-well plate). Various concentrations of the chemical compound or extract being studied are added to the wells. After a certain time period, a colour reagent that interacts with live cells only is added. A colour reaction (often pink or purple) shows up only in those wells where the cells are still alive; the absence of colour indicates that the cells are dead. An advantage of this method is that large numbers of compounds and concentrations can be tested simultaneously on human cells without the need to sacrifice animals. Unfortunately, *in vitro* studies do not necessarily give an accurate picture of what would happen in the human body.

Valuable pharmacological and toxicological knowledge has been gained (and is still being generated today) from animal and laboratory studies with drugs extracted from plants, such as atropine, nicotine and salicylic acid.

References
1. **Hardman, J.G., Gilman, A.G. & Limbird, L.E. 1996.** *Goodman & Gilman's The Pharmacological Basis of Therapeutics*, 9th edition. McGraw-Hill, New York.
2. **Rang, H.P., Dale, M.M., & Ritter, J.M. 1999.** *Pharmacology*. Churchill-Livingstone, Edinburgh.
3. **Folb, P.I., 1980.** *The Safety of Medicines*. Springer-Verlag, Berlin.

Test for cyanogenic glycosides – cyanide gas turns the test strips bright blue

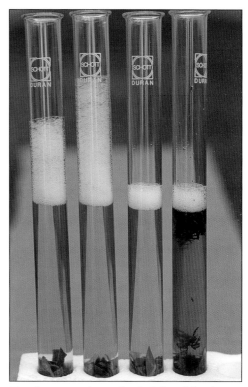

Test for saponins – the height of the foam layer is measured

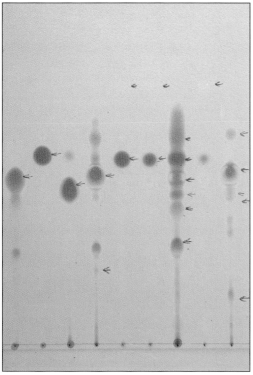

TLC plate with toxic compounds showing as spots

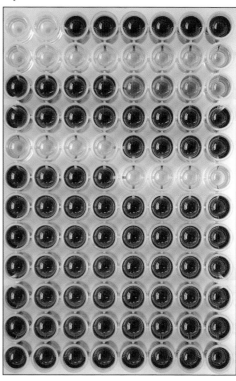

A 96-well plate, used for toxicity testing in live cell cultures

Extraction and isolation of toxins

Plants, in common with other living organisms, consist of a complex mixture of chemical compounds. The toxicity of most plants can be attributed to the presence of only a single active principle or of a small collection of structurally closely related substances. For researchers to investigate the biological effect of a toxic compound, it is necessary to extract the compound from the plant material, separate it from the mixture of all the other compounds present in the extract (chromatographic methods), and determine its chemical structure. Furthermore, it is also necessary to develop quick methods (analytical methods) to determine whether certain material contains the toxic substance or not. These methods are essential for forensic scientists, food scientists and the pharmaceutical industry.

The most common method of extraction is solvent extraction. The plant material is left in contact with a solvent, either at room temperature or at an elevated temperature, for a period of time (often for 24 hours). Extraction at higher temperatures can be done in a specialised glass perculator known as a soxhlet apparatus. The nature of the toxin will determine which solvent is used for the extraction. If the toxin is non-polar (such as gomphoside, see p. 48), methanol is used. For more polar compounds (proteins, lectins, glycosides) water or a buffer solution will be used. Alkaloids, which form a water-soluble salt under acidic conditions, will be extracted with an acidic solution in order to separate them from other non-polar constituents. Treatment of the acidic salt of the alkaloid with a base will give us the parent alkaloids again. Once the extraction is completed, the liquid extract is separated (filtered) from the plant material and the solvent removed by evaporation to give us a solid extract containing, amongst others, our toxic compound.

The next step will be to separate the toxic compound from all the other components. A process called chromatography is most often used for this step. In column chromatography, a glass tube is filled with a solid stationary material. The extract is applied to the top of the column and a liquid, called the mobile phase, is allowed to move down the column. The different types of constituents in the mixture will move at different rates down the column. Fractions are collected at the bottom of the column and the different fractions now contain the different compounds. For larger substances, such as proteins and lectins, size-exclusion chromatography will be used, that is the stationary phase has pores of a specific size. Smaller molecules will be trapped in the pores and larger molecules will then move faster through the column. The most common stationary phase used for smaller molecules is silica gel. The silica gel is polar and the more polar a compound is, the stronger it will be adsorbed onto the silica. The less polar constituents will elute much faster from the column than more polar ones. Once the toxin is isolated in a pure form by chromatography, it is possible to determine its chemical structure and investigate its biological effects.

The extraction methods described above are lengthy and time-consuming processes. Often it is necessary to analyse a large number of samples for the presence of a toxin. Analytical methods such as thin layer chromatography (TLC), gas chromatography (GC) or high performance liquid chromatography (HPLC) are then used. In gas chromatography, which is used for the analysis of terpenes and other volatile compounds, a gas is the mobile phase. GC and HPLC systems are computer controlled and are often equipped with autosamplers. The results are obtained in the form of a chromatogram, in which each chemical compound appears as a peak at a certain retention time (the time at which the compound is eluted from the column). The area under each peak is related to the concentration of the compound. Not only do we confirm that a specific toxin is present (by looking at the retention time) but we can also tell how much of the toxin is present.

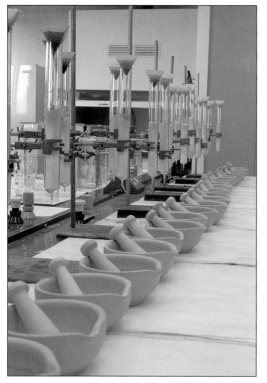

Crude extracts are filtered before analysis

Solvent extraction and column chromatography

A soxhlet apparatus is used for extraction

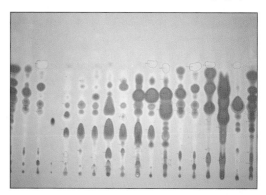

TLC plate showing toxins as spots

GC system, used to analyse volatile compounds

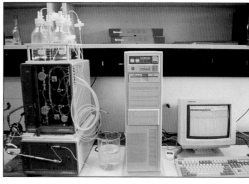

HPLC system, for analysis of non-volatiles

Poisonous principles and their effects

ALKALOIDS

Alkaloids are nitrogen-containing compounds known for their medicinal and toxic effects. True alkaloids are synthesised by the plant from amino acids. An amazing diversity of structural types is found in nature. Alkaloids are classified according to the structure of the nitrogen-containing ring in the molecule – for example, we have a pyridine ring system in pyridine alkaloids and a tropane ring system in tropane alkaloids.

Tobacco Alkaloids (piperidine & pyridine types)

Tobacco alkaloids are derived from the amino acid lysine. There are two basic types, namely piperidine and pyridine alkaloids.

Piperidine   Coniine   Pyridine   Nicotine

An example of a piperidine alkaloid is coniine, one of several extremely toxic compounds in the hemlock plant (*Conium maculatum*). Hemlock was used by the Greeks to execute criminals. Coniine causes paralysis of the motor nerve endings. An example of a pyridine alkaloid is nicotine. This alkaloid is absorbed through the mucous membranes of the nose, mouth and lungs. It acts on the central nervous system, smooth muscle of the intestine and the cardiovascular system through vasoconstriction and increase in blood pressure. It has an oral LD_{50} of 250 mg/kg in mice and the fatal dose in humans is said to be 50 mg. Tobacco consumption has far-reaching effects on the health economy and the social and cultural aspects of a country.

Tropane Alkaloids (atropine type)

Atropine-type alkaloids contain a tropane nucleus that is derived from the amino acid ornithine. Tropane alkaloids occur mainly in members of the Solanaceae family and are particularly well known.

Tropane   Hyoscyamine   Scopolamine

The alkaloids in the deadly nightshade (*Atropa belladonna*) have been known for centuries as poisonous substances. The main alkaloids, hyoscyamine and atropine (racemic hyoscyamine), have an effect on the autonomic nervous system by increasing the heart rate, decreasing intestinal tone and peristalsis, and decreasing secretions such as saliva, gastric and from the eye. Acute poisoning leads to hallucinations and delirium. In South Africa the most common plant containing tropane alkaloids is the thorn apple, jimson weed or *stinkblaar* (*Datura stramonium*). It has a pharmacological action similar to *Atropa*, and all parts of the plant are also poisonous. The presence of scopolamine leads to raving manifestation of delirium (the seeds are called *malpitte*). The oral LD_{50} is 622 mg/kg in rats. Cocaine, an alkaloid from the coca plant (*Erythroxylum coca*) also falls in this group.

Solanum tabacum – tobacco

Conium maculatum – poison hemlock

Atropa belladonna – deadly nightshade

Erythroxylum coca – the coca plant

Isoquinoline Alkaloids

There are several different types of isoquinoline alkaloids in nature, all derived from the amino acids phenylalanine and tyrosine. Morphine is the most well-known isoquinoline alkaloid and occurs in the opium poppy (*Papaver somniferum*). Morphine has a very complex pharmacological action, such as a central nervous system effect of which a pain-relieving, analgesic effect is its main property; uncontrolled use of morphine leads to addiction. The euphoria and passing sensation of well-being explains its physiological dependence. It quickly leads to tolerance and the dose must be increased to have the same effect. Heroin is a synthetic derivative of morphine.

Isoquinoline	Morphine	(+)-Tubocurarine

The famous curares (forest hunting poisons) contain bisbenzyltetrahydroisoquinoline alkaloids, such as the Menispermaceae alkaloids. A typical example is curare, more correctly known as (+)-tubocurarine. This alkaloid has a powerful muscle-relaxing activity, so that the prey animals (monkeys, parrots) cannot flee, are unable to hold onto the branches and conveniently fall to the ground. Curare is only poisonous when injected and the meat of the prey animals is safe to eat. *Erythrina* alkaloids (present in *Erythrina* species) also have curare-like activity. Other examples are the protoberberidines and related types, such as sanguinarine.

Quinoline Alkaloids

Quinoline alkaloids are biosynthetically derived from anthranilic acid. Quinine from cinchona plants (mainly *Cinchona pubescens*) is well known as an anti-malaria preparation. Although replaced by synthetic drugs in the treatment of malaria it is still used in life-threatening cases of cerebral malaria. The major use of quinine is in the beverage industry as the bitter substance in tonic water for 'gin and tonic'.

Quinoline	Anthranilic acid	Quinine

Indole Alkaloids

These alkaloids are all derived from tryptamine, and occur mainly in four plant families – the Apocynaceae, Strychnaceae, Gelsemiaceae and Rubiaceae. Famous examples are reserpine (from *Rauvolfia*), gelsemine (see *Gelsemium*, p. 239), vincristine (from Madagascar periwinkle, *Catharanthus roseus*) and strychnine (from *Strychnos* species). The seeds of *Strychnos nux-vomica* contain the very bitter and extremely poisonous alkaloid strychnine. The LD_{50} is 0,96 mg/kg intravenously in rats. The symptoms of strychnine poisoning include anxiety, increased sensitivity to noise and light followed by convulsive attacks. Death follows asphyxia due to the contraction of the diaphragm.

Indole	Tryptamine		Harmine

Strychnine

Closely related are the tryptamines or so-called β-carboline alkaloids. A famous example is the hallucinogenic harman alkaloids (harmine and related compounds) that were used as 'truth serum' by the Nazis. The source is Syrian rue (*Peganum harmala*, family Zygophyllaceae). It is known that psychoactive vapours are released when seeds are thrown into a fire.

Papaver somniferum – the opium poppy

Cinchona pubescens – a source of quinine

Strychnos nux-vomica – the source of strychnine

Peganum harmala – Syrian rue

Pyrrolizidine Alkaloids (*Senecio* alkaloids)

These alkaloids are found in various plant families as amino alcohols (necines, such as retronecine) or as macrocyclic ring structures, such as retrorsine. The base is saturated in less harmful macrocyclic pyrrolizidines such as platyphylline, and unsaturated in all hepatotoxic compounds (see retrorsine below). In South Africa, pyrrolizidine alkaloids of *Senecio* (Asteraceae) and *Crotalaria* (Fabaceae) cause chronic poisoning of livestock.

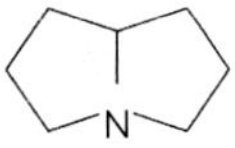

Pyrrolizidine 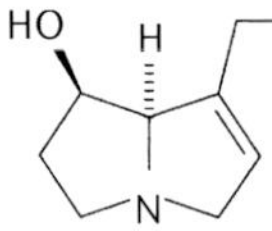   Retronecine 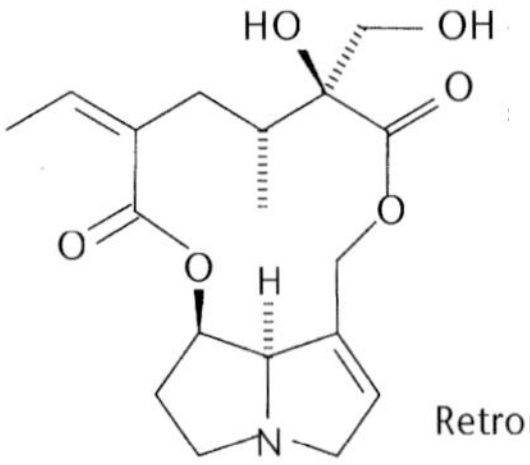   Retrorsine 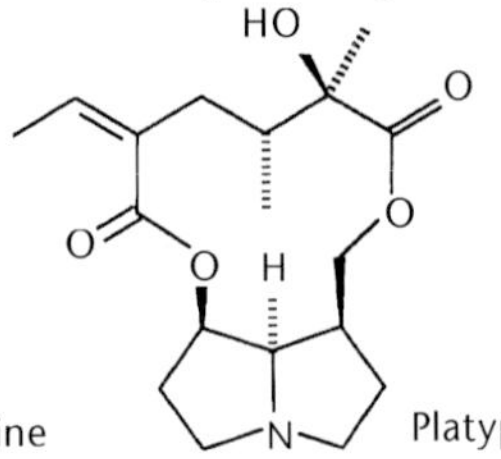   Platyphylline

Plants containing pyrrolizidine alkaloids are rarely responsible for acute poisoning in humans. There are cases where the use of traditional medicines of *Crotalaria* caused chronic intoxication. No contamination of fodder and grain has recently been reported in South Africa. The symptoms associated with chronic poisoning are abdominal pain, loss of appetite and oedema of the extremities.

Quinolizidine Alkaloids (lupin alkaloids)

Quinolizidine alkaloids are derived from the amino acid lysine via cadaverine. These alkaloids are common in the legume family (Fabaceae), where several structural types are found. Examples are lupinine (bicyclic), cytisine (tricycilic) and tetracyclic ones such as sparteine (found in indigenous legumes, including *Lebeckia* species) and anagyrine.

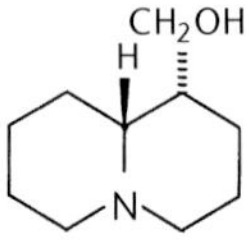

Lupinine 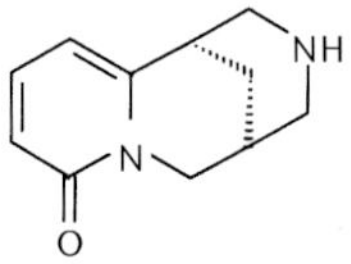   Cytisine 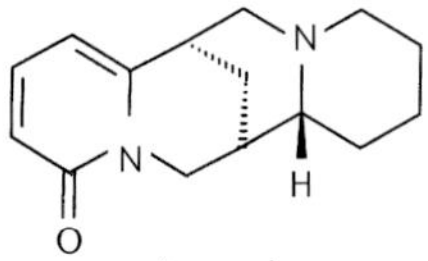   Anagyrine 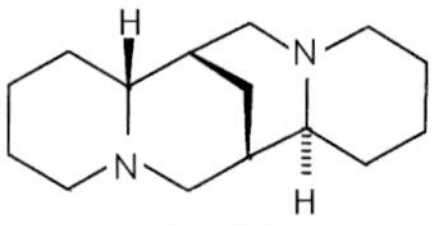   Sparteine

Sparteine has known effects on the heart and is also an oxytocic compound (it causes an increase in the tone and strength of the contractions of the uterus). Cytisine and anagyrine are quite toxic and cause hypersalivation and vomiting in humans (in severe cases, convulsions and respiratory arrest). Teratogenic effects in cattle have been reported, and human poisoning through contaminated milk is possible.

Steroid Alkaloids & Terpenoid Alkaloids

There are two main types of steroidal alkaloids: C_{21} alkaloids derived from pregnane (common in Apocynaceae) and C_{24} alkaloids that are closely related to steroidal saponins (common in Solanaceae and Melanthiaceae, formerly part of Liliaceae). An example from Melanthiaceae with toxic steroidal alkaloids is *Veratrum album*, the white hellebore of Europe. The steroidal alkaloid, solanine, is present in very small quantities in members of the Solanaceae, including potatoes, tomatoes and black nightshade (*nastergal*). The aglycone, solanidine, is shown below. The symptoms of intoxication with solanine are irritation of the throat, headache, fatigue, diarrhoea, coma and convulsions. The action is thought to be through inhibition of cholinesterase.

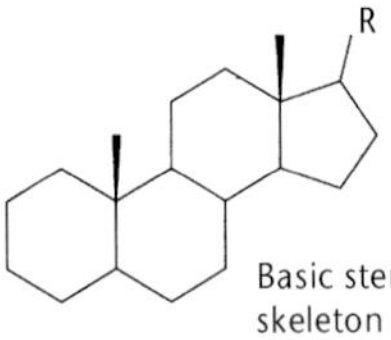

Basic steroid skeleton 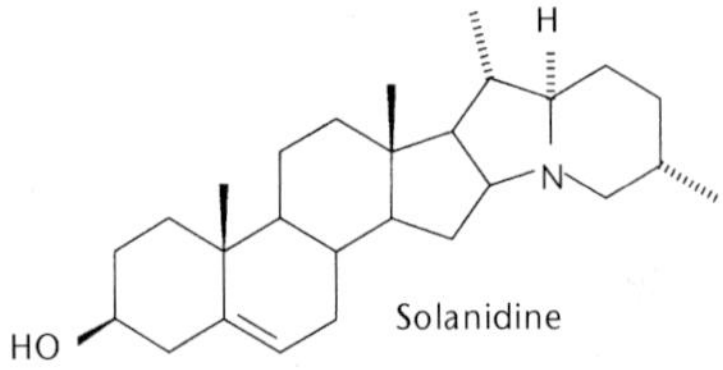   Solanidine 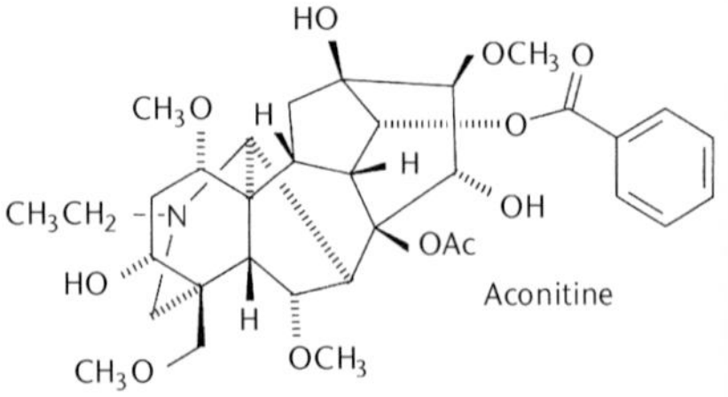   Aconitine

Terpenoid alkaloids are sometimes considered to be pseudoalkaloids, because they are not derived from amino acids but from terpenoids, which incorporate a nitrogen atom during biosynthesis. Aconite or monkshood (*Aconitum napellus*) is one of the most poisonous of all plants – a mere 10 g of root is sufficient to kill an adult. The main alkaloid, aconitine, is very poisonous – the lethal dose is 3–6 mg. Terpenoid alkaloids are also found in *Delphinium* species (larkspur) and *Erythrophleum* species (the famous war and ordeal poisons of Africa).

Crotalaria capensis – a known source of pyrrolizidine alkaloids

Lebeckia cytisoides – a known source of sparteine

Veratrum album – white hellebore

Aconitum napellus – aconite or monkshood

CYANOGENIC GLYCOSIDES

A sugar molecule is often attached to some other molecule, and the resultant compound is then known as a glycoside. If the sugar part of the molecule is glucose, we call it a glucoside; when it is fructose, it is known as a fructoside, and so on. Cyanogenic glycosides are compounds that release the lethal gas hydrogen cyanide (HCN, prussic acid) after enzymatic breakdown of the glycoside. The process is known as cyanogenesis and is a fine example of the intricate ways in which plants protect themselves against herbivores. The cyanogenic glycosides and the enzymes are found in different parts of the plant cell. When the plant cells are damaged (through chewing, wilting or some other cause) the glycosides mix with the enzymes and cyanide gas is released. This type of poisoning is known as prussic acid poisoning (*geilsiekte* or *blousuurvergiftiging*) and livestock losses are commonly recorded in South Africa. *Dimorphotheca cuneata* (*bietou*) is one of many culprits (see p. 261 for a list of known cyanogenic plants).

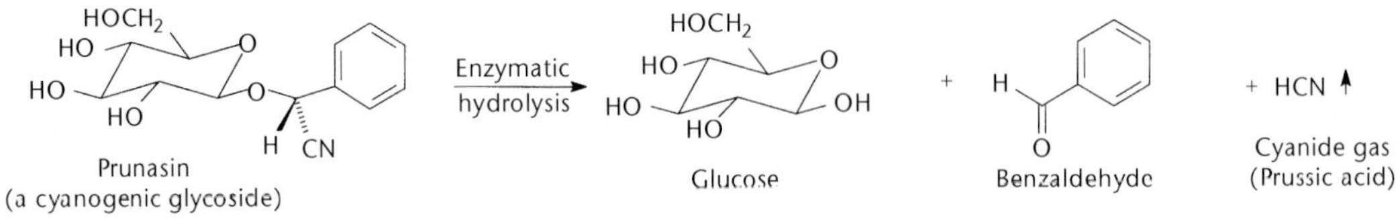

Prunasin (a cyanogenic glycoside) — Enzymatic hydrolysis → Glucose + Benzaldehyde + HCN Cyanide gas (Prussic acid)

Cassava starch (manioc) obtained from *Manihot esculenta*, which is the chief starch source for millions of people in tropical regions, contains a cyanogenic glycoside, linamarin. Although the method of preparation of the starch will remove the glycosides, detoxification is rarely complete. The neuropathological conditions that follow ingestion of this starch can be seen in many tropical regions. The fruit of bitter almonds (*Prunus dulcis* var. *amara*) contains 2–3% of a cyanogenic glycoside, amygdalin.

COUMARINS

Coumarins are aromatic compounds with a specific ring structure. There are simple coumarins, such as coumarin itself and umbelliferone (see structures below) or furanocoumarins, where there is an additional so-called furan ring attached to the first ring of the basic coumarin structure. Xanthotoxin is an example of this type of coumarin, which is known to cause severe light-induced dermatitis (a severe allergic reaction that may result in painful blistering of the skin – see *Peucedanum galbanum*, p. 168). Furanocoumarins are classified as linear (e.g. xanthotoxin) or angular (e.g. angelicin). Coumarins are sometimes present in essential oils because they are sufficiently volatile to be extracted through the process of steam distillation.

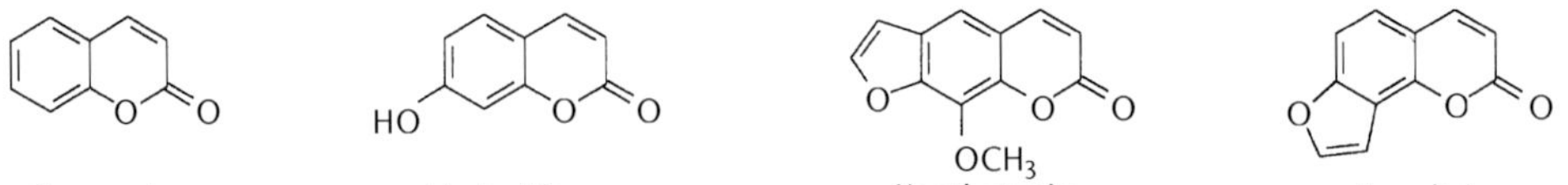

Coumarin   Umbelliferone   Xanthotoxin   Angelicin

The flowering tops of *Melilotus* are used in traditional medicine in blood circulatory disorders; they contain small quantities of the lactone coumarin. If the plant is infected with fungi it forms dicoumarol, which is toxic through its anticoagulant properties (see *Melilotus alba*, p. 150). The synthetic coumarin-type anticoagulants (such as warfarin) were designed with dicoumarol as a model. These are mainly used as rat poison. Other rich sources of coumarins are lace flower fruits (*Ammi majus*), cabbages (*Brassica* species), wild parsley (*Peucedanum* species) and rue (*Ruta graveolens*). These plants may cause dermatitis in sensitive people.

Manihot esculenta – cassava

Dimorphotheca cuneata – *bietou*

Ammi majus – lace flower

Ruta graveolens – rue or *wynruit*

TERPENOIDS

Terpenoids are formed in nature by isoprene units (five carbon units) that are linked together. The various classes of terpenoids have the following numbers of isoprene units: Monoterpenoids have two units – an example is 1,8-cineole, also known as eucalyptol (see *Eucalyptus cladocalyx*, p. 237). Tuliposide A is a rare example of a toxic hemiterpene (formed from a single isoprene unit) that is found as one of the skin irritant compounds in tulip bulbs. Sesquiterpenoids have three units – an example is lasiosperman, a toxic component of *Lasiospermum* species. Sesquiterpenoids may be further linked to form larger molecules – an example is gossypol, the toxic component of the seed cake of cotton (*Gossypium* species). Triterpenoids have six units and often occur in nature as glycosides (see below). They may be modified to a steroidal skeleton, so that the number of isoprene units is not immediately obvious. An example of a steroidal triterpene is diosgenin, present in *Dioscorea* species.

Isoprene

Eucalyptol
(terpene)

Tuliposide A
(hemiterpene)

Lasiosperman
(sesquiterpene)

Phorbol
(diterpene)

Another large group of terpenoids is the diterpenoids. They are made up of four isoprene units but various modifications can occur. Examples are the toxic daphnane orthoesters (such as kraussianin, p. 120) present in *Gnidia* and other members of the Thymelaeaceae. Toxic diterpenes (phorbol-derived compounds) also occur in members of the Euphorbiaceae – in the latex and in the seeds (e.g. oil of *Croton*, made from *Croton tiglium*). The effects of *Euphorbia* latex reported in young children are inflammation of the mouth and throat, diarrhoea and vomiting, which could lead to delirium and convulsions. If the latex ever gets into an eye, immediate and profuse rinsing is necessary as well as medical attention. Poinsettia (*Euphorbia pulcherrima*) is often used as a houseplant but the milky latex is fortunately not very toxic. Pyrethrins (see *Chrysanthemum cinerariifolium*, p. 228) are monoterpenoids with an irregular structure. Sesquiterpene lactones are a large class of modified sesquiterpenes that occur in many members of the Asteraceae. Some of these lactones are responsible for allergic reactions and dermatitis in gardeners and farmers (see *Chrysanthemum xmorifolium*, p. 229).

SAPONINS

Both triterpenoids and steroids are often present in plants in the form of saponins. This means that they have one or more sugar molecules attached to them, which make them water soluble and soaplike (hence the name saponin). Their presence in a watery extract is immediately evident from the foam that forms when the solution is shaken vigorously. Saponins, like other glycosides, can be hydrolysed to yield the triterpenoid or steroid as aglycone (the part of the molecule that is attached to the sugar).

Diosgenin
(aglycone of
steroidal saponin)

Oleanoglycotoxin A
(triterpenoid saponin)

Forty years ago, very large quantities of *Dioscorea* were collected in the Lydenburg district. It was exported to the USA for the extraction of diosgenin, which was used in the partial synthesis of the hormones used in the production of oral contraceptives. Saponin-containing plants are only mildly toxic *per se*. Liquid extracts of the plants given intravenously will lead to haemolysis and death. Saponin glycosides have an anti-inflammatory and anti-oedema action. Other examples of plants containing saponins are inkberry (*Phytolacca* species, Phytolaccaceae) and lucerne or alfalfa (*Medicago sativa*, Fabaceae). Oleanoglycotoxin occurs in *Phytolacca dodecandra*.

Artemisia absinthium – used to flavour absinthe

Gossypium herbaceum – cotton

Croton tiglium – the source of croton oil

Euphorbia pulcherrima – poinsettia

Tulipa hybrid – tulips

Dioscorea elephantipes – the elephant's foot

HEART GLYCOSIDES

Cardiac glycosides are a specific group of steroidal glycosides comprising two basic types, the so-called cardenolides and bufadienolides. The cardenolides have a five-member ring above the basic steroid skeleton – examples are ouabain (present in *Strophanthus gratus*) and digitoxin (present in *Digitalis purpurea*, see p. 234). Bufadienolides differ in the presence of a six-member ring above the steroid skeleton. An example is cotyledoside (present in *Tylecodon wallichii* that is, with other members of the *plakkie* family (Crassulaceae), such as the well-known *Cotyledon orbiculata*, responsible for *krimpsiekte* in livestock). In South Africa, heart glycosides are the most important of all causes of livestock poisoning.

Ouabain	Cotyledoside

The most famous plant containing heart glycosides, digoxin and digitoxin, is the foxglove, *Digitalis* species. Concoctions containing *Digitalis* have been used in European traditional medicine for centuries. The use of the plant in heart conditions was formally described in 1785 for treatment of 'dropsy' or congestive heart failure. Symptoms of cardiac glycoside poisoning are nausea and vomiting, vision disorders, extra-systoles; in severe cases complete heart block with bradycardia. Death occurs due to ventricular fibrillation. The oral LD_{50} of digitoxin in rats is 8,3 mg/kg. Other plants containing poisonous cardiac glycosides are *Nerium*, *Thevetia*, *Bowiea*, *Cotyledon* and *Scilla*. Although heart glycosides are in the top 10 of most frequently prescribed medicines, they are also amongst the most poisonous of all prescription drugs.

LECTINS (haemagglutinins, phytotoxins)

Some proteins and glycoproteins in legume seeds are able to attach themselves to red blood cells and cause their precipitation or agglutination. Animal studies have demonstrated that their toxicity does not parallel haemagglutination. Prolonged cooking or dry heating destroys the activity of legume lectins and the associated toxic effect. Poisonous plants that contain lectins are, for example, mistletoe (*Viscum album*) and castor oil seeds (*Ricinus communis*).

OXALATES

Oxalic acid is present as oxalate salts in rhubarb (*Rheum*) and sorrel (*Oxalis*), hence the sour acidic taste of these plants. Excessive ingestion of leaves can lead to stomach pain, heartburn, nausea and vomiting. Calcium oxalate occurs in many toxic plants and sharp crystals (raffides) may cause severe irritation of mucous membranes in the mouth and throat (see dumb cane, *Dieffenbachia maculata*, p. 233). The arum lily (*Zantedeschia aethiopica*) is not really toxic but the oxalate crystals may cause distress if leaves are eaten.

MISCELLANEOUS COMPOUNDS (selenium, molybdenum, heavy metals, nitrate, fluoroacetates, amides, and others)

There are several classes of compounds that are not covered by the above discussion. These are dealt with under the individual plants in which they occur. Inorganic salts are of importance in livestock poisoning, resulting in a loss of productivity rather than acute toxicity. They are rarely implicated in human poisoning. A study of metal concentrations in plants and urine from patients treated with traditional remedies showed that metal contamination from plants is not a problem in traditional South African remedies.

Strophanthus gratus – a commercial source of ouabain

Cotyledon orbiculata – *plakkie*

Viscum album – the European mistletoe

Zantedeschia aethiopica – arum lily

ABRUS PRECATORIUS

Fabaceae

crab's eyes, jequirity, lucky bean, love bean (English); minnie-minnies (Afrikaans)

DESCRIPTION The plant is a climbing shrub (creeper) with woody stems and pinnately compound leaves, each with about 10 to 15 pairs of small, oblong leaflets[1,2]. Pale purple, inconspicuous flowers are borne in dense groups, followed by clusters of fruits (pods). Each pod produces up to four or five seeds of about 5 mm in diameter. The bright red seeds have a black patch around the hilum, and a hard, impermeable seed coat, so that they are only poisonous when scarified or damaged in some way.

TYPE OF TOXIN Lectin.

IMPORTANCE *Abrus* seeds are highly toxic – a single seed (if removed from the tough seed coat and broken up or chewed well) is reported to be sufficient to cause death[3-7]. When used as beads in necklaces, seeds are known to cause dermatitis. Children are attracted to the brightly coloured seeds and may be poisoned if they swallow damaged or punctured seeds.

POISONOUS INGREDIENTS The seeds contain one of the most deadly plant toxins known – a lectin called abrin[8], which inhibits protein synthesis in cells. Abrin consists of two polypeptide chains joined by disulphide bonds – the one peptide is able to inactivate ribosomes, the other is known to bind the toxin to the cell surface[9]. Abrin may be confused with abrine, an indole alkaloid also found in seeds of *A. precatorius*[5]. Seeds of another common legume climber, *Wisteria sinensis* (wistaria or bloureën) contain a poisonous lectin called wistarin.

PHARMACOLOGICAL EFFECTS Fatal poisoning in both humans and domestic animals has been reported[3-7]. Symptoms always appear after a latent period of several hours, and include loss of appetite, diarrhoea and vomiting, followed by intestinal inflammation and haemorrhage. The LD_{50} in mice is reported to be a mere 2 mg/kg body-weight[4]. Despite their toxicity, the seeds are traditionally used as aphrodisiacs, oral contraceptives or emetics[3]. Powdered seeds are used to treat ophthalmia, eye infections, snakebite, ulcers and intestinal worms[3]. Abrin is antigenic and animals can thus be immunised with small doses before being allowed to graze on pastures infested with *Abrus*[7]. The leaves and roots are used medicinally and are known to contain the sweetening agent glycyrrhizin.

DISTRIBUTION *A. precatorius* has a wide distribution in the tropics[1,2] and grows naturally in the eastern and northern parts of South Africa.

1. **Verdcourt, B. 1970.** A reappraisal of the species of the genus *Abrus* Adans. *Kew Bull.* 24: 235-253.
2. **Verdcourt, B. 1971.** Leguminosae. Papilionoideae. *Flora of Tropical East Africa* 3(1): 113-118.
3. **Watt, J.M. & Breyer-Brandwijk, M.G. 1962.** *The Medicinal and Poisonous Plants of Southern and Eastern Africa*, 2nd edition. Livingstone, London.
4. **Harborne, J.B., Baxter, H. & Moss, G.P. (eds) 1997.** *Dictionary of Plant Toxins.* John Wiley & Sons, Chichester.
5. **Merck 1989.** *The Merck Index.* 11th edition. Merck, Rahway.
6. **Verdcourt, B. & Trump, E.C. 1969.** *Common Poisonous Plants of East Africa.* Collins, London.
7. **Kellerman, T.S., Coetzer, J.A.W. & Naudé, T.W. 1988.** *Plant Poisonings and Mycotoxicoses of Livestock in Southern Africa.* Oxford University Press, Cape Town.
8. **Wei, C.H., Hartman, F.C., Pfuderer & Yang, W.-K. 1974.** Purification and characterization of two toxic proteins from seeds of *Abrus precatorius*. *J. Biol. Chem.* 249: 3061-3067.
9. **Olsnes, S. 1978.** Toxic and non-toxic lectins from *Abrus precatorius*. *Methods Enzymol.* 50: 323-330.

Abrus precatorius

Lucky beans or love beans, the poisonous seeds of *Abrus precatorius*

ACACIA SIEBERIANA VAR. *WOODII*

Fabaceae

---

paper-bark thorn (English); papierbasdoring (Afrikaans)

DESCRIPTION This thorn tree has a characteristic flat-topped crown, flaking, papery bark and velvety stems bearing straight thorns[1,2]. The leaves are doubly compound and the fluffy, rounded flower heads are cream-coloured. The fruit is an oblong, woody pod. Several other species of *Acacia* are also known to be poisonous to stock, particularly *A. erioloba* (camel thorn), *A. caffra* (common hook-thorn) and *A. nilotica* (scented thorn).

TYPE OF TOXIN Cyanogenic glycoside.

IMPORTANCE *A. sieberiana* and several other species such as *A. caffra* and *A. erioloba* cause prussic acid poisoning (*geilsiekte*) in stock[3-6]. Since *A. sieberiana* has relatively soft thorns, sufficient quantities of the young shoots may be grazed to cause poisoning. Milled pods of *A. erioloba* are sometimes fed to cattle or sheep during droughts. After hailstorms, poisoning may occur when animals eat the wilted young shoots of *A. caffra* or *A. sieberiana*. *A. nilotica* does not appear to be cyanogenic, but large quantities of pods are known to cause acute toxicity and abortion in goats[6].

POISONOUS INGREDIENTS The major cyanogenic glycoside isolated from *A. sieberiana* is proacacipetalin, but it also contains other minor ones such as 3-hydroxyheterodendrin[7-9]. The glycoside acacipetalin[7] was first thought to be the major toxin, but it was later shown[8,9] that this compound is an artefact that resulted from the treatment of the isomeric procacipetalin with $CaCO_3$ during the original isolation process.

PHARMACOLOGICAL EFFECTS *Acacia* species produce typical symptoms of prussic acid poisoning in stock, known in Afrikaans as *geilsiekte*[3-6]. Prussic acid is present as cyanogenic glycosides but these occur in separate parts of the plant cell than the hydrolysing enzymes (such as β-glucosidases). When cells are damaged (e.g. through grazing and digestion by animals), the enzymes react with the glycosides to form hydrogen cyanide (a lethal gas). A more detailed discussion of cyanogenesis is given elsewhere. A large number of plants contain cyanogenic compounds (see list on p. 261).

DISTRIBUTION *A. sieberiana* is widely distributed in the north-eastern parts of South Africa and is particularly common in overgrazed areas of the KwaZulu-Natal midlands[1,2]. The distribution areas of South African *Acacia* species are well documented[1,2].

Proacacipetalin   3-Hydroxyheterodendrin

---

1. **Ross, J.H. 1975.** Subfamily Mimosoideae. *Flora of Southern Africa* 16(1). Botanical Research Institute, Pretoria.
2. **Smit, N. 1999.** *Guide to the Acacias of South Africa.* Briza Publications, Pretoria.
3. **Steyn, D.G. 1934.** *The Toxicology of Plants in South Africa.* Central News Agency, South Africa.
4. **Steyn, D.G. 1949.** *Die Vergiftiging van Mens en Dier.* Van Schaik, Pretoria.
5. **Vahrmeijer, J. 1981.** *Poisonous Plants of Southern Africa That Cause Stock Losses.* Tafelberg Publishers, Cape Town.
6. **Kellerman, T.S., Coetzer, J.A.W. & Naudé, T.W. 1988.** *Plant Poisonings and Mycotoxicoses of Livestock in Southern Africa.* Oxford University Press, Cape Town.
7. **Rimington, C. 1935.** The chemical constitution of acacipetalin, a new cyanogenic glucoside isolated from *Acacia stolonifera* Burch. *S. Afr. J. Sci.* 32: 154-171.
8. **Ettlinger, M.G., Jaroszewski, J.W., Jensen, S.R., Nielsen, B.J. & Nartey, F. 1977.** Proacacipetalin and acacipetalin. *J. Chem. Soc., Chem. Commun.* 952-953.
9. **Brimer, L., Christensen, S.B., Jaroszewski, J.W. & Nartey, F. 1981.** Structural elucidation and partial synthesis of 3-hydroxyheterodendrin, a cyanogenic glucoside from *Acacia sieberiana* var. *woodii*. *Phytochemistry* 20: 2221-2223.

Acacia sieberiana var. *woodii*

Flower heads of *Acacia sieberiana* var. *woodii*

Elongated flower heads of *Acacia caffra*

ACOKANTHERA OPPOSITIFOLIA
Apocynaceae

bushman's poison bush (English); boesmangif, gewone gifboom (Afrikaans);
uhlunguyembe (Zulu); nthunguyembe (Xhosa)

DESCRIPTION *A. oppositifolia* was previously known as *A. venetum*. It is an evergreen shrub or small tree of up to 5 m in height. The leaves are thick in texture, glossy green, tinged with red and the secondary veins are quite prominent[1]. Attractive and sweetly scented, white or pale pink flowers are borne in dense clusters. The fleshy, plum-like fruits are red to purple and up to 20 mm long when mature. Two other species occur in South Africa: *A. oblongifolia* has larger fruits (more than 20 mm long), while *A. schimperi* has very broad, almost rounded leaves without conspicuous secondary veins[1].

TYPE OF TOXIN Cardiac glycoside (cardenolide).

IMPORTANCE *A. oppositifolia* and other species are well known throughout Africa as a traditional source of extremely toxic arrow poisons[2-4]. The poison is usually obtained from the leaves, roots or wood after boiling in water for a long period until a gum-like substance is obtained. An arrow wound in humans may lead to death within 15 minutes. Cases of murder and suicide have been recorded. Fruits appear to be variable in their toxicity, but accidental poisoning of children has been recorded. Several medicinal uses are known, including treatment of abdominal pain, headache and snakebite[5]. Poisoning of animals is surprisingly rare but cattle are sometimes at risk during droughts[6].

POISONOUS INGREDIENTS Members of the genus *Acokanthera* contain several toxic cardiac glycosides such as ouabain[7,8]. The major toxic component of both *A. oppositifolia* and *A. oblongifolia* is acovenoside A. Ouabain is the famous arrow poison from East Africa but it is not known if southern African *A. schimperi* also has ouabain as major glycoside.

PHARMACOLOGICAL EFFECTS Concentrated decoctions may lead to death within a few minutes due to heart failure. Symptoms include nausea, salivation, retching, purging and exhaustion, with the usual respiratory and cardiac abnormalities associated with heart glycosides. In animals typical *krimpsiekte*-like symptoms will be evident[6] and the identification of the source of poisoning may be confirmed by pieces of the leathery leaves in the rumen[4,6].

DISTRIBUTION *A. oppositifolia* is the most widely distributed species (see map) and occurs over large parts of central and southern Africa. *A. oblongifolia* is confined to sand dunes along the eastern coast, while *A. schimperi* occurs mainly in Mpumalanga, Swaziland and along the border between Mozambique and KwaZulu-Natal.

Acovenoside A

Ouabain

1. **Kupicha, F.K. 1982.** Studies on African Apocynaceae: the genus *Acokanthera*. *Kew Bull.* 37: 40-67.
2. **Verdcourt, B. & Trump, E.C. 1969.** *Common Poisonous Plants of East Africa.* Collins, London.
3. **Neuwinger, H.D. 1996.** *African Ethnobotany: Poisons and Drugs: Chemistry, Pharmacology,Toxicology.* Chapman & Hall, Germany.
4. **Steyn, D.G. 1934.** *The Toxicology of Plants in South Africa.* Central News Agency, South Africa.
5. **Watt, J.M. & Breyer-Brandwijk, M.G. 1962.** *The Medicinal and Poisonous Plants of Southern and Eastern Africa*, 2nd edition. Livingstone, London.
6. **Kellerman, T.S., Coetzer, J.A.W. & Naudé, T.W. 1988.** *Plant Poisonings and Mycotoxicoses of Livestock in Southern Africa.* Oxford University Press, Cape Town.
7. **Schlegel, W., Tamm Ch. & Reichstein, T. 1955.** The constitution of acovenoside A. *Helv. Chim. Acta* 38: 1013-1025.
8. **De Villiers, J.P. 1962.** The cardiac glycosides of *Acokanthera oblongifolia*. *J. S. Afr. Chem. Inst.* 15: 82-84.

Fruits of *Acokanthera oppositifolia*

Flowers of *Acokanthera oppositifolia*

ADENIA DIGITATA

Passifloraceae

bobbejaangif (Afrikaans); kamam (?); motsatsa (Tswana)

DESCRIPTION *A. digitata* is a herbaceous climber with slender stems arising from a tuber below the ground[1]. The tendrils used in climbing are a distinct feature of this species. The exceptionally variable leaves are deeply lobed to digitate, and the tubular flowers develop into attractive but highly toxic, yellow or bright red, berry-like capsules[1]. At least two other species are known to be poisonous. *A. glauca* (*bobbejaangif*) lacks tendrils and has a peculiar thick, tuberous, bright green, bottle-shaped base. *A. gummifera* (*impinda* in Zulu, *slangklimop* in Afrikaans) has thick, woody, green stems.

TYPE OF TOXIN Cyanogenic glycoside, lectin.

IMPORTANCE *A. digitata* is exceptionally poisonous and may cause death in humans within a few hours after ingestion[2]. The bulbous stems are sometimes confused with other edible tubers, resulting in fatal poisoning (about 30 g of root are said to be sufficient to kill an adult). The brightly coloured fruits are attractive to children and numerous deaths have been recorded. The thick, green stem of *A. gummifera* is very poisonous but is popular as an emetic and for treating leprosy and malaria[2] or it is sprinkled around the house as a traditional disinfectant. Species of *Adenia* have been used as fish poisons[3] and have also been implicated in stock losses, homicide and suicide[2-6].

POISONOUS INGREDIENTS The toxicity of *Adenia* species is due to a combination of a highly toxic protein, modeccin, and cyanogenic glycosides[7-9]. The structure and activity of modeccin are similar to that of the lectins abrin (*Abrus precatorius*) and ricinin (*Ricinus communis*). The major cyanogenic glycoside of *A. digitata* and *A. glauca* is tetraphyllin B. *Passiflora* species (alien invaders in South Africa) also contain cyanogenic glycosides.

PHARMACOLOGICAL EFFECTS The symptoms of *A. glauca* poisoning include vomiting, diarrhoea and fits, with kidney and liver damage[2]. Modeccin is exceptionally poisonous (injection of 0,01 mg/kg is said to be sufficient to kill a rabbit[2]). The type of poisoning and the likelihood of recovery depend on whether cyanogenic glycosides or the toxic protein predominates[2]. If a person is poisoned by *Adenia*, recovery from the glycosides is more likely than from modeccin.

DISTRIBUTION *A. digitata* is widely distributed in the subtropical regions of southern Africa (see map)[1]. *A. glauca* has a fairly restricted distribution in the northern parts of South Africa and the adjoining parts of Botswana, while *A. gummifera* has a very wide distribution, from the Eastern Cape Province northwards to eastern Africa and Somalia[1].

Tetraphyllin B

1. De Wilde, W.J.J.O. 1976. Passifloraceae. *Flora of Southern Africa* 22: 106-117.
2. Watt J.M. & Breyer-Brandwijk, M.G. 1962. *The Medicinal and Poisonous Plants of Southern and Eastern Africa*. 2nd edition. Livingstone, London.
3. Verdcourt, B. & Trump, E.C. 1969. *Common Poisonous Plants of East Africa*. Collins, London.
4. Steyn, D.G. 1934. *The Toxicology of Plants in South Africa*. Central News Agency, South Africa.
5. Steyn, D.G. 1949. *Die Vergiftiging van Mens en Dier*. Van Schaik, Pretoria.
6. Kellerman, T.S., Coetzer, J.A.W. & Naudé, T.W. 1988. *Plant Poisonings and Mycotoxicoses of Livestock in Southern Africa*. Oxford University Press, Cape Town.
7. Gasperi-Campani, A., Barbieri, L., Lorenzoni, E., Montanaro, L., Sperti, S., Bonetti, E. & Stirpe, F. 1978. Modeccin, the toxin of *Adenia digitata*. Purification, toxicity and inhibition of protein synthesis *in vitro*. *Biochem. J.* 174: 491-496.
8. Spencer, K.C. & Seigler, D.S. 1982. Tetraphyllin B and *epi*-tetraphyllin B from *Adenia glauca* Schinz. *Onderstepoort J. Vet. Sci.* 49: 137-138.
9. Spencer, K.C. & Seigler, D.S. 1982. Tetraphyllin B from *Adenia digitata*. *Phytochemistry* 21: 653-655.

Flowers of *Adenia digitata*

Fruits of *Adenia digitata*

Adenia glauca

Fruit of *Adenia glauca*

Adenia gummifera

Adenia gummifera stems as sold at muti markets

ADENIUM MULTIFLORUM

Apocynaceae

---

impala lily (English); impalalelie (Afrikaans)

DESCRIPTION *A. multiflorum* is a thick-stemmed shrub of up to 3 m in height. The stem and branches contain a watery sap[1,2]. Glossy green leaves are crowded on the branch ends. The flowers are large and showy – bright red with pale pink or white in the central part. The cigar-shaped fruits split open to release numerous cylindrical, hairy seeds. The plant was previously known as *A. obesum* var. *multiflorum*[1,2].

TYPE OF TOXIN Cardiac glycoside (cardenolide).

IMPORTANCE The impala lily is known in Africa and in southern Africa as a source of fish poison and arrow poison[3,4]. Poison is prepared from the bark and fleshy parts of the trunk but it is always used in combination with other poisons[4]. Leaves and flowers are poisonous to goats and cattle[4], but the plant is sometimes heavily browsed[2] and is not considered to be of much toxicological significance[5]. In contrast, *A. boehmianum* from northern Namibia

is the source of an extremely toxic arrow poison[6,7]. The vernacular name *ouzuwo* is the Herero word for poison[7]. The latex of the cultivated *Plumeria rubra* (frangipani) is a skin irritant and is considered to be poisonous when swallowed.

POISONOUS INGREDIENTS The stem and roots of *A. multiflorum* contain more than 30 different cardiac glycosides[8,9] (cardenolides and pregnane glycosides). The major cardiac glycoside[9] in this species is obebioside B.

PHARMACOLOGICAL EFFECTS There does not seem to be much specific information on the toxicity of *Adenium* cardenolides. It may be interesting to investigate the main compounds of *A. boehmianum*, a species known to be highly toxic[6].

DISTRIBUTION *A. multiflorum* occurs only in the extreme eastern parts of South Africa but it is widely distributed in the central and eastern parts of Africa.

Obebioside B

1. **Plaizier, A.C. 1980.** A revision of *Adenium* Roem. & Schult. and of *Diplorhynchus* Welw. ex Fic. & Hiern (Apocynaceae). *Mededelingen van de Landbouwhogeschool te Wageningen* 80(12): 9-13.
2. **Coates Palgrave, K. 1977.** *Trees of Southern Africa.* Struik, Cape Town.
3. **Watt, J.M. & Breyer-Brandwijk, M.G. 1962.** *The Medicinal and Poisonous Plants of Southern and Eastern Africa*, 2nd edition. Livingstone, London.
4. **Verdcourt, B. & Trump, E.C. 1969.** *Common Poisonous Plants of East Africa.* Collins, London.
5. **Kellerman, T.S., Coetzer, J.A.W. & Naudé, T.W. 1988.** *Plant Poisonings and Mycotoxicoses of Livestock in Southern Africa.* Oxford University Press, Cape Town.
6. **Neuwinger, H.D. 1996.** *African Ethnobotany: Poisons and Drugs: Chemistry, Pharmacology, Toxicology.* Chapman & Hall, Germany.
7. **Malan, J. S. & Owen-Smith, G. L. 1974.** The ethnobotany of Kaokoland. *Cimbebasia* Ser. B 2,5: 131-178.
8. **Hoffmann, J.J. & Cole, J.R. 1977.** Phytochemical investigations of *Adenium obesum* Forskal (Apocynaceae): isolation and identification of cytotoxic agents. *J. Pharm. Sci.* 66: 1336-1338.
9. **Yamauchi, T. & Abe, F. 1990.** Cardiac glycosides and pregnanes from *Adenium obesum* (Studies on the constituents of *Adenium*. I). *Chem. Pharm. Bull.* 38: 669-672.

Adenium multiflorum

Flowers of *Adenium multiflorum*

Adenium boehmianum

ALBIZIA VERSICOLOR
Fabaceae

---

poison-pod albizia (English); grootblaarvalsdoring (Afrikaans)

DESCRIPTION *A. versicolor* is an attractive tree of about 10 m in height with a rounded or spreading crown and greyish-brown, rough bark[1,2]. The twigs, leaf stalks and undersides of the very large leaflets have a dense layer of rusty-red hairs. Fluffy, cream-coloured flowers are followed by large, reddish-brown pods. *A. tanganyicensis* (the paperbark albizia) has much smaller leaflets and smooth (hairless) twigs and is easily recognised by the attractive red, papery bark that peels off to reveal a beautiful smooth, whitish underbark[1,2].

TYPE OF TOXIN Pyridine alkaloid.

IMPORTANCE *A. versicolor* and *A. tanganyicensis* cause cattle losses through albiziosis[3-6]. This type of poisoning usually occurs in late winter or early spring when the unripe pods are blown down by wind[2-6]. Poisoned animals develop hypersensitivity, intermittent convulsions, high temperature, and may ultimately die from heart failure[5]. As little as half a kilogram *A. versicolor* pods can be fatal to cattle and ripe pods of *A. tanganyicensis* at a dose of 5 g/kg body-weight proved fatal to sheep[5]. Albiziosis may be confused with other types of poisoning or even with the disease *hartwater*, but remains of pods and seeds are found in the rumen of dead animals[5].

POISONOUS INGREDIENTS Two neurotoxins have been isolated from the seeds of *A. tanganyicensis*, viz. 4'-*O*-methylpyridoxine (the major compound) and 5'-*O*-acetyl-4'-*O*-methylpyridoxine[7]. The former compound also occurs in the seeds of *Ginkgo biloba*[8]. The structures are similar to that of pyridoxine, better known as vitamin B$_6$.

PHARMACOLOGICAL EFFECTS The neurotoxicity of the two *Albizia* species is caused by the presence of methylpyridoxine, which is a pyridoxine antagonist. The severity of the antivitamin B$_6$ activity can be judged from the LD$_{50}$ in humans, which is about 11 mg/kg body-weight by oral route[8]. Symptoms of poisoning can be prevented or reversed by dosing with vitamin B$_6$. Experiments with sheep have confirmed the value of this treatment in preventing stock losses from *Albizia* poisoning[9].

DISTRIBUTION *A. versicolor* occurs in the extreme eastern parts of South Africa (see map) and *A. tanganyicensis* is found mainly in Limpopo Province, but the distributions of both species extend northwards into the subtropical parts of southern Africa[1,2].

4'-*O*-Methylpyridoxine: R=H
5'-*O*-Acetyl-4'-*O*-methylpyridoxine: R=Ac

Pyridoxine
(Vitamin B$_6$)

1. **Ross, J.H. 1975.** Subfamily Mimosoideae. *Flora of Southern Africa* 16(1). Botanical Research Institute, Pretoria.
2. **Coates Palgrave, K. 1977.** *Trees of Southern Africa.* Struik, Cape Town.
3. **Needham, A.J.E. & Lawrence, J.A. 1966.** The toxicity of *Albizia versicolor*. *The Rhodesian Agricultural Journal* 63: 137-140.
4. **Basson, P.A., Adelaar, T.F., Naude, T.W. & Minnie, J.A. 1970.** *Albizia* poisoning: report of the first outbreak and some experimental work in South Africa. *J. S. Afr. Med. Assoc.* 41: 117-130.
5. **Kellerman, T.S., Coetzer, J.A.W. & Naudé, T.W. 1988.** *Plant Poisonings and Mycotoxicoses of Livestock in Southern Africa.* Oxford University Press, Cape Town.
6. **Vahrmeijer, J. 1981.** *Poisonous Plants of Southern Africa That Cause Stock Losses.* Tafelberg Publishers, Cape Town.
7. **Steyn, P.S., Vleggaar, R. & Anderson, L.A.P. 1987.** Structure elucidation of two neurotoxin from *Albizia tanganyicensis*. *S. Afr. J. Chem.* 40: 191-192.
8. **Harborne, J.B., Baxter, H. & Moss, G.P. (eds) 1997.** *Dictionary of Plant Toxins.* John Wiley & Sons, Chichester.
9. **Gummow, B., Bastianello, S.S., Labuschagne, L. & Erasmus, G.L. 1992.** Experimental *Albizia versicolor* poisoning in sheep and its successful treatment with pyridoxine hydrochloride. *Onderstepoort J. Vet. Res.* 59: 111-118.

Albizia versicolor

Albizia tanganyicensis

Leaves and flowers of *Albizia versicolor*

AMARANTHUS HYBRIDUS
Amaranthaceae

---

marog (Sotho); pigweed (English); misbredie (Afrikaans)

DESCRIPTION *A. hybridus* is a weedy annual with erect, leafy stems and soft, broad, pointed leaves on long stalks. Flowers are minute and inconspicuous, and are borne in plumes or spikes[1,2]. The plants grow well in fertile soils and are therefore often found as weeds on refuse heaps and abandoned cattle pens. The closely related *A. thunbergii* has purple leaves.

TYPE OF TOXIN Nitrate.

IMPORTANCE *Amaranthus* species often contain large amounts of nitrate and sometimes cause fatal nitrate poisoning (also known as nitrite poisoning) in domestic animals[3-5]. Ruminants such as cattle and sheep are particularly vulnerable, but nitrate poisoning may also occur in other animals and even, under exceptional circumstances, in infants. Fatalities are most likely when hungry animals are allowed to consume large quantities of the fresh or dried plants in a short period[3-5]. It is not only *Amaranthus* species that cause nitrate poisoning. Several cultivated food and fodder plants, including beetroot, rapeseed, Sudan grass, sorghum, oats, rye, wheat and even maize may accumulate high levels of nitrate[4]. Soil type, soil nitrate level, the growth stage of the plant, even temperature and rainfall may influence the nitrate concentration in the fodder. Plants are actually only a minor source of nitrate poisoning when compared to contaminated water[4].

POISONOUS INGREDIENTS It is ironic that a highly nutritious leaf vegetable[6] such as *A. hybridus* should be the cause of lethal poisoning in ruminants. High levels of nitrate are responsible for the toxic effects, but *A. reflexus* is reported to also contain high levels of calcium oxalate[7] (see *Oxalis* species, p. 162).

PHARMACOLOGICAL EFFECTS Poisoning occurs when microorganisms in the rumen of the animal convert the relatively non-toxic nitrate to nitrite[4]. Nitrite is usually converted to ammonia, but if the balance is disturbed by large quantities of nitrate, then nitrite may accumulate to toxic levels. It may be absorbed into the bloodstream, where it adversely affects the oxygen transport capacity of red blood cells (through oxidation of haemoglobin). This leads to a typical dark-brown discolouration of the blood and carcass evident in post-mortem examinations[4,5]. Nitrate may also cause dilation of blood vessels and a drop in blood pressure[4].

DISTRIBUTION *Amaranthus* species are cosmopolitan weeds that are widely distributed in many parts of the world. The wild form of *A. hybridus* occurs over most of southern Africa (see map), but introduced forms and other species (mainly of South American origin) are commonly encountered, particularly in disturbed places[1,2].

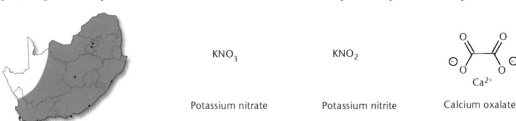

KNO₃

Potassium nitrate

KNO₂

Potassium nitrite

Ca²⁺

Calcium oxalate

1. **Brenan, J.P.M. 1981.** The genus *Amaranthus* in southern Africa. *Jl S. Afr. Bot.* 47: 451-492.
2. **Henderson, M. & Anderson, J.G. 1966.** *Common Weeds in South Africa. Memoirs of the Botanical Survey of South Africa* 37.
3. **Steyn, D.G. 1949.** *Die Vergiftiging van Mens en Dier.* Van Schaik, Pretoria.
4. **Kellerman, T.S., Coetzer, J.A.W. & Naudé, T.W. 1988.** *Plant Poisonings and Mycotoxicoses of Livestock in Southern Africa.* Oxford University Press, Cape Town, and references cited therein.
5. **Vahrmeijer, J. 1981.** *Poisonous Plants of Southern Africa That Cause Stock Losses.* Tafelberg Publishers, Cape Town.
6. **Van Wyk, B-E. & Gericke, N. 2000.** *People's Plants. A Guide to Useful Plants of Southern Africa,* Chapter 4 (Vegetables). Briza Publications, Pretoria.
7. **Harborne, J.B., Baxter, H. & Moss, G.P. (eds) 1997.** *Dictionary of Plant Toxins.* John Wiley & Sons, Chichester.

Young plant of *Amaranthus hybridus* (wild form)

Amaranthus hybridus (wild form)

Amaranthus thunbergii

AMARYLLIS BELLADONNA

Amaryllidaceae

March lily, belladonna lily (English); Maartblom, belladonnalelie (Afrikaans)

DESCRIPTION The March lily is a robust bulbous plant with strap-shaped leaves that die down each year. In late summer and autumn, when the bulbs are leafless, the thick, bright red flowering stalk emerges from the ground. The spectacular flowers are large, trumpet-shaped and pale to dark pink[1]. Another toxic bulb of the Amaryllidaceae is *Ammocharis coranica*. It is similar to *Amaryllis* but the leaves are present during flowering.

TYPE OF TOXIN Isoquinoline alkaloids (Amaryllidaceae type).

IMPORTANCE *Amaryllis* bulbs and seeds are very poisonous – 200 g of fresh bulb result in fatal poisoning of sheep[2]. Schoolchildren are known to have died from eating bulbs of Amaryllidaceae, but the plants were not properly identified[2]. There are no clearly recorded cases of fatal poisoning in humans[2-4], but care should be taken when growing the plant as an ornamental bulb and cut flower. *Ammocharis coranica* is highly toxic but rarely leads to poisoning. In the Kalahari, the pounded bulb is mixed with water and taken as an emetic.

POISONOUS INGREDIENTS Ambelline is known to be the major alkaloid *of A. belladonna*[5,6], but the plant also contains lycorine, caranine, acetylcaranine

and undulatine. Some sources[4] consider lycorine (see *Clivia*, p. 70) to be the major alkaloid, and it is possible that there are regional and seasonal variations. The major alkaloid of *Ammocharis* is lycorine, but it also contains acetylcaranine, caranine, crinamine and other alkaloids[5,7].

PHARMACOLOGICAL EFFECTS The major alkaloid of *Amaryllis*, ambelline, has analgesic activity similar to that of morphine but it is much too toxic to be used in modern medicine[8]. When injected into mice, the LD_{50} was found to be 5 mg/kg body-weight[8]. Lycorine is highly toxic, and is frequently responsible for accidental poisoning by daffodil bulbs. The LD_{50} in dogs is 41 mg/kg body-weight[8]. One of the alkaloids, anhydrolycorinium chloride, has significant antineoplastic activity[9]. Acetylcaranine is a uterine stimulant and is active against some forms of leukaemia, while caranine causes respiratory paralysis and death in animals[8].

DISTRIBUTION *A. belladonna* occurs naturally only in the winter rainfall region of the south Western and Eastern Cape Provinces[1], while *Ammocharis* is widely distributed in the eastern and central interior of South Africa. *A. belladonna* is popular as a garden ornamental and is now cultivated in so many parts of the world that few people are aware of its origin.

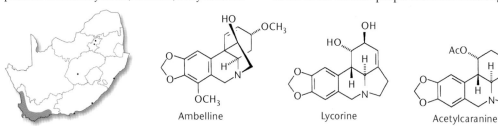

Ambelline   Lycorine   Acetylcaranine

1. **Dyer, R.A. 1955.** *Amaryllis belladonna. Flowering Plants of Africa* 30: t.1200.
2. **Steyn, D.G. 1934.** *The Toxicology of Plants in South Africa.* Central News Agency, South Africa.
3. **Steyn, D.G. 1949.** *Die Vergiftiging van Mens en Dier.* Van Schaik, Pretoria.
4. **Watt, J.M. & Breyer-Brandwijk, M.G. 1962.** *The Medicinal and Poisonous Plants of Southern and Eastern Africa,* 2nd edition. Livingstone, London.
5. **Mason, L.H., Puschett, E.R. & Wildman, W.C. 1955.** Alkaloids of the Amaryllidaceae. IV. Crystalline alkaloids of *Ammocharis coranica* (Ker-Gawl.) Herb., *Brunsvigia rosea* (Lam.) Hannibal and two *Crinium* species. *J. Amer. Chem. Soc.* 77: 1253-1256.
6. **Naegeli, P., Warnhoff, E.W., Fales, H.M., Lyle, R.E. & Wildman W.C. 1963.** Ambelline. *J. Org. Chem.* 28: 206-210.
7. **Koorbanally, N., Mulholland, D.A. & Crouch, N. 2000.** Alkaloids and triterpenoids from *Ammocharis coranica* (Amaryllidaceae). *Phytochemistry* 54: 93-97.
8. **Harborne, J.B., Baxter, H. & Moss, G.P. (eds) 1997.** *Dictionary of Plant Toxins.* John Wiley & Sons, Chichester.
9. **Pettit, G.R., Gaddamidi, V., Goswami, A. & Cragg, G.M. 1984.** Antineoplastic agents, 99. *Amaryllis belladonna. J. Nat. Prod.* 47: 796-801.

Amaryllis belladonna

Ammocharis coranica

ARGEMONE OCHROLEUCA
Papaveraceae

---

prickly poppy, Mexican poppy (English); bloudissel (Afrikaans)

DESCRIPTION This troublesome weed is a robust annual herb of up to 1 m in height, with prickly grey stems and leaves containing a bright yellow sap[1]. The flowers are pale yellow or cream-coloured and the thorny fruit capsules are oblong in shape. They contain numerous black seeds. *A. mexicana* also occurs as a weed in South Africa. It is easily distinguished from *A. ochroleuca* (previously known as *A. subfusiformis*) by the bright yellow flowers, the more thinly textured leaves and the broader fruit capsules[1].

TYPE OF TOXIN Isoquinoline alkaloid.

IMPORTANCE *Argemone* seeds are known to have caused human fatalities in the north-western parts of the Cape as a result of wheat contamination[2,3]. The plants are prickly and unpalatable to domestic animals, so that it does not really pose a serious threat[4]. Chickens, however, are vulnerable when they are fed on contaminated grain[2,3]. The bright yellow sap of the plant has been widely used for medicinal purposes[3]. In South Africa it has been used for its narcotic properties, and also against eczema, itch and other skin disorders. The seeds are narcotic, emetic, sedative and purgative[3]. In India, the seed is a common adulterant of both mustard seed and mustard seed oil, resulting in a condition known as epidemic dropsy[2,3].

POISONOUS INGREDIENTS The whole plant of *Argemone* species contains the toxic isoquinoline alkaloids berberine and protopine[3,5], while sanguinarine is concentrated in the seeds[6].

PHARMACOLOGICAL EFFECTS In humans, poisoning by seeds may lead to vomiting, diarrhoea, blurred vision, and in chronic cases, swollen legs and other serious symptoms[2,3]. About 8,8 ml seed oil per kg body-weight is required to produce toxic effects, and symptoms tend to appear only after seeds or seed oil have been ingested over a period of a week or more[3]. In poultry, the tips of the wattles become purple and swollen, and there may be extensive oedema and congestion of the internal organs[2]. Berberine is moderately toxic but has pronounced effects on the respiratory system[3]. Protopine has powerful stimulation effects on the heart and uterus[3]. Sanguinarine is toxic and has an LD_{50} of about 18 mg/kg when injected into mice and has been linked to the development of glaucoma in India in people who consume adulterated mustard oil[3,6,7].

DISTRIBUTION *A. ochroleuca* is exceptionally common and occurs practically throughout southern Africa. It often forms dense stands on old lands. The closely related *A. mexicana* is found mainly along the coastal parts of KwaZulu-Natal[1].

Berberine   Sanguinarine

1. **Henderson, L. 2001.** *Alien Weeds and Invasive Plants.* Plant Protection Research Institute Handbook no. 12, Agricultural Research Council, Pretoria.
2. **Steyn, D.G. 1949.** *Die Vergiftiging van Mens en Dier.* Van Schaik, Pretoria.
3. **Watt, J.M. & Breyer-Brandwijk, M.G. 1962.** *The Medicinal and Poisonous Plants of Southern and Eastern Africa,* 2nd edition. Livingstone, London.
4. **Kellerman, T.S., Coetzer, J.A.W. & Naudé, T.W. 1988.** *Plant Poisonings and Mycotoxicoses of Livestock in Southern Africa.* Oxford University Press, Cape Town.
5. **Stermitz, F.R. 1967.** Alkaloids of the Papaveraceae. V. Muramine and berberine from *Argemone squarrosa. J. Pharm. Sci.* 56: 760-762.
6. **Dalvi, R.R. 1985.** Sanguinarine: its potential as a liver toxic alkaloid present in the seeds of *Argemone mexicana. Experientia* 41: 77-78.
7. **Harborne, J.B., Baxter, H. & Moss, G.P. (eds) 1997.** *Dictionary of Plant Toxins.* John Wiley & Sons, Chichester.

Flowers and fruits of *Argemone ochroleuca*

The yellow sap of *Argemone ochroleuca*

Argemone mexicana

Argemone ochroleuca

ASCLEPIAS FRUTICOSA
Asclepiadaceae

milkweed (English); melkbos, tontelbos (Afrikaans); umsinga-lwesalukazi (Zulu); lebegana, lereke-la-ntja (Sotho); modimolo (Southern Sotho)

DESCRIPTION The common milkweed is an erect, multi-stemmed shrub of up to 2 m in height, with long, thin stems and narrow, opposite leaves[1]. All parts of the plant produce white latex when broken. Greenish-yellow flowers are borne in pendulous clusters, followed by large, bladdery fruits. The fruit is inflated, has a narrow tip and sparse, wiry hairs occur on the surface. The silky hairs on the seeds have been used for tinder (*tontel* in Afrikaans). A second species, *A. physocarpa*, is also known to be poisonous. It differs from *A. fruticosa* in the white, not yellow flowers and globose fruits that lack narrow tips.

TYPE OF TOXIN Cardiac glycoside (cardenolide).

IMPORTANCE *Asclepias* species are toxic to cattle and sheep but cases of poisoning are rare, because the plants are unpalatable and animals do not normally feed on them[2-7]. Some stock losses have occurred under extreme conditions of drought. *A. physocarpa* is known to have caused the death of calves in KwaZulu-Natal[3]. Powdered leaves and roots of both species have been used as snuff to treat headache and tuberculosis[7].

POISONOUS INGREDIENTS The major compounds of *A. fruticosa* are gomphoside and afroside[8] and it is likely that these or similar cardiac glycosides are also present in *A. physocarpa*.

PHARMACOLOGICAL EFFECTS *A. fruticosa* is toxic to animals but only in large quantities. Animals develop respiratory problems and severe gastro-enteritis[2,3,7]. *A. physocarpa* is quite toxic[2-7] and about 300 g[3] (or 1 772 g fed over a period of five days[6]) are said to be sufficient to kill a sheep. The symptoms are fever, paralysis, respiratory problems, and a rapid but weak heartbeat[2,3,7].

DISTRIBUTION *A. fruticosa* is an indigenous plant but has become a troublesome weed over most parts of South Africa[1]. It is usually found in disturbed places such as roadsides and abandoned fields. *A. physocarpa* has a more limited distribution in the eastern parts of South Africa.

Gomphoside: R=H
Afroside: R=OH

1. **Henderson, M. & Anderson, J.G. 1966.** *Common Weeds in South Africa. Memoirs of the Botanical Survey of South Africa* 37.
2. **Steyn, D.G. 1934.** *The Toxicology of Plants in South Africa.* Central News Agency, South Africa.
3. **Steyn, D.G. 1949.** *Die Vergiftiging van Mens en Dier.* Van Schaik, Pretoria.
4. **Kellerman, T.S., Coetzer, J.A.W. & Naudé, T.W. 1988.** *Plant Poisonings and Mycotoxicoses of Livestock in Southern Africa.* Oxford University Press, Cape Town.
5. **Vahrmeijer, J. 1981.** *Poisonous Plants of Southern Africa That Cause Stock Losses.* Tafelberg Publishers, Cape Town.
6. **Verdcourt, B. & Trump, E.C. 1969.** *Common Poisonous Plants of East Africa.* Collins, London.
7. **Watt, J.M. & Breyer-Brandwijk, M.G. 1962.** *The Medicinal and Poisonous Plants of Southern and Eastern Africa*, 2nd edition. Livingstone, London.
8. **Cheung, H.T.A., Coombe, R.G., Sidwell, W.L.T. & Watson, T.R. 1981.** Afroside, a 15β-hydroxycardenolide. *J. Chem. Soc. Perkin Trans. I*, 1981: 64-72, and references cited therein.

Asclepias fruticosa

Asclepias physocarpa

ATHANASIA MINUTA

Asteraceae

---

vuursiektebossie (Afrikaans); fire sickness bush (English)

DESCRIPTION The plant is a woody, much-branched, untidy shrub of about 50 cm in height and has the branch tips modified to form sharp spines. The leaves are long, very narrow and somewhat fleshy. A distinct feature is the stalkless (sessile) flower heads, which bear inconspicuous, yellowish flowers[1]. The plant was previously known as *Asaemia minuta* or *Asaemia axillaris* but has now been included in the genus *Athanasia*[1]. It is interesting to note that *Athanasia trifurcata*, a weedy species from the south-western parts of the Cape, is also known to cause stock losses and photosensitisation in sheep[2]. This plant is common on old lands and is well known by the Afrikaans name *Klaaslouwbos*. It has an erect growth form and long narrow leaves with distinctive forked tips[1].

TYPE OF TOXIN Unknown.

IMPORTANCE The plant causes outbreaks of poisoning known as *vuursiekte* ('fire sickness') that may lead to photosensitivity, liver damage and death in sheep[2,3]. Animals would not normally feed on *A. minuta* except when forced to do so by drought – outbreaks of poisoning therefore do not occur very often[3]. The value and agricultural potential of grazing farms are lowered by the presence of dense stands of the shrubs. Cases of poisoning by *A.*

trifurcata are also quite rare. Sheep grazing on old lands infested with *A. trifurcata* may become photosensitive and develop symptoms not unlike that of *vuursiekte*[2].

POISONOUS INGREDIENTS Nothing appears to be known about the chemical compounds of *A. minuta*. Several terpenoids are known from *Athanasia* species and terpenoids or coumarins may possibly be responsible for the photosensitivity observed in sheep.

PHARMACOLOGICAL EFFECTS The symptoms and clinical signs of *Athanasia* poisoning are well documented[2-6]. Symptoms can become evident three days after animals are introduced into a camp containing *A. minuta* (or after two days in the case of *A. trifurcata*). Signs of poisoning include apathy, icterus (jaundice), intensely yellow urine and photosensitivity, with serious liver damage.

DISTRIBUTION *A. minuta* occurs naturally over large parts of the dry western half of South Africa and into southern Namibia[1]. It is usually found in low-lying areas (vleis and pans), often near permanent or temporary water. *A. trifurcata* occurs only in the fynbos and adjoining renosterveld areas of the Cape[1].

1. **Kallersjo, M. 1991.** The genus *Athanasia* (Compositae-Anthemideae). *Opera Bot.* 106: 15-75.
2. **Kellerman, T.S., Coetzer, J.A.W. & Naudé, T.W. 1988.** *Plant Poisonings and Mycotoxicoses of Livestock in Southern Africa*. Oxford University Press, Cape Town.
3. **Vahrmeijer, J. 1981.** *Poisonous Plants of Southern Africa That Cause Stock Losses*. Tafelberg Publishers, Cape Town.
4. **Kellerman, T.S., Basson, P.A., Naudé, T.W., Van Rensburg, I.B.R. & Welman, W.G. 1973.** Photosensitivity in South Africa. I. A comparative study of *Asaemia axillaris* (Thunb.) Harv. ex Jackson and *Lasiospermum bipinnatum* (Thunb.) Druce poisoning in sheep. *Onderstepoort J. Vet. Res.* 40: 115-126.
5. **Kellerman, T.S., Coetzer, J.A.W., Schneider, D.J. & Welman, W.G. 1983.** Photosensitivity in South Africa. III. Ovine hepatogenous photosensitivity caused by the plant *Athanasia trifurcata* L. (Asteraceae). *Onderstepoort J. Vet. Res.* 50: 47-52.
6. **Coetzer, J.A.W. & Bergh T. 1983.** Photosensitivity in South Africa. IV. Pathological changes in the liver in ovine photosensitivity caused by the plant *Asaemia axillaris* (Thunb.) Harv. ex Jackson. *Onderstepoort J. Vet. Res.* 50: 55-58.

Athanasia minuta

Flower heads of *Athanasia minuta*

Athanasia trifurcata

BOOPHANE DISTICHA
Amaryllidaceae

bushman poison bulb (English); gifbol (Afrikaans); incotha (Zulu);
incwadi (Xhosa); leshoma (Southern Sotho, Tswana); muwandwe (Shona)

DESCRIPTION This distinctive plant has a large bulb growing partly above the ground, from which the symmetrically arranged leaves emerge after flowering[1]. The bulb is easily recognised by the thick layers of papery scales surrounding the fleshy inner part. Attractive pink to reddish flowers are borne in a rounded inflorescence but the plants do not flower every year.

TYPE OF TOXIN Isoquinoline alkaloid (Amaryllidaceae type).

IMPORTANCE *B. disticha* is perhaps the most important and interesting of all southern African poisonous plants. It is extremely toxic and has been the cause of several human fatalities resulting from murder, suicide or accidental poisoning by traditional medicine[2,3]. It is one of the most prominent arrow poisons of southern Africa[4-6] and of considerable ethnobotanical[6] interest as a hallucinogen and in traditional medicine. One of the main medicinal uses is the treatment of painful wounds[2]. A recent discovery of 2 000-year-old human (Khoi-San) remains mummified with *Boophane* bulb scales[7], testifies to the historical and cultural importance of the plant in South Africa.

POISONOUS INGREDIENTS The main toxin is buphanidrine, but the bulb yields at least 10 other alkaloids, such as undulatin, buphanisine, acetyl-nerbowdine and buphanimine[8,9].

PHARMACOLOGICAL EFFECTS Buphanidrine is a powerful analgesic, hallucinogen[10] and neurotoxin, with a lethal dose of less that 10 mg/kg in mice. Symptoms of poisoning are well documented[2] and include dizziness, restlessness, impaired vision, unsteady gait, visual hallucinations, and finally coma and death.

DISTRIBUTION *B. disticha* is widely distributed in the southern and eastern parts of South Africa and further north into tropical Africa. It is usually found in open grassland.

Buphanidrine   3-Acetylnerbowdine

1. **Leighton, F.M. 1947.** Plantae novae africanae. *Jl S. Afr. Bot.* 13: 59-60.
2. **Watt, J.M. & Breyer-Brandwijk, M.G. 1962.** *The Medicinal and Poisonous Plants of Southern and Eastern Africa*, 2nd edition. Livingstone, London.
3. **Gordon, I. 1947.** A case of fatal buphanine poisoning. *Clin. Proc.*, Cape Town 6: 90-93.
4. **Schapera, I. 1925.** Bushmen arrow poisons. *Bantu Stud.* 2: 190-214.
5. **Neuwinger, H.D. 1996.** *African Ethnobotany: Poisons and Drugs: Chemistry, Pharmacology, Toxicology.* Chapman & Hall, Germany.
6. **Van Wyk, B-E. & Gericke, N. 2000.** *People's Plants. A Guide to Useful Plants of Southern Africa.* Briza Publications, Pretoria.
7. **Binneman, J. 1999.** Mummified human remains from the Kouga mountains, Eastern Cape. *The Digging Stick* (Newsletter of the Archaeological Society of South Africa) 16: 1-2.
8. **Hauth, H. and Stauffacher, D. 1961.** Die Alkaloide von *Buphane disticha* (L.F.) Herb. *Helv. Chim. Acta*, 44: 491-497.
9. **Hauth, H. & Stauffacher, D. 1963.** The structure of acetylnerbowdine. *Helv. Chim. Acta* 46: 810-812.
10. **De Smet, P.A. 1996.** Some ethnopharmacological notes on African hallucinogens. *J. Ethnopharmacol.* 50: 141-146.

Boophane disticha

Flowers of *Boophane disticha*

Bulb of *Boophane disticha*

BOWIEA VOLUBILIS

Hyacinthaceae

---

climbing potato (English); knolklimop (Afrikaans); igibisila (Zulu); umagaqana (Xhosa)

DESCRIPTION *B. volubilis* is a peculiar plant with greenish-white, fleshy bulbs borne partly above the ground. The bulb scales are not papery or fibrous but fleshy. An interesting feature is the succulent, twining, leafless flowering stems (inflorescence) that form the main above-ground part of the plant. It bears small, greenish flowers[1] that eventually turn into small, two-locular capsules with numerous black seeds.

TYPE OF TOXIN Cardiac glycoside (bufadienolide).

IMPORTANCE *Bowiea* bulbs are extremely toxic and have been the cause of numerous fatalities in humans and animals[2-5]. Death may occur within a few minutes. The bulbs are commonly sold as traditional medicine and are used for a variety of ailments[6]. As a result, it often leads to fatal poisoning through overdose[4]. Cases of livestock poisoning are rare[7].

POISONOUS INGREDIENTS Several cardiac glycosides are known from *Bowiea*, all structurally related to bovoside A, the main bufadienolide[8].

PHARMACOLOGICAL EFFECTS Symptoms of poisoning are vomiting, purging, excessive salivation, and irregular heart palpitations[4]. The major heart glycoside, bovoside A, has an LD_{50} in cats of 0,12 mg/kg body-weight[9]. In sheep, a mere half an ounce (*ca.* 15 g) of fresh bulb can be fatal[3].

DISTRIBUTION *B. volubilis* is widely distributed in the eastern parts of South Africa. A closely related species, *B. gariepensis*, occurs on the border between South Africa and Namibia[1].

Bovoside A

---

1. **Van Jaarsveld, E.J. 1983.** *Bowiea gariepensis & Bowiea volubilis. Jl. S. Afr. Bot.* 49: 343-346.
2. **Steyn, D.G. 1934.** *The Toxicology of Plants in South Africa.* Central News Agency, South Africa.
3. **Steyn, D.G. 1949.** *Die Vergiftiging van Mens en Dier.* Van Schaik, Pretoria.
4. **Watt, J.M. & Breyer-Brandwijk, M.G. 1962.** *The Medicinal and Poisonous Plants of Southern and Eastern Africa*, 2nd edition. Livingstone, London.
5. **Verdcourt, B. & Trump, E.C. 1969.** *Common Poisonous Plants of East Africa.* Collins, London.
6. **Van Wyk, B-E., Van Oudtshoorn, B. & Gericke, N. 2000.** *Medicinal Plants of South Africa*, 2nd edition. Briza Publications, Pretoria, and references cited therein.
7. **Kellerman, T.S., Coetzer, J.A.W. & Naudé, T.W. 1988.** *Plant Poisonings and Mycotoxicoses of Livestock in Southern Africa.* Oxford University Press, Cape Town.
8. **Katz, A. 1954.** Über die Glykoside von *Bowiea volubilis* Harv. *Helv. Chim. Acta* 37: 832-836.
9. **Harborne, J.B., Baxter, H. & Moss, G.P. (eds) 1997.** *Dictionary of Plant Toxins.* John Wiley & Sons, Chichester.

Bulbs of *Bowiea volubilis*

Flowers of *Bowiea volubilis*

Fruits of *Bowiea volubilis*

BRABEJUM STELLATIFOLIUM

Proteaceae

---

wild almond (English); wilde amandel (Afrikaans)

DESCRIPTION Wild almond is a robust shrub with characteristic toothed leaves arranged in groups of four to nine at each node[1]. Clusters of small, white flowers are followed by golden brown, velvety fruits. Jan van Riebeeck, the first Dutch settler at the Cape, planted a famous hedge of wild almond in 1660. Parts of this hedge are still visible at the National Botanical Gardens, Kirstenbosch, and have been declared a national monument.

TYPE OF TOXIN Cyanogenic glycoside.

IMPORTANCE Wild almonds are said to have been a popular food in the Cape, but a lengthy leaching process was needed to make them edible and to wash out the toxic substances[2,3]. Seeds have also been used as a coffee substitute after soaking, boiling and then roasting[2,3]. Some fatalities have occurred after eating wild almonds[3,4]. The first death was reported in 1655, when one of Van Riebeeck's men died from eating too many wild almonds. In 1862, a six-year-old girl died after ingesting an unspecified number of kernels[3]. In Europe and America, numerous cases and some fatalities are regularly reported, resulting from the ingestion of bitter almonds (*Prunus dulcis* var. *amara*, family Rosaceae) and seed kernels of other fruits such as plum and peach containing amygdalin and other cyanogenic glycosides[5].

POISONOUS INGREDIENTS Wild almond is thought to contain cyanogenic glycosides but the active compounds appear to be unknown[2,3]. Bitter almonds and seed kernels of the genus *Prunus* contain two cyanogenic glycosides, amygdalin and prunasin[5]. Amygdalin is also known from the underground parts of *Gerbera jamesonii* cultivars[6].

PHARMACOLOGICAL EFFECTS Symptoms of poisoning are poorly known but do not appear to be typical of hydrocyanic acid poisoning[3].

DISTRIBUTION *B. stellatifolium* is restricted to the Western Cape Province[1].

Amygdalin

Prunasin

1. **Rebelo, T. 1995.** *Sasol Proteas: a Field Guide to the Proteas of Southern Africa.* Fernwood Press, Cape Town.
2. **Steyn, D.G. 1949.** *Die Vergiftiging van Mens en Dier.* Van Schaik, Pretoria.
3. **Watt, J.M. & Breyer-Brandwijk, M.G. 1962.** *The Medicinal and Poisonous Plants of Southern and Eastern Africa*, 2nd edition. Livingstone, London.
4. **Van Wyk, B-E. & Gericke, N. 2000.** *People's Plants. A Guide to Useful Plants of Southern Africa.* Briza Publications, Pretoria.
5. **Bruneton, J. 1999.** *Toxic Plants Dangerous to Humans and Animals.* Intercept, Hampshire.
6. **Harborne, J.B., Baxter, H. & Moss, G.P. (eds) 1997.** *Dictionary of Plant Toxins.* John Wiley & Sons, Chichester.

Flowers of *Brabejum stellatifolium*

Fruits of *Brabejum stellatifolium*

Seeds (nuts) of *Brabejum stellatifolium*

CALLILEPIS LAUREOLA

Asteraceae

---

impila, ihlmvu (Zulu); ox-eye daisy (English)

DESCRIPTION *Impila* is an attractive shrub of about 50 cm in height, with erect, leafy branches arising from a permanent woody base. The large and striking flower heads have dark purple central florets and a ring of pale yellow to white ray florets[1]. The thick, tapering taproots are harvested and sold on muti markets.

TYPE OF TOXIN Diterpenoid.

IMPORTANCE *C. laureola* is well known by the Zulu name *impila*, which means health. It is a popular traditional medicine[2] but is also a common cause of human fatalities[3,4]. According to a newspaper report (*The Star*, 21 August 1979) 263 known deaths were recorded in the King Edward Hospital in Durban between 1958 and 1977. Death occurs within five days and results from acute liver and kidney damage. Half the recorded fatalities were children below the age of 15. The symptoms are severe vomiting, abdominal pain, headache, convulsions, and rapid progression into coma. *Impila* is commonly sold on street markets as a cough remedy and there are regular casualties, because it is no longer used within the safeguards of traditional cultural practices[4]. Traditionally, *impila* is

never given to children under the age of 10. It should not be administered as an enema, but only orally as a weak solution that is completely expelled through emesis (*phalaza*) immediately after being drunk[4].

POISONOUS INGREDIENTS The main poisonous principle is atractyloside, a kaurene glycoside[5] that is structurally related to carboxyparquin and parquin, the toxic metabolites of *Cestrum parqui* (see p. 62). Three other kaurenoid glucosides (all derivatives of atractyloside) have been found in the plant[6].

PHARMACOLOGICAL EFFECTS Atractyloside is highly toxic in mammals and produce strychnine-like symptoms[7]. The LD_{50} is reported to be 431 mg/kg body-weight when administered intra-muscularly to rats[7,8]. The pure compound is used in scientific experiments because it is a specific inhibitor of ADP transport at the mitochondrial membrane[7,8].

DISTRIBUTION *C. laureola* occurs in the eastern and north-eastern parts of South Africa, from the Eastern Cape Province to Mpumalanga.

Atractyloside

1. **Hilliard, O.M. 1977.** *Compositae in Natal*. University of Natal Press, Pietermaritzburg.
2. **Watt, J.M. & Breyer-Brandwijk, M.G. 1962.** *The Medicinal and Poisonous Plants of Southern and Eastern Africa*, 2nd edition. Livingstone, London.
3. **Wainwright, J., Schonland, M.M. & Candy, H.A. 1977.** Toxicity of *Callilepis laureola*. *S. Afr. Med. J.* 52: 313-315.
4. **Popat, A., Shear, N.H., Malkiewicz, I, Stewart, M.J., Steenkamp, V., Thomson, S. & Neuman, M.G. 2001.** The toxicity of *Callilepis laureola*, a South African traditional herbal medicine. *Clinical Biochem.* 34: 229-236, and references cited therein.
5. **Candy, H.A., Pegel, K.H., Brookes, B. & Rodwell, M. 1977.** The occurrence of atractyloside in *Callilepis laureola*. *Phytochemistry* 16: 1308-1309.
6. **Brookes, K.B., Candy, H.A. & Pegel, K.H. 1983.** Atractylosides in *Callilepis laureola* (Asteraceae). *S. Afr. J. Chem.* 36: 65-68.
7. **Harborne, J.B., Baxter, H. & Moss, G.P. (eds) 1997.** *Dictionary of Plant Toxins*. John Wiley & Sons, Chichester.
8. **Merck 1989.** *The Merck Index*, 11th edition. Merck, Rahway.

Callilepis laureola

Flower heads of *Callilepis laureola*

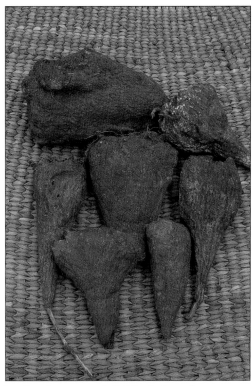

Impila, the roots of *Callilepis laureola*

CATHARANTHUS ROSEUS

Apocynaceae

Madagascar periwinkle (English); isisushlungu (Zulu); begraafplaasblom (Afrikaans)

DESCRIPTION *C. roseus* is a perennial herb with dark green, glossy leaves and attractive flowers ranging from white to pink or purple in colour[1]. It has become a popular ornamental plant and several colour forms have been developed by plant breeders.

TYPE OF TOXIN Indole alkaloid.

IMPORTANCE *C. roseus* (previously known as *Vinca rosea*) contains highly toxic alkaloids but cases of human or livestock poisoning are rare. It is better known as a source of medicinally important alkaloids, the so-called vinca alkaloids, used in the treatment of diabetes and cancer. *Catharanthus* was traditionally used to treat diabetes, and the anticancer activity was discovered quite by chance while scientists were studying the antihypoglycemic effects of extracts from the plant[2]. A tricyclic *Catharanthus* alkaloid, norharman, occurs in *Tribulus terrestris* and causes locomotor effects in sheep[3].

POISONOUS INGREDIENTS The plant contains a complex mixture of indole alkaloids. Some of these, such as catharanthine, leurosine and vindolinine have antidiabetic effects[4]. Binary alkaloids such as vincristine and vinblastine are used in cancer chemotherapy[2,5].

PHARMACOLOGICAL EFFECTS The indole alkaloids of *Catharanthus* are highly active and have a range of biological effects. Catharanthine and related alkaloids are hypoglycemic. Vinblastine has central and peripheral neurotoxic effects[2,3]. It is an irritant of the skin and respiratory tract and causes damage to the cornea of the eye. Medically it is used to treat Hodgkin's disease and other lymphomas. Vincristine is used in combined therapy to treat leukaemia, Hodgkin's disease and other forms of cancer. Vincristine and vinblastine are both extremely poisonous, with an LD_{50} of a mere 1 mg/kg when injected into rats[2,3], with slightly higher values reported in mice[6].

DISTRIBUTION This popular garden plant originally comes from Madagascar but has become a weed in tropical and subtropical regions of the world. It is also grown in gardens in South Africa and is nowadays commonly found as a roadside weed, particularly in KwaZulu-Natal and Mpumalanga.

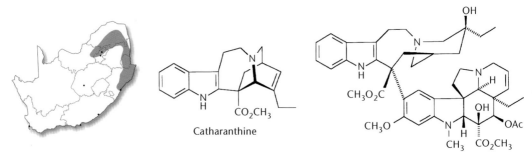

Catharanthine

Vinblastine

1. **Codd, L.E. 1963.** Apocynaceae. 7. *Catharanthus. Flora of Southern Africa* 26, pp. 267-268. Botanical Research Institute, Pretoria.
2. **Noble, R.L. 1990.** The discovery of the vinca alkaloids – chemotherapeutic agents against cancer. *Biochem. Cell. Biol.* 68: 1344-1351.
3. **Harborne, J.B., Baxter, H. & Moss, G.P. (eds) 1997.** *Dictionary of Plant Toxins.* John Wiley & Sons, Chichester.
4. **Marles, R.J. & Farnsworth, N.R. 1995.** Antidiabetic plants and their active constituents. *Phytomedicine* 2: 137-189.
5. **Bruneton, J. 1999.** *Pharmacognosy, Phytochemistry, Medicinal Plants,* 2nd edition. Intercept, Hampshire.
6. **Merck 1989.** *The Merck Index.* 11th edition. Merck, Rahway.

Catharanthus roseus – normal wild form

Catharanthus roseus – white form

Catharanthus roseus – garden form

CESTRUM LAEVIGATUM

Solanaceae

inkberry (English); inkbessie (Afrikaans)

DESCRIPTION The plant is usually a shrub of about 2 m in height but it may become a small tree. The leaves are about 50 mm wide and emit a strong unpleasant smell. Clusters of tubular, greenish-yellow flowers are produced in the axils of the leaves. They are followed by small, oval berries of about 10 mm long, which turn from green to purple-black when they ripen. *C. laevigatum* is closely related to *C. parqui* and differs only in the narrower leaves (up to 25 mm wide) and the fact that the flower clusters are borne on the branch tips as well as the leaf axils[1]. *C. aurantiacum* has orange-yellow flowers and white berries.

TYPE OF TOXIN Diterpenoid.

IMPORTANCE *C. laevigatum* and other species commonly cause livestock poisoning[2-6]. Stock losses have been ascribed to *C. aurantiacum*[4], *C. laevigatum* and *C. parqui*. Several cases were reported from the Chase Valley near Pietermaritzburg, where the poisoning is known as Chase Valley Disease[2,3]. Plants produce young growth and green berries in June and July (a time when grazing is scarce) so that livestock losses usually occur during this period[2,3,5,6]. The toxin is not lost in dried plant material and hedge clippings may be particularly dangerous. Human poisoning is rare, but green berries are said to have caused fatalities in children[2].

POISONOUS INGREDIENTS The toxicity of *Cestrum* species can be attributed to carboxyparquin, an extremely poisonous terpenoid. It is one of two kaurene glycosides isolated from dried leaves of *C. parqui* (the other is parquin, said to be much less toxic)[7]. There is a close similarity between the structures of these two compounds and the structure of atractyloside, the toxic principle of *Callilepis laureola*. The toxic compounds of *Cestrum laevigatum* have not been studied in detail.

PHARMACOLOGICAL EFFECTS Poisoning with *C. laevigatum* usually produces death within a few hours[2,5]. Symptoms in cattle include salivation, watery eyes, colic, arched back, weakness, staggering gait and abdominal pain, with characteristic lesions of the liver. Cattle are fatally poisoned by as little as 200 g of dried leaves, while a daily dose of 15 g proved fatal to goats[5]. The LD_{50} of carboxyparquin in mice was found to be 4,3 mg/kg[7].

DISTRIBUTION *Cestrum* species were imported as ornamentals from South America but have become troublesome weeds. *C. laevigatum* now occurs over a large part of the eastern half of South Africa (see map), while *C. parqui* and *C. aurantiacum* occur sporadically, mainly in the central and extreme eastern parts of the country.

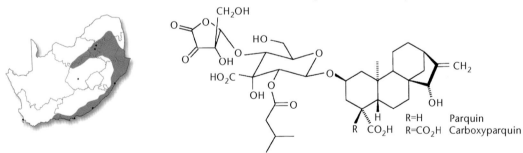

1. **Henderson, L. 2001.** *Alien Weeds and Invasive Plants.* Plant Protection Research Institute Handbook no. 12, Agricultural Research Council, Pretoria.
2. **Steyn, D.G. 1949.** *Die Vergiftiging van Mens en Dier.* Van Schaik, Pretoria.
3. **Watt, J.M. & Breyer-Brandwijk, M.G. 1962.** *The Medicinal and Poisonous Plants of Southern and Eastern Africa,* 2nd edition. Livingstone, London.
4. **Verdcourt, B. & Trump, E.C. 1969.** *Common Poisonous Plants of East Africa.* Collins, London.
5. **Kellerman, T.S., Coetzer, J.A.W. & Naudé, T.W. 1988.** *Plant Poisonings and Mycotoxicoses of Livestock in Southern Africa.* Oxford University Press, Cape Town.
6. **Vahrmeijer, J. 1981.** *Poisonous Plants of Southern Africa That Cause Stock Losses.* Tafelberg Publishers, Cape Town.
7. **Pearce, C.M., Skelton, N.J., Naylor, S., Kanaan, R., Kelland, J., Oelrichs, P.B., Sanders, J.K.M. & Williams, D.H. 1992.** Parquin and carboxyparquin, toxic glycosides from the shrub *Cestrum parqui. J. Chem. Soc., Perkin Trans. I,* 1992: 593-600.

Cestrum laevigatum

Flowers and berries of *Cestrum laevigatum*

Cestrum parqui

CHENOPODIUM MUCRONATUM

Chenopodiaceae

---

stinking goosefoot (English)

DESCRIPTION The plant is a spreading herb with green or red stems and small, greyish-green leaves. Clusters of inconspicuous flowers are produced on the branch ends. A unique feature of this species is that it emits a strong odour of decaying fish[1] – it can therefore easily be distinguished from similar-looking species. In Europe, the plant is known as *C. vulvaria*. The white goosefoot or common goosefoot (*C. album*) is an erect herb with larger leaves and no odour[2]. The latter is often used as traditional spinach (*marog*) in South Africa. *C. multifidum* is also known as stinking goosefoot in South Africa, but it has a completely different smell and is easily recognised by the deeply dissected leaves[2]. *C. ambrosioides* (wormseed goosefoot) is a native of tropical America that is known to produce essential oil with toxic components. This species has long, narrow leaves with toothed margins[2]. Another member of the family is *Beta vulgaris*, the common beetroot from temperate Europe and Asia.

TYPE OF TOXIN Amine (*C. mucronatum*), oxalate (*C. album*), essential oil (*C. ambrosioides*) and nitrate (*Beta vulgaris*).

IMPORTANCE Nothing seems to have been documented about the potential danger of *C. mucronatum* to livestock. The plant recently killed 70 sheep in the Western Cape Province (Bredasdorp-Napier area), when large quantities of material were grazed on fallow lands. Stinking goosefoot is known to be poisonous but is rarely ingested in sufficient quantity to cause problems[1]. *C. ambrosioides* is a traditional medicine, used mainly to dispel worms. It is known to be toxic if too much is taken. Beetroot leaves are sometimes the cause of nitrite poisoning in livestock in South Africa (see *Amaranthus hybridus*, p. 42).

POISONOUS INGREDIENTS The smell of the plant results from high levels of trimethylamine, a compound that is widespread in nature. The characteristic smell of fish is also due to derivatives of trimethylamine. Other compounds present are mono- and dimethylamine, as well as 1,14% betain[1]. The possibility that *Chenopodium* causes nitrite poisoning should be considered, as *Beta vulgaris* is a known culprit. The main compound in *C. ambrosioides* oil is a monoterpenoid, ascaridole.

PHARMACOLOGICAL EFFECTS The symptoms of poisoning by trimethylamine are similar to that recorded for nitrate poisoning: cerebral cramps, titanic convulsions, rapid breathing, increased blood pressure and death due to respiratory failure[1]. (For nitrate poisoning see *Amaranthus*.) Ascaridole is toxic to mammals[3].

DISTRIBUTION *Chenopodium* species occur as weeds in gardens, old lands and disturbed places over most parts of South Africa. The distribution of *C. mucronatum* is shown here.

$$H_3C - \underset{\underset{CH_3}{|}}{N} - CH_3$$

Trimethylamine

Ascaridole

Calcium oxalate

1. **Roth, L., Daunderer, M. & Kormann, K. 1994.** *Giftpflanzen Pflanzengifte,* 4th edition. Nikol, Hamburg.
2. **Henderson, M. & Anderson, J.G. 1966.** *Common Weeds in South Africa. Memoirs of the Botanical Survey of South Africa* 37.
3. **Harborne, J.B., Baxter, H. & Moss, G.P. (eds) 1997.** *Dictionary of Plant Toxins.* John Wiley & Sons, Chichester.

Chenopodium mucronatum – form with green stems

Chenopodium mucronatum – form with red stems

Chenopodium album

Chenopodium ambrosioides

CHRYSOCOMA CILIATA
Asteraceae

---

bitterbos (English); bitterbos, bitterkaroo (Afrikaans)

DESCRIPTION The *bitterbos* is a dense, rounded shrub of about 50 cm in height. The small, needle-shaped leaves are yellowish green, sticky to the touch, with a bitter taste. Bright yellow flower heads, with only central disc florets and no ray florets, are produced on the branch tips. The plant is exceptionally common and was previously known as *C. tenuifolia*[1].

TYPE OF TOXIN Unknown.

IMPORTANCE *C. ciliata* is responsible for at least two troublesome diseases in animals[2-5]. It causes *kaalsiekte* (alopecia) in lambs and kids, and *lakseersiekte* (purging disease) in adult animals (sheep, goats and cattle)[2-5]. *Kaalsiekte* occurs when pregnant goats or sheep ingest large quantities of the plant before they give birth. The toxin is passed to the young lambs through the milk, and they usually develop the disease within two weeks of birth. A characteristic symptom is hair loss, which may lead to secondary problems such as skin damage by the sun and subsequent infections, pneumonia as a result of exposure to cold and also diarrhoea[5]. Skin irritation leads to licking, and ingested hair often forms hairballs (trichobezoars) that can obstruct the rumen. *Kaalsiekte* may reach epidemic proportions in wet years when succulent

new growth makes the plants more palatable. *Lakseersiekte* (purging disease), on the other hand, is seen mostly in the winter or during droughts, when adult animals grazing on degraded veld are forced to ingest large quantities of *bitterbos*[4,5]. This disease is characterised by severe diarrhoea and the animals either die suddenly or develop chronic diarrhoea and weakness. A third condition, known as *valsiekte* (falling disease) is also associated with *C. tenuifolia*[5,6]. Young lambs develop ataxia of the hindquarters, so that they typically fall and drag their hind legs behind them[5,6]. It remains to be proven, however, that *Chrysocoma* is indeed the cause.

POISONOUS INGREDIENTS Unknown.

PHARMACOLOGICAL EFFECTS The symptoms of *kaalsiekte*[2-5], *lakseersiekte*[2-5] and *valsiekte*[5,6] have been described in detail and are only briefly summarised above, but the chemical compound(s) responsible and their physiological effects are not yet known.

DISTRIBUTION The plant is an indigenous species that has become invasive in overgrazed parts of the Karoo. It is a natural component of the vegetation but increases rapidly under conditions of overgrazing or poor veld management[7].

1. **Bayer, E. 1981.** Revision der Gattung *Chrysocoma* L. (Asteraceae – Astereae). *Mitt. Bot. Staatssaml., München* 17: 259.
2. **Steyn, D.G. 1949.** *Die Vergiftiging van Mens en Dier.* Van Schaik, Pretoria.
3. **Watt, J.M. & Breyer-Brandwijk, M.G. 1962.** *The Medicinal and Poisonous Plants of Southern and Eastern Africa*, 2nd edition. Livingstone, London.
4. **Vahrmeijer, J. 1981.** *Poisonous Plants of Southern Africa That Cause Stock Losses.* Tafelberg Publishers, Cape Town.
5. **Kellerman, T.S., Coetzer, J.A.W. & Naudé, T.W. 1988.** *Plant Poisonings and Mycotoxicoses of Livestock in Southern Africa.* Oxford University Press, Cape Town.
6. **Van der Vyfer, F.H., Kellerman, T.S., Bastianello, S.S., de Wet, J.A.L., Joubert, J.P.J. & Faul, A. 1985.** Valsiekte (falling disease): a nervous disorder in lambs suspected of being caused by the plant *Chrysocoma tenuifolia*. *J. S. Afr. Vet. Assoc.* 56: 65-68.
7. **Milton, S.J. & Dean, W.R.J. 1996.** *Karoo Veld. Ecology and Management.* Agricultural Research Institute, Pretoria.

Chrysocoma ciliata

Flower heads of *Chrysocoma ciliata*

CISSAMPELOS CAPENSIS

Menispermaceae

dawidjies, dawidjiewortel (Afrikaans)

DESCRIPTION *C. capensis* (previously known as *Antizoma capensis*) is a perennial climber with twining stems and small, heart-shaped leaves[1]. Inconspicuous, hairy, greenish flowers are produced in clusters, followed by small orange berries. *Zehneria scabra* (Cucurbitaceae) is sometimes also known as *dawidjiewortel*, but the latter is cucumber-like and can be distinguished by the coiled tendrils.

TYPE OF TOXIN Isoquinoline alkaloid (bisbenzyl-isoquinoline type).

IMPORTANCE The leaves of *C. capensis* are known to be toxic to cattle[2]. The rhizomes are used as a popular traditional remedy in the Cape, but there appear to be no records of any human poisoning. Various medicinal uses are known[2-4]. Tinctures or decoctions of the rhizome are used as blood purifiers, and also against bladder ailments, diarrhoea, dysentery, colic and glandular swellings. Leaves are applied to sores and snakebites. The leaves and rhizomes are almost certainly toxic to humans, as the latter has been used as emetics and purgatives[2]. Species such as the pantropical *C. perreira* and the closely related *C. mucronata* have been used as ingredients of arrow poisons.

POISONOUS INGREDIENTS Both the roots and leaves contain alkaloids[5]. The major component of the leaves is the proaporphine known as glaziovine, whereas the major compound in rhizomes is insularine, a bisbenzyltetrahydroisoquinoline alkaloid[5].

PHARMACOLOGICAL EFFECTS Nothing appears to be known about the effects of the main compounds in *C. capensis*. Menispermaceae alkaloids are however famous for their potent muscle relaxant properties and their use as dart and arrow poisons in forests[6]. In this way, the prey animals (typically monkeys or parrots) release their grip on the perch and fall to the ground where they can be collected. Other poisons may cause spasms so that the animal would clasp tightly onto the branches when hit by the dart or arrow and remain out of reach of the hunter. The meat is safe to eat, because the alkaloids are not absorbed in the stomach and have no effect unless they are injected into the bloodstream.

DISTRIBUTION The plant is widely distributed in the western parts of South Africa and in the southern parts of Namibia[1].

Glaziovine

Insularine

1. **Botha, D.J. 1975.** A Taxonomic Study of the South African Representatives of the Menispermaceae, pp. 80-85. Unpublished Ph.D. thesis, University of Pretoria.
2. **Watt, J.M. & Breyer-Brandwijk, M.G. 1962.** *The Medicinal and Poisonous Plants of Southern and Eastern Africa*, 2nd edition. E & S Livingstone, London.
3. **Van Wyk, B-E., Van Oudtshoorn, B. & Gericke, N. 2000.** *Medicinal Plants of South Africa*, 2nd edition. Briza Publications, Pretoria.
4. **Van Wyk, B-E. & Gericke, N. 2000.** *People's Plants. A Guide to Useful Plants of Southern Africa.* Briza Publications, Pretoria.
5. **Van Heerden, F.R., Van Wyk, B-E. & Viljoen, A.M. 2002.** Cissacapine, a new bisbenzylisoquinoline alkaloid from *Cissampelos capensis* with antiplasmodial activity. (unpublished manuscript).
6. **Lewis, W.H. & Elvin-Lewis, M.P.F. 1977.** *Medical Botany.* John Wiley, New York.

Cissampelos capensis

Flowers of *Cissampelos capensis*

Rhizomes of *Cissampelos capensis* (*dawidjiewortel*)

Cissampelos mucronata

CLIVIA MINIATA

Amaryllidaceae

bush lily, orange lily (English); boslelie (Afrikaans); umayime (Zulu)

DESCRIPTION *Clivia* species are attractive shade-loving perennials with fleshy, tuberous rhizomes and dark-green, strap-shaped leaves. The flowers of *C. miniata* are relatively large, usually dark to pale orange but sometimes yellow and all arise from the same point on the flowering stalk[1,2]. The plant is a popular garden ornamental and it is grown indoors as a pot plant in many parts of the world.

TYPE OF TOXIN Isoquinoline alkaloid (lycoranan type).

IMPORTANCE *C. miniata* rhizomes and leaves are toxic and there is a danger that children and domestic animals may be poisoned in the house. The plant is widely used in traditional medicine to help with and hasten childbirth, to treat fever and snake bite and to relieve pain[3-5]. The traditional use may lead to accidents through overdose.

POISONOUS INGREDIENTS *C. miniata* produces several alkaloids of the isoquinoline type. The best

known of these is lycorine, a toxic substance also found in other members of the family, and known to occur in *Clivia* in concentrations of up to 0,4% of the dry weight[6]. Alkaloids such as cliviamine, clivonine and cliviamartine have been isolated from the roots and leaves[7]. A structurally related alkaloid, hippeastrine, has also been reported from the plant[8].

PHARMACOLOGICAL EFFECTS Lycorine is highly toxic, with an LD_{50} in dogs of 41 mg/kg[8]. Symptoms of poisoning are salivation, vomiting and diarrhoea, leading to paralysis and collapse[6]. The leaves of *C. miniata* have uterotonic effects[9] which help to explain the traditional medicinal uses of the plant. Hippeastrine is a feeding inhibitor of butterfly larvae[8].

DISTRIBUTION *C. miniata* occurs naturally along the eastern coastal parts of South Africa, from the Eastern Cape Province to Swaziland and Mpumalanga.

Hippeastrine

Lycorine

1. **Dyer, R.A. 1921.** *Clivia miniata. Flowering Plants of Africa* 1: t. 13.
2. **Dyer, R.A. 1931.** *Clivia miniata* var. *flava. Flowering Plants of Africa* 11: t. 411.
3. **Watt, J.M. & Breyer-Brandwijk, M.G. 1962.** *The Medicinal and Poisonous Plants of Southern and Eastern Africa*, 2nd edition. Livingstone, London.
4. **Hutchings, A., Scott, A.H., Lewis, G. & Cunningham, A.B. 1996.** *Zulu Medicinal Plants. An Inventory.* University of Natal Press, Pietermaritzburg.
5. **Van Wyk, B-E., Van Oudtshoorn, B. & Gericke, N. 2000.** *Medicinal Plants of South Africa*, 2nd edition. Briza Publications, Pretoria.
6. **Bruneton, J. 1999.** *Pharmacognosy, Phytochemistry, Medicinal Plants*, 2nd edition. Intercept, Hampshire.
7. **Ieven, M., Vlietinck, A.J., Vanden Berghe, D.A. & Totte, J. 1982.** Plant antiviral agents. III. Isolation of alkaloids from *Clivia miniata* Regel (Amaryllidaceae). *J. Nat. Prod.* 45: 564-573.
8. **Harborne, J.B., Baxter, H. & Moss, G.P. (eds) 1997.** *Dictionary of Plant Toxins.* John Wiley & Sons, Chichester.
9. **Veale, D.J.H., Oliver, D.W., Arangies, N.S. & Furman, K.I. 1989.** Preliminary isolated organ studies using an aqueous extract of *Clivia miniata* leaves. *J. Ethnopharmacol.* 27: 341-346.

Clivia miniata

Flowers of *Clivia miniata*

Rhizome and leaves of *Clivia miniata*

CONIUM MACULATUM

Apiaceae

---

hemlock, poison hemlock (English)

DESCRIPTION Hemlock is a robust, biennial herb of up to 2 m in height, with stems characteristically blotched with purple or sometimes with yellow spots[1]. The large, compound leaves have oblong, pointed segments. Small white flowers are borne in typical umbels and the small, dry fruits are distinctly ribbed. *C. maculatum* is not indigenous to South Africa but has been recorded only as a weed of cultivation[1]. There are, however, five indigenous species of *Conium* in South Africa but none of them have the characteristic spotted stems of *C. maculatum*[1]. Hemlock is easily recognised by the distinctive mousy odour that remains on the hands after handling the plant.

TYPE OF TOXIN Piperidine alkaloid.

IMPORTANCE This famous plant is reputed to be the hemlock given as a death potion to Socrates. Poisoning as an official state method of execution and for political or financial objectives was a common practice in Greek and Roman times and only culminated in the Middle Ages[2]. All parts of the plant are highly toxic and fatalities have occurred after eating the roots, leaves or fruits. The small, dry fruits (often referred to as seeds) have an alkaloid concentration of up to 3,5% of the dry weight[3,4]. In Europe, hemlock has been used medicinally as a sedative and antispasmodic. In South Africa, the plant is highly localised and poorly known, and no human or animal poisoning has been recorded. The indigenous species are equally poorly known but some have been used in traditional medicine[1].

POISONOUS INGREDIENTS The monounsaturated piperidine alkaloid γ-coniceine is the major toxin of *C. maculatum*[3,4]. It is the precursor of the other alkaloids in poison hemlock, namely coniine and N-methylconiine. γ-Coniceine is seven times more toxic that coniine and also much more toxic than pseudoconhydrine and N-methylconiine, but all of these alkaloids contribute to the toxicity of the plant[5,6]. It has been shown that there are rapid changes in the plant and that γ-coniceine can be converted to coniine[4]. The chemical composition of the South African species has not been accurately recorded but they are also known to contain hemlock alkaloids[1].

PHARMACOLOGICAL EFFECTS γ-Coniceine and coniine are extremely toxic, causing paralysis of motor nerve endings that leads to drowsiness, nausea, vomiting, breathing difficulty and finally asphyxia, paralysis and death[4-6]. Hemlock may cause teratogenic effects in cattle and pigs when they ingest the plant during pregnancy[4].

DISTRIBUTION *C. maculatum* occurs only in the Western Cape Province as a rare weed of cultivation[1]. The indigenous species are widely distributed, especially in the southern and eastern parts of the country[1].

γ-Coniceine

R=H, Coniine
R=CH₃, N-Methylconiine

1. **Hilliard, O.M. & Burtt, B.L. 1985.** *Conium* (Umbelliferae) in South Africa. *S. Afr. J. Bot.* 51: 465-474.
2. **Gallo, M.A. & Doull, J. 1991.** History and scope of toxicology. Chapter 1 in Casarett and Doull's *Toxicology*, 4th edition. Pergamon Press, New York
3. **Fairbairn, J.W. & Suwal, P.N. 1961.** The alkaloids of hemlock (*Conium maculatum* L.) – II. Evidence for rapid turnover of the major alkaloids. *Phytochemistry* 1: 38-46.
4. **López, T.A., Cid, M.S. & Bianchini, M.L. 1999.** Biochemistry of hemlock (*Conium maculatum* L.) alkaloids and their acute and chronic toxicity in livestock. A review. *Toxicon* 37: 841-865.
5. **Harborne, J.B., Baxter, H. & Moss, G.P. (eds) 1997.** *Dictionary of Plant Toxins.* John Wiley & Sons, Chichester.
6. **Merck 1989.** *The Merck Index.* 11th edition. Merck, Railway.

Flower heads of *Conium maculatum*

Conium maculatum

Spotted stem of *Conium maculatum*

COTULA NIGELLIFOLIA

Asteraceae

---

staggers weed (English); stootsiektebossie, rivierals, waterkerwel (Afrikaans)

DESCRIPTION The plant is a straggling and creeping annual or perennial herb with greyish-green stems and leaves[1]. The leaves are up to twice compound and have deeply dissected lobes. Single flower heads are borne on slender stalks – they have yellow disc florets in the middle and a circle of very short, pure white ray florets around the edge. There are two varieties. *C. nigellifolia* var. *nigellifolia* has relatively large flower heads of about 10 mm in diameter and the involucral bracts are 2 mm wide. The rare var. *tenuior* has smaller flower heads (about 5 mm in diameter), narrower involucral bracts of 1 mm broad and more finely dissected leaves[1]. The plant was previously known as *Matricaria nigellifolia*.

TYPE OF TOXIN Unknown.

IMPORTANCE The plant causes a fatal nervous disorder in cattle known as *stootsiekte* (pushing disease), sometimes also called bovine staggers, brain staggers or brain disease[2-5]. Feeding studies have shown that as little as 10 g dried plant material per kg body-weight may cause pushing disease in cattle[5], while 370 g/kg fed to sheep did not result in any symptoms[6]. This confirmed that sheep are resistant to the disease.

POISONOUS INGREDIENTS Nothing appears to be known about the chemical compounds of *C. nigellifolia*.

PHARMACOLOGICAL EFFECTS The symptoms of *stootsiekte* are described as apathy, aimless wandering and pushing of the head against solid objects, together with a reduced response to stimuli, bulging eyes, a stumbling gait and difficulty in drinking, salivation, running eyes and diarrhoea[2-5]. The condition is usually fatal but the symptoms may only appear after a latent period of several weeks. The brains of poisoned cattle show lesions and marked encephalitis[7] (inflammation of the brain).

DISTRIBUTION *C. nigellifolia* occurs in the eastern and northern parts of South Africa but is particularly common in the Eastern Cape Province and KwaZulu-Natal[1]. The var. *tenuior* is found in these two provinces only[1]. Plants usually grow in wet places or near water, often in the shade.

1. **Hilliard, O.M. 1977.** *Compositae in Natal.* University of Natal Press, Pietermaritzburg.
2. **Steyn, D.G. 1949.** *Die Vergiftiging van Mens en Dier.* Van Schaik, Pretoria.
3. **Watt, J.M. & Breyer-Brandwijk, M.G. 1962.** *The Medicinal and Poisonous Plants of Southern and Eastern Africa*, 2nd edition. Livingstone, London.
4. **Vahrmeijer, J. 1981.** *Poisonous Plants of Southern Africa That Cause Stock Losses.* Tafelberg Publishers, Cape Town.
5. **Kellerman, T.S., Coetzer, J.A.W. & Naudé, T.W. 1988.** *Plant Poisonings and Mycotoxicoses of Livestock in Southern Africa.* Oxford University Press, Cape Town.
6. **Newsholme, S.J. & Kellerman, T.S. 1984.** Resistance of sheep to poisoning by the plant *Matricaria nigellifolia* DC. *Onderstepoort J. Vet. Res.* 51: 277-278.
7. **Newsholme, S.J., Kellerman, T.S. & Welman, W.G. 1984.** Pathology of a nervous disorder (pushing disease or 'stootsiekte') in cattle caused by the plant *Matricaria nigellifolia* DC. (Asteraceae). *Onderstepoort J. Vet. Res.* 51: 119-127.

Plant of *Cotula nigellifolia*

Cotula nigellifolia

Flower heads and leaves of *Cotula nigellifolia*

COTYLEDON ORBICULATA

Crassulaceae

---

plakkie, kouterie (Afrikaans); pig's ears (English); imphewula (Xhosa); seredile (Sotho)

DESCRIPTION *C. orbiculata* is a succulent shrub with woody branches and thick, fleshy leaves of variable shape. They are bright green to grey, often with reddish margin and usually covered with a waxy layer on the surface. Attractive red to orange, tubular, pendulous flowers are borne on a long stalk. *C. orbiculata* is a very variable species and several different varieties have been described, of which some were formerly treated as distinct species[1].

TYPE OF TOXIN Cardiac glycoside (bufadienolide).

IMPORTANCE *C. orbiculata* is one of several Crassulaceae species (see *Kalanchoe*, p. 132, and *Tylecodon*, p. 212) that cause *krimpsiekte* ('shrinking disease'), regarded as one of the most important poisonings of small stock in South Africa[2-5]. The plants are succulent in the dry season and are eaten by livestock when other grazing is unpalatable. The meat of the poisoned animal may cause secondary poisoning of dogs and even humans. Two types of *krimpsiekte* have been described[4]. Acute or *'opblaas' krimpsiekte* results in sudden death of hungry animals that have consumed large quantities of the plant. Chronic or *'dun' krimpsiekte* occurs after acute attacks or after the animal has been exposed to the poison for long periods. The symptoms may appear weeks or months after exposure and may only be evident after the animal has been disturbed or chased. All animals, including horses, dogs and chickens are susceptible, but sheep and goats are more commonly affected[4].

POISONOUS INGREDIENTS Four bufadienolides have been isolated[5] from *C. orbiculata*, namely orbicusides A, B and C and tyledoside C.

PHARMACOLOGICAL EFFECTS Symptoms of *krimpsiekte* poisoning are very different from those normally seen with cardiac glycoside poisoning: exhaustion, paralysis of the head and neck, convulsions, respiratory paralysis and finally death[4]. Poisoned animals may sometimes lie paralysed but fully conscious on their sides for several weeks before they die. As little as 14 g of dried leaves given over a period of 25 days have produced *krimpsiekte* in a goat and it has been shown that the toxins have a cumulative effect[4]. The LD_{50} of the major bufadienolides of *C. orbiculata* (subcutaneous injection in guinea-pigs) was found to vary between 0,1 and 0,25 mg/kg[5].

DISTRIBUTION *C. orbiculata* is widely distributed over practically the whole of southern Africa[1].

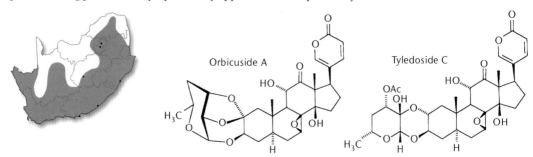

1. **Tölken, H.R. 1985.** Crassulaceae. *Flora of Southern Africa* 14. Botanical Research Institute, Pretoria.
2. **Terblanche, M. & Adelaar, T.F. 1965.** A note on the toxicity of *Cotyledon orbiculata* L. *J. S. Afr. Vet. Med. Ass.* 36: 555-559.
3. **Vahrmeijer, J. 1981.** *Poisonous Plants of Southern Africa That Cause Stock Losses.* Tafelberg Publishers, Cape Town.
4. **Kellerman, T.S., Coetzer, J.A.W. & Naudé, T.W. 1988.** *Plant Poisonings and Mycotoxicoses of Livestock in Southern Africa.* Oxford University Press, Cape Town.
5. **Anderson, L.A.P., Schultz, R.A., Kellerman, T.S., Kotze, S.M., Prozesky, L., Erasmus, G.L. & Labuschagne, L. 1985.** Isolation and characterization of and some observations on poisoning by bufadienolides from *Cotyledon orbiculata* L. var. *orbiculata*. *Onderstepoort J. Vet. Res.* 52: 21-24.
6. **Steyn, P.S., Van Heerden, F.R., Vleggaar, R. & Anderson, L.A.P. 1986.** Bufadienolide glycosides of the Crassulaceae. Structure and stereochemistry of orbicusides A-C, novel toxic metabolites of *Cotyledon orbiculata*. *J. Chem. Soc., Perkins Trans. I,* 1986: 1633-1636.

Cotyledon orbiculata

Cotyledon orbiculata – narrow-leaved form

Cotyledon orbiculata – Magaliesberg form

CRINUM BULBISPERMUM

Amaryllidaceae

---

river lily (English); rivierlelie (Afrikaans); umduze (Zulu)

DESCRIPTION This is an attractive bulbous plant with long, slender, curving leaves and large, pink and white, trumpet-shaped flowers. A distinctive feature of *C. bulbispermum* is the blunt leaf tips. This results from the leaves that typically die back in winter and grow out again each year. Several other species of *Crinum* occur in South Africa. *C. macowanii* is relatively well known because it is an important Zulu traditional medicine, known as *umduze*[2].

TYPE OF TOXIN Isoquinoline alkaloid (Amaryllidaceae type).

IMPORTANCE *Crinum* species are used as traditional medicine[2,3] and there is a danger of poisoning through accidental overdose. *C. bulbispermum* is an old remedy for colds and scrofula, while *C. macowanii* is used for various complaints, including fever, scrofula, micturition, rheumatic fever, blood cleansing, kidney and bladder ailments, glandular swelling and for skin problems[2,3].

POISONOUS INGREDIENTS The major alkaloids of *C. bulbispermum* were found to be crinine and

powelline[4], lycorine and crinamine[5] or bulbispermine[6]. Regional or seasonal variation may possibly explain the different results that have been reported. At least 10 other alkaloids have been isolated from *C. bulbispermum*[4-7], including acetylcaranine, ambelline, crinasiadine, crinasiatine, galanthamine and hippeastrine[7]. Various other *Crinum* species (including *C. macowanii*) are also rich sources of alkaloids.

PHARMACOLOGICAL EFFECTS *Crinum* species have not been clearly implicated in human poisoning in South Africa despite the presence of toxic alkaloids. Stock losses have been reported in East Africa[8] but *Crinum* appears to be of little toxicological importance in South Africa[9]. Crinamine is nevertheless highly toxic, with an oral LD_{50} in dogs a mere 10 mg/kg body-weight[7]. It is a powerful transient hypotensive in dogs and also shows respiratory depressant activity[7].

DISTRIBUTION *C. bulbispermum* occurs naturally over large parts of southern Africa and often grows along rivers and other seasonally wet areas[1].

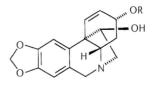

Bulbispermine: R=H
Crinamine: R=CH$_3$

1. **Verdoorn, I.C. 1973**. The genus *Crinum* in southern Africa. *Bothalia* 11: 27-52.
2. **Van Wyk, B-E., Van Oudtshoorn, B. & Gericke, N. 2000**. *Medicinal Plants of South Africa*, 2nd edition. Briza Publications, Pretoria.
3. **Watt, J.M. & Breyer-Brandwijk, M.G. 1962**. *The Medicinal and Poisonous Plants of Southern and Eastern Africa*, 2nd edition. Livingstone, London.
4. **Kobayashi, S., Tokumoto, T., Kihara, M., Imakura, Y., Shingu, T. & Taira, Z. 1984**. Alkaloidal constituents of *Crinum latifolium* and *Crinium bulbispermum* (Amaryllidaceae). *Chem. Pharm. Bull.* 32: 3015-3022
5. **El Moghazi, A.M. & Ali, A.A. 1976**. Investigation of the alkaloid constituents of *Crinum bulbispermum*. Part II. Isolation and identification of crinamine, and other three alkaloids. *Planta Med.* 29: 156-159.
6. **Elgorashi, E.E., Drewes, S.E. & Van Staden, J. 1999**. Alkaloids of *Crinum bulbispermum*. *Phytochemistry* 52: 533-536.
6. **Harborne, J.B., Baxter, H. & Moss, G.P. (eds) 1997**. *Dictionary of Plant Toxins*. John Wiley & Sons, Chichester.
7. **Verdcourt, B. & Trump, E.C. 1969**. *Common Poisonous Plants of East Africa*. Collins, London.
8. **Steyn, D.G. 1949**. *Die Vergiftiging van Mens en Dier*. Van Schaik, Pretoria.

Crinum bulbispermum

Crinum macowanii

CROTALARIA SPARTIOIDES

Fabaceae

---

dune bush (English); besembossie, duinebos, Januariebos (Afrikaans)

DESCRIPTION *Crotalaria* species can be distinguished by the pointed keel (beak) formed by the lowermost two petals of the flower and by the strongly inflated pods[1]. *C. spartioides* has thin, erect branches, uniformly yellow flowers and narrow leaflets, while the related *C. virgultalis* that grows in the same area, has flowers marked with white and red and slightly wider leaflets (usually broader than 2,5 mm)[1]. *C. dura* is similar to *C. globifera*, and both are known as wild lucerne, *wilde lusern* or *jaagsiektebossie*. *C. dura* has more densely hairy leaves and shorter, more rounded pods. *C. burkeana* (rattle bush, *stywesiektebos* or *styfsiektebos*) is easily recognised by the long red hairs on the pods[1].

TYPE OF TOXIN Pyrrolizidine alkaloid.

IMPORTANCE *Crotalaria* species are responsible for at least three types of poisoning in livestock[2-4]. *Crotalariosis* is an acute or chronic condition resulting from the ingestion of large quantities of *Crotalaria* in a short period, or smaller amounts over a long period, resulting in serious liver and lung damage (see also *Senecio*, p. 190). *C. spartioides* is particularly toxic[4]. *Jaagsiekte* is a chronic and often fatal lung condition in horses associated with *C. dura*, *C. globifera* and *C. juncea*[2-4]. These species may also cause liver damage in horses, cattle and sheep, and *C. juncea* is known to cause hair loss in sheep. A third condition is *stywesiekte* ('stiffsickness') caused by *C.*

burkeana[2-4]. The condition occurs mainly in cattle – inflammation of the horn-forming membrane of the hoof, leading to an abnormal stance and gait (hence the name *stywesiekte*)[2-4]. Due to the abnormal gait, the hoofs lose touch with the ground and become elongated and the tips turn up. In severe cases the animals lie down, lose condition and die, but with careful nursing there are usually no fatalities.

POISONOUS INGREDIENTS A large number of pyrrolizidine alkaloids occur in *Crotalaria* species. *C. spartioides* contains retrorsine[5], while dicrotaline is the major compound in *C. dura* and *C. globifera*[6,7]. The toxin in *C. burkeana* is unknown.

PHARMACOLOGICAL EFFECTS The symptoms of crotalariosis and seneciosis are well known and manifest mainly in severe lung and liver damage[8]. *Jaagsiekte* is usually fatal and is characterised by fever and shallow, rapid breathing due to lung damage. The symptoms of *stywesiekte* are unusual (see above) and the disease is poorly understood.

DISTRIBUTION *C. spartioides* is found only in the Kalahari dune region of the northern Cape Province (see map)[1]. *C. globifera* occurs over large parts of KwaZulu-Natal, southern Mpumalanga and northern Gauteng, while *C. dura* is confined to KwaZulu-Natal[1]. *Crotalaria burkeana* occurs over most of the northern parts of South Africa[1].

Dicrotaline

Retrorsine

1. **Polhill, R.M. 1982.** Crotalaria *in Africa and Madagascar.* Balkema, Rotterdam.
2. **Steyn, D.G. 1949.** *Die Vergiftiging van Mens en Dier.* Van Schaik, Pretoria.
3. **Vahrmeijer, J. 1981.** *Poisonous Plants of Southern Africa That Cause Stock Losses.* Tafelberg Publishers, Cape Town.
4. **Kellerman, T.S., Coetzer, J.A.W. & Naudé, T.W. 1988.** *Plant Poisonings and Mycotoxicoses of Livestock in Southern Africa.* Oxford University Press, Cape Town.
5. **Harborne, J.B., Baxter, H. & Moss, G.P. (eds) 1997.** *Dictionary of Plant Toxins.* John Wiley & Sons, Chichester.
6. **Marais, J.S.C. 1944.** Dicrotaline: the toxic alkaloid from *Crotalaria dura* (Wood and Evans) and *Crotalaria globifera* (E. Mey). *Onderstepoort J. Vet. Sci. Anim. Ind.* 20: 61-65.
7. **Adams, R. & van Duuren, B.L. 1953.** Dicrotaline. The structure and synthesis of dicrotalic acid. *J. Amer. Chem. Soc.* 75: 2377-2379.
8. **Mattocks, A.R. 1986.** *The Chemistry and Toxicology of Pyrrolizidine Alkaloids.* Academic Press, London.

Flowers and pods of *Crotalaria spartioides*

Growth form of *Crotalaria spartioides*

Pods of *Crotalaria burkeana*

Flowers of *Crotalaria globifera*

CUCUMIS AFRICANUS

Cucurbitaceae

---

wild cucumber (English); wildekomkommer (Afrikaans)

DESCRIPTION *C. africanus* is a perennial creeper with trailing, hairy stems. The leaves are divided into five lobes, have toothed margins and rough hairs. The small, yellow, male and female flowers occur on the same plant. Male flowers are borne in clusters of five or more, while the female flowers are solitary. The characteristic fruits are oblong to ellipsoid, with sparse, stiff bristles on the surface. Oblong fruits are said to be non-bitter, while the smaller, ellipsoid fruit are usually bitter and poisonous. *C. myriocarpus* subsp. *myriocarpus* is similar to *C. africanus* but it is an annual plant, the female flowers are minutely hairy inside, the leaf stalks have three different hair types and the fruits are smaller, more rounded and with more prominent longitudinal stripes. *C. myriocarpus* subsp. *leptodermis* (previously considered to be a separate species, *C. leptodermis*) has fruits that are uniformly yellow when mature, with fewer bristles on their surfaces.

TYPE OF TOXIN Triterpenoid (Cucurbitacin).

IMPORTANCE *Cucumis* species have caused fatal and near-fatal human poisoning[2-4]. The use of bitter fruits or bitter fruit juice of wild cucumbers and wild watermelons as purgatives and enemas is potentially lethal, and has resulted in death[2-4]. *C. myriocarpus* and *C. africanus* have been responsible for stock losses[4,5]. Animals usually die suddenly without any symptoms but diarrhoea and weakness is evident in less severe cases[4,5].

POISONOUS INGREDIENTS A series of structurally related triterpenoids known as cucurbitacins occur in bitter fruits of the pumpkin family, including wild cucumbers, pumpkins and calabashes. Cucurbitacins are extremely bitter and very toxic. An example is cucurbitacin B, a widely distributed compound that has been isolated from fruits of *C. africanus*[6,7].

PHARMACOLOGICAL EFFECTS Cucurbitacins are amongst the most bitter of all substances known to man[7]. Cucurbitacin B has an LD_{50} of 0,5 mg/kg (when injected into a rabbit) or when given orally to mice, the LD_{50} is 5 mg/kg body-weight[7]. The compound has antitumour activity but is too toxic to be used in medicine[7].

DISTRIBUTION *C. africanus* (see map) and *C. myriocarpus* are widely distributed throughout the interior of South Africa. The latter occurs as a weed on old lands and disturbed places.

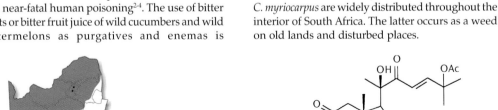

Cucurbitacin B

1. **Kirkbride, J.H. 1993.** *Biosystematic Monograph of the Genus Cucumis.* Parkway Publishers, Boone, North Carolina.
2. **Steyn, D.G. 1934.** *The Toxicology of Plants in South Africa.* Central News Agency, South Africa.
3. **Steyn, D.G. 1949.** *Die Vergiftiging van Mens en Dier.* Van Schaik, Pretoria.
4. **Watt, J.M. & Breyer-Brandwijk, M.G. 1962.** *The Medicinal and Poisonous Plants of Southern and Eastern Africa,* 2nd edition. Livingstone, London.
5. **Kellerman, T.S., Coetzer, J.A.W. & Naudé, T.W. 1988.** *Plant Poisonings and Mycotoxicoses of Livestock in Southern Africa.* Oxford University Press, Cape Town.
6. **Lavie, D. & Glotter, E. 1971.** The Cucurbitanes, a group of tetracyclic triterpenes. *Fortschr. Chem. Org. Naturst.* 29: 307-362.
7. **Harborne, J.B., Baxter, H. & Moss, G.P. (eds) 1997.** *Dictionary of Plant Toxins.* John Wiley & Sons, Chichester.

Cucumis africanus

Cucumis myriocarpus

CYNANCHUM AFRICANUM

Asclepiadaceae

bobbejaantou, klimop (Afrikaans)

DESCRIPTION C. africanum is a climber with slender, twining stems and bright green, glossy and somewhat succulent leaves occurring in opposite pairs[1]. All parts of the plant exude milky latex. Small, brown and white flowers are borne in clusters. The characteristic fruits have two oblong, pointed capsules that burst open at maturity to release the plumed seeds. C. obtusifolium and C. capense (previously known as C. ellipticum) are climbers with broad leaves and whitish flowers. C. obtusifolium can be distinguished from C. capense by the five-lobed corona in the middle of each flower – in C. capense, the corona is cup-shaped and similar to that of C. africanum[1].

TYPE OF TOXIN Steroid glycoside.

IMPORTANCE C. africanum, C. obtusifolium and C. capense are highly toxic and cause a poisoning syndrome known as cynanchosis, klimop poisoning, krampsiekte or krimpsiekte (this form of krimpsiekte is more acute than Cotyledon krimpsiekte)[2-6]. Poisoning occurs mainly along the coastal parts and cattle or sheep are most commonly affected.

POISONOUS INGREDIENTS Several toxic pregnane glycosides have been isolated from C. africanum[7,8]. The major component is cynafoside B (lethal dose to guinea-pigs: 65 mg/kg) while the most toxic component is cynafoside H (lethal dose to guinea-pigs: 10 mg/kg). The chemical compounds of C. obtusifolium and C. capense appear to be as yet unknown. Pregnane glycosides occur in several Cynanchum species from other parts of the world but phenanthroindolizidine alkaloids are also present (e.g. in C. vincetoxicum).

PHARMACOLOGICAL EFFECTS Cynanchosis is characterised by a staggering gait and tremors[3-6], followed by spasms and convulsions (usually with stiff legs and the head pulled backwards) and finally paralysis, which may last for days or even weeks. Depending on the amount of material ingested, death may occur rapidly, but animals sometimes recover.

DISTRIBUTION C. africanum occurs from Namaqualand to Port Elizabeth (see map)[1]. C. obtusifolium is the most abundant species and grows from the Cape Peninsula eastwards along the entire east coast[1]. C. capense is quite common in the Eastern Cape Province but the distribution extends eastwards to KwaZulu-Natal and further north[1].

Cynafoside B

1. **Liede, S. 1993.** A taxonomic revision of the genus *Cynanchum* L. (Asclepiadaceae) in southern Africa. *Bot. Jahr. Syst.* 114: 503-550.
2. **Steyn, D.G. 1934.** *The Toxicology of Plants in South Africa.* Central News Agency, South Africa.
3. **Steyn, D.G. 1949.** *Die Vergiftiging van Mens en Dier.* Van Schaik, Pretoria.
4. **Watt, J.M. & Breyer-Brandwijk, M.G. 1962.** *The Medicinal and Poisonous Plants of Southern and Eastern Africa,* 2nd edition. Livingstone, London.
5. **Vahrmeijer, J. 1981.** *Poisonous Plants of Southern Africa That Cause Stock Losses.* Tafelberg Publishers, Cape Town.
6. **Kellerman, T.S., Coetzer, J.A.W. & Naudé, T.W. 1988.** *Plant Poisonings and Mycotoxicoses of Livestock in Southern Africa.* Oxford University Press, Cape Town.
7. **Tsukamoto, S., Hayashi, K., Mitsuhashi, H., Snyckers, F.O. and Fourie, T.G. 1985.** Studies on the constituents of Asclepiadaceae Plants. LXII. The structures of two glycosides, cynafoside A and B, with a novel sugar chain containing a pair of optically isomeric sugars, D- and L-cymaroses, from *Cynanchum africanum. Chem. Pharm. Bull.* 33: 4807-4811.
8. **Steyn, P.S., Van Heerden, F.R., Vleggaar, R., Erasmus, G.L. & Anderson, L.A.P. 1989.** Toxic constituents of the Asclepiadaceae. Structure elucidation of the cynafosides, toxic pregnane glycosides of *Cynanchum africanum* R. Br. *S. Afr. J. Sci.* 42: 29-37.

Flowers of *Cynanchum africanum*

Fruit of *Cynanchum africanum*

Cynanchum obtusifolium

DATURA STRAMONIUM

Solanaceae

thorn apple, jimson weed (English); stinkblaar, malpitte
(Afrikaans); ijoyi (Xhosa); iloyi (Zulu); lethsowe (Sotho)

DESCRIPTION *D. stramonium* is a common weed of roadsides and waste places. It is a robust annual plant with thick stems, large irregularly lobed, hairless leaves and large, attractive white or pale purple flowers[1]. The distinctive fruits are thorny capsules that split open to release numerous small, kidney-shaped black seeds. *D. ferox* is very similar to *D. stramonium* and is often confused with it, but the capsules have fewer, larger and thicker spines. *D. innoxia* is a less common species, easily identified by the large white flowers and hairy leaves[1].

TYPE OF TOXIN Tropane alkaloid.

IMPORTANCE The seeds and less often the leaves of *Datura* species are a common cause of human poisoning in South Africa[2-4]. Seeds may be accidentally eaten by small children or deliberately as a dangerous prank amongst schoolchildren (the seeds are known as *malpitte*), sometimes with fatal results. Poisoning may also result from the seeds contaminating grain and flour, or from leaves accidentally collected as wild spinach (*marog*)[3,4]. The plants have numerous medicinal uses in South Africa, mainly to treat asthma and to reduce pain[4,5]. Cases of livestock poisoning are rare and most

animals (unlike humans) can tolerate high levels of atropine without any ill effect[6]. *Atropa belladonna* (deadly nightshade), the original source of atropine, has commonly been used for poisoning in Europe. The berries are poisonous to children but less so to adults. Other parts of the plant are extremely poisonous.

POISONOUS INGREDIENTS Several alkaloids occur in *Datura* species, the most important being hyoscyamine, scopolamine (hyoscine) and atropine (racemic hyoscyamine)[7].

PHARMACOLOGICAL EFFECTS Atropine is a highly toxic substance and has a lethal dose in humans of only 100 mg[7]. It has anticholinergic activity and causes blurred vision, suppressed salivation, vasodilation and delirium[7,8]. In modern medicine it is used in anaesthesia and as an ingredient of eye drops. Hyoscine is used to treat motion sickness, Parkinsonism and spasms[7,8].

DISTRIBUTION *D. stramonium* (see map) and *D. ferox* probably originate from tropical America but are now cosmopolitan weeds[1]. Both species are widely distributed in South Africa.

Scopolamine
(hyoscine)

Hyoscyamine

1. **Henderson, L. 2001.** *Alien Weeds and Invasive Plants.* Plant Protection Research Institute Handbook no. 12, Agricultural Research Council, Pretoria.
2. **Steyn, D.G. 1949.** *Die Vergiftiging van Mens en Dier.* Van Schaik, Pretoria.
3. **Watt, J.M. & Breyer-Brandwijk, M.G. 1962.** *The Medicinal and Poisonous Plants of Southern and Eastern Africa*, 2nd edition. Livingstone, London.
4. **Verdcourt, B. & Trump, E.C. 1969.** *Common Poisonous Plants of East Africa.* Collins, London.
5. **Van Wyk, B-E., Van Oudtshoorn, B. & Gericke, N. 2000.** *Medicinal Plants of South Africa*, 2nd edition. Briza Publications, Pretoria.
6. **Kellerman, T.S., Coetzer, J.A.W. & Naudé, T.W. 1988.** *Plant Poisonings and Mycotoxicoses of Livestock in Southern Africa.* Oxford University Press, Cape Town.
7. **Seeger, R. & Neumann, H.G. 1986.** Hyoscyamine – atropine. Hyoscine (scopolamine). *Deutsch. Apoth. Ztg.* 126: 1930-1934.
8. **Bruneton, J. 1999.** *Toxic Plants Dangerous to Humans and Animals.* Intercept, Hampshire.
9. **Harborne, J.B., Baxter, H. & Moss, G.P. (eds) 1997.** *Dictionary of Plant Toxins.* John Wiley & Sons, Chichester.

Datura stramonium – purple-flowered form

Datura ferox

Datura innoxia

Seeds of *Datura*, known as *malpitte*

DICHAPETALUM CYMOSUM
Dichapetalaceae

---

poison leaf (English); gifblaar (Afrikaans); makhouw (Tswana); umkauzaan (Ndebele)

DESCRIPTION *Gifblaar* is an enormous woody plant that grows underground except for the numerous branch tips that emerge above the ground[1]. The leaves are oblong, bright green above and below, with the secondary veins forming loops near the leaf margin. At the base of each leaf stalk are two very small stipules. Young leaves are hairy but become more or less smooth with age. Clusters of white flowers are produced in early spring. On rare occasions, large, orange fruits are formed. *Gifblaar* is superficially similar to numerous other plants with the same distinctive growth form, such as *Pygmaeothamnus* (*goorappel*) and *Pachystigma* (*gousiekte*). It is, however, easily recognised by the alternate leaves (not opposite) and the same bright green colour of the upper and lower leaf surfaces. The colour and shape of the flowers are also distinctive.

TYPE OF TOXIN Monofluoroacetic acid[2].

IMPORTANCE *Gifblaar* is a common cause of serious livestock losses in South Africa, Botswana, Namibia and Zimbabwe[3-7]. Because it is such a deep-rooted plant, it sprouts at a time when no other green pasture is available. Young, newly emerged shoots are particularly toxic.

POISONOUS INGREDIENTS *D. cymosum* contains monofluoroacetic acid[2]. Fluoroacetic acid is relatively harmless but is converted in the body of the animal to highly toxic fluorocitrate[7-9].

PHARMACOLOGICAL EFFECTS Monofluoroacetic acid interferes with the metabolism of acetic acid in the Krebs cycle and causes a fatal loss of cellular respiration[7-9]. It mimics the action of acetic acid, so that fluorocitric acid is formed instead of citric acid. Fluorocitric acid inhibits the activity of aconitase enzymes[8,9]. The lethal oral dose of monofluoroacetate is less than 0,5 mg/kg body-weight in most animals. As little as 20 g of fresh leaves may kill a sheep[3]. Ruminants typically die of heart failure within 24 hours of ingesting the plants, without showing any symptoms[7].

DISTRIBUTION *D. cymosum* has a limited distribution and occurs from Gauteng northwards and westwards, with an isolated area in the extreme north of KwaZulu-Natal[1,6,7]. Plants are usually found on northern slopes or sandy flats. The veld type in which *gifblaar* is found characteristically include trees such as *Burkea africana* (wild seringa) and *Ochna pulchra* (*lekkerbreek*) and is known amongst farmers as *gifveld* (poison veld)[6,7].

$$H-\overset{\displaystyle F}{\underset{\displaystyle H}{C}}-\overset{\displaystyle O}{C}-OH$$

Monofluoroacetic acid

1. **Breteler, F.J. 1978.** The African Dichapetalaceae VI. A taxonomic revision. Species c-f. *Mededelingen van de Landbouwhogeschool te Wageningen* 72(10): 1-84.
2. **Marais, J.S.C. 1943.** Monofluoroacetic acid, the toxic principle of 'Gifblaar' *Dichapetalum cymosum* (Hook). Engl. *Onderstepoort J. Vet. Sci. Anim. Ind.* 20: 67-73.
3. **Steyn, D.G. 1934.** *The Toxicology of Plants in South Africa.* Central News Agency, South Africa.
4. **Steyn, D.G. 1949.** *Die Vergiftiging van Mens en Dier.* Van Schaik, Pretoria.
5. **Watt, J.M. & Breyer-Brandwijk, M.G. 1962.** *The Medicinal and Poisonous Plants of Southern and Eastern Africa*, 2nd edition. Livingstone, London.
6. **Vahrmeijer, J. 1981.** *Poisonous Plants of Southern Africa That Cause Stock Losses.* Tafelberg Publishers, Cape Town.
7. **Kellerman, T.S., Coetzer, J.A.W. & Naudé, T.W. 1988.** *Plant Poisonings and Mycotoxicoses of Livestock in Southern Africa.* Oxford University Press, Cape Town.
8. **Peters, R. 1954.** Biochemical light upon an ancient poison: a lethal synthesis. *Endeavour* 13: 147-154.
9. **Vickery, B. & Vickery, M.L. 1973.** Toxicity for livestock of organofluorine compounds present in *Dichapetalum* plant species. *Vet. Bull.* 43: 537-542.

Typical growth form of *Dichapetalum cymosum*

Leaves and flowers of *Dichapetalum cymosum*

Flowers of *Dichapetalum cymosum*

DIMORPHOTHECA CUNEATA

Asteraceae

Karoo bietou (English); witgousblom, witbietou (Afrikaans)

DESCRIPTION *D. cuneata* is a woody shrublet of about 50 cm in height. The leaves are oblong and characteristically toothed along the margins, and are sticky and aromatic when young. Attractive flower heads are borne on the tips of the branches, usually in early spring. They have yellow disc florets in the middle, surrounded by numerous pure white (or rarely purple) ray florets that fold open in the daytime. Two types of one-seeded fruits are formed (hence the name *Dimorphotheca*): a larger, rounded, flat, winged fruit and a much smaller, narrow, wingless one with a warty surface[1]. There are several *Dimorphotheca* species in South Africa and they are not always easy to identify if fruits are not available[1,2]. Species known to be poisonous include *D. nudicaulis*, *D. zeyheri* and *D. spectabilis*[3-5]. The last-mentioned is an attractive herb with large purple flower heads, known as blue *bietou* or Transvaal *bietou* (previously classified as *Castalis spectabilis*, but nowadays included in *Dimorphotheca*)[2]. Several species from other genera are also considered to be toxic, such as *Arctotheca calendula* (previously *Cryptostemma calendulaceum*), *Epaltes gariepinia* (previously *E. alata*) and *Osteospermum ecklonis* (previously *Dimorphotheca ecklonis*)[3,4].

TYPE OF TOXIN Cyanogenic glycoside.

IMPORTANCE *Dimorphotheca* species and other plants from the family loosely referred to as *bietou* or *gousblom* are well known for causing prussic acid poisoning in stock[3,7]. There may be severe losses in sheep in some years[7].

POISONOUS INGREDIENTS The presence of the toxic cyanogenic glycoside, linamarin, from several *Dimorphotheca* species has been reported[8,9].

PHARMACOLOGICAL EFFECTS Poisoning with *bietou* causes the same symptoms as observed in other cyanogenic plants. Typical symptoms include respiratory distress, breathing difficulty and blue discoloration of the skin. The low stomach pH of non-ruminants inhibits the release of prussic acid.

DISTRIBUTION *D. cuneata* is one of the most widely distributed species of the genus and occurs over most of the dry interior of South Africa[6,7]. Other species, such as *D. nudicaulis*, are limited to the Cape fynbos region, while *D. spectabilis* occurs in the grasslands of the summer rainfall region.

HO—
HO—
HO—
HO—
O
CH₃
O
CH₃
CN
Linamarin

1. **Norlindh, T. 1943.** *Studies in Calenduleae.* C.W.K. Gleerup, Lund. p. 38-97.
2. **Nordenstam, B. 1994.** New combinations in the Calenduleae. *Compositae Newsletter* 25: 46-49.
3. **Steyn, D.G. 1934.** *The Toxicology of Plants in South Africa.* Central News Agency, South Africa.
4. **Steyn, D.G. 1949.** *Die Vergiftiging van Mens en Dier.* Van Schaik, Pretoria.
5. **Watt, J.M. & Breyer-Brandwijk, M.G. 1962.** *The Medicinal and Poisonous Plants of Southern and Eastern Africa*, 2nd edition. Livingstone, London.
6. **Vahrmeijer, J. 1981.** *Poisonous Plants of Southern Africa That Cause Stock Losses.* Tafelberg Publishers, Cape Town.
7. **Kellerman, T.S., Coetzer, J.A.W. & Naudé, T.W. 1988.** *Plant Poisonings and Mycotoxicoses of Livestock in Southern Africa.* Oxford University Press, Cape Town.
8. **Butler, G.W. 1965.** The distribution of the cyanoglucosides linamarin and lotaustralin in higher plants. *Phytochemistry* 4: 127-131.
9. **Marais, J.S.C. & Rimington, C. 1934.** Isolation of the poisonous principle of *Dimorphotheca cuneata* Less. *Onderstepoort J. Vet. Sci. Animal Ind.* 3: 111-117.

Dimorphotheca cuneata

Dimorphotheca spectabilis

Flower heads of *Dimorphotheca cuneata*

Leaves of *Dimorphotheca cuneata*

DIOSCOREA DREGEANA
Dioscoreaceae

---

wild yam (English); isidakwa (Zulu); wildejam (Afrikaans)

DESCRIPTION *D. dregeana* is a perennial, herbaceous creeper with slender, twining, slightly thorny stems growing annually from a fleshy, tuberous rootstock. The large leaves have three pointed leaflets and are somewhat hairy. Male and female flowers are borne on separate plants. The inconspicuous flowers are borne in slender, branched clusters that hang down from the stems, followed by oblong capsules[1]. The southern African species of *Dioscorea* are not well known[1] but only three species (*D. dregeana, D. dumetorum* and *D. cochleari-apiculata*) have compound leaves[2].

TYPE OF TOXIN Piperidine alkaloid; steroid glycoside.

IMPORTANCE *Dioscorea* species are widely used in traditional medicine in South Africa and some are also used as a starch food, usually after leaching in water for several days to remove the water-soluble poison[2,3]. Human deaths have been reported after the use of the plant as famine food or as medicine[3]. *D. dregeana* is reported to make a person 'mad drunk' (hence the Zulu name *isidakwa*)[3,5,6] and

has been used in poison bait to destroy monkeys. It is used to treat hysteria, convulsions and epilepsy and to pacify psychotic patients[5,6].

POISONOUS INGREDIENTS The toxic principle of several *Dioscorea* species is the piperidine alkaloid dioscorine[7,8]. Also present are steroidal saponins, such as glycosides of diosgenin, that may be partly responsible for the medicinal uses of the plant but at the same time have been implicated in sheep losses[7]. Numerous other compounds are known from *Dioscorea* species, including dioscin, deltonin, deltoside, hircinol and demethylbatatstin[7].

PHARMACOLOGICAL EFFECTS Dioscorine is highly toxic to humans[7]. It has an LD_{50} of 60 mg/kg in mice when administered by injection. Derivatives of plant-derived steroids are nowadays used as oral contraceptives, anti-inflammatory agents and as androgens, estrogens and progestins[8]. The hallucinogenic effect of the plant is well known.

DISTRIBUTION *D. dregeana* is limited to the moist, eastern parts of South Africa.

Dioscorine

Diosgenin

HO

1. **Von Teichman, I., Van der Schijff, H.P. & Robbertse, P.J. 1975**. The genus *Dioscorea* L. in South Africa. *Boissiera* 24: 215-224.
2. **Wilkin, P. 1999**. A revision of the compound-leaved yams (*Dioscorea*, Dioscoreaceae) of Africa. *Kew Bull.* 54: 19-39.
3. **Watt, J.M. & Breyer-Brandwijk, M.G. 1962**. *The Medicinal and Poisonous Plants of Southern and Eastern Africa*, 2nd edition. Livingstone, London.
4. **Verdcourt, B. & Trump, E.C. 1969**. *Common Poisonous Plants of East Africa*. Collins, London.
5. **Van Wyk, B-E., Van Oudtshoorn, B. & Gericke, N. 2000**. *Medicinal Plants of South Africa*, 2nd edition. Briza Publications, Pretoria.
6. **Van Wyk, B-E. & Gericke, N. 2000**. *People's Plants. A Guide to Useful Plants of Southern Africa*. Briza Publications, Pretoria.
7. **Harborne, J.B., Baxter, H. & Moss, G.P. (eds) 1997**. *Dictionary of Plant Toxins*. John Wiley & Sons, Chichester.
8. **Bruneton, J. 1999**. *Toxic Plants Dangerous to Humans and Animals*. Intercept, Hampshire.

Leaves and flowers of *Dioscorea dregeana*   Tuber and stem of *Dioscorea dregeana*

Isidakwa, the tubers of *Dioscorea dregeana*

DIPCADI GLAUCUM

Hyacinthaceae

poison onion, wild onion (English); dronk-ui, gif-ui, groenlelie, malkop-ui, wilde-ui (Afrikaans)

DESCRIPTION The plant is a perennial bulb, often occurring in large groups of several hundred individuals[1]. Broad, somewhat fleshy leaves emerge annually from the bulbs. They are variable in size and shape but are often quite broad. An erect flowering stem of up to 2 m in height develops in the summer months. The numerous pendulous flowers are inconspicuous and brownish green in colour. Rounded capsules, containing numerous black seeds are formed after flowering. *Dipcadi* species are easily recognised by the distinctive flower shape (see photograph of *D. viride*).

TYPE OF TOXIN Unknown.

IMPORTANCE The plant is known as a cause of sporadic but serious sheep losses, mainly in the Northern Cape Province (Griqualand West region)[2-6]. Other species such as *D. viride* are considered to be poisonous but no details have been recorded.

POISONOUS INGREDIENTS No information on the toxic principle of *D. glaucum* is available.

Kellerman[6] speculated that the compound might be a cardiac glycoside.

PHARMACOLOGICAL EFFECTS The symptoms are similar to those seen in poisoning with *Urginea* species[2,3]. Fatal poisoning resulted after feeding sheep 100 g of fresh bulbs for three consecutive days[2]. When harvested in the post-seeding stage, the bulbs were found to be more toxic than when they are flowering[2]. Sheep show loss of appetite, diarrhoea, weakness, high fever, accelerated and weak pulse, gastro-intestinal irritation, abortion in ewes, and a characteristic pressing of the head against objects (hence '*malkop-ui*')[2]. The term *malkop* has also been used for stomach staggers, caused by *Senecio* species[7].

DISTRIBUTION *D. glauca* is widely distributed in the northern parts of South Africa but is particularly common in that part of the Northern Cape Province known as Griqualand West (Douglas and Kimberley districts) and also in the adjoining parts of the Free State (Luckhoff , Fauresmith and Koffiefontein)[1,5].

1. **Obermeyer, A.A. 1963.** The South African species of *Dipcadi. Bothalia* 8: 117-137.
2. **Steyn, D.G. 1934.** *The Toxicology of Plants in South Africa.* Central News Agency, South Africa.
3. **Steyn, D.G. 1949.** *Die Vergiftiging van Mens en Dier.* Van Schaik, Pretoria.
4. **Watt, J.M. & Breyer-Brandwijk, M.G. 1962.** *The Medicinal and Poisonous Plants of Southern and Eastern Africa*, 2nd edition. Livingstone, London.
5. **Vahrmeijer, J. 1981.** *Poisonous Plants of Southern Africa That Cause Stock Losses.* Tafelberg Publishers, Cape Town.
6. **Kellerman, T.S., Coetzer, J.A.W. & Naudé, T.W. 1988.** *Plant Poisonings and Mycotoxicoses of Livestock in Southern Africa.* Oxford University Press, Cape Town.
7. **Walsh, L.H. 1909.** *South African Poisonous Plants.* Maskew Miller, Cape Town.

Fruiting plant of *Dipcadi glaucum*

Flowers of *Dipcadi viride*

Single flower of *Dipcadi glaucum*

The onion-like bulbs of *Dipcadi glaucum*

DRIMIA ROBUSTA

Hyacinthaceae

---

indongana-zibomvana, isiklenama (Zulu); brandui (Afrikaans)

DESCRIPTION *Drimia* species are bulbous plants with strap-shaped leaves and long, slender, flowering stalks bearing small, greenish-purplish flowers. The flowers are tubular, with the stamens fused into a tube and the petals characteristically reflexed and bent backwards onto the base of the flower[1]. *Drimia* is often confused with *Urginea* (see p. 214) because the two genera are sometimes combined into one[1]. However, *Urginea* species generally have straight petals and free, spreading stamens. *Drimia* species could possibly be confused with the poisonous *Ornithoglossum viride* (Cape poison onion or *slangkop* in Afrikaans), which also has strongly reflexed petals and which is also a well-known cause of *slangkop* poisoning. It belongs to the family Colchicaceae and is easily recognised by the small size of the plant and the drooping flowers.

TYPE OF TOXIN Cardiac glycoside (bufadienolide).

IMPORTANCE *D. robusta* is a popular traditional medicine, especially in KwaZulu-Natal[2-4]. There is a danger of accidental poisoning or that people may be harmed if the bulbs are used indiscriminately.

The plant has long been suspected of being poisonous to stock[2].

POISONOUS INGREDIENTS The suspicion that *D. robusta* is poisonous was confirmed recently when a cardiac glycoside, 12β-hydroxyscillirosidin, was isolated from the bulbs[5]. Symptoms typical of '*slangkop* poisoning' (see *Urginea sanguinea*, p. 214) appear when *Ornithoglossum viride* is grazed by animals[6,7] but the chemical principles appear to be unknown.

PHARMACOLOGICAL EFFECTS The symptoms of cardiac glycoside poisoning were discussed on p. 28. The effects of *Drimia* poisoning are likely to be similar to those of *Urginea*, as the two genera are closely related. When bulb scales or leaves are rubbed on bare skin, a stinging effect and a rash is produced[3], hence the name *brandui* ('burning onion').

DISTRIBUTION The known distribution of *D. robusta* is shown on the map. *O. viride* is abundant all over South Africa except for the moist eastern regions.

12β —Hydroxyscillirosidin

1. **Jessop, J.P. 1977.** Studies in the bulbous Liliaceae in South Africa: 7. The taxonomy of *Drimia* and certain allied genera. *Jl S. Afr. Bot.* 43: 265-319.
2. **Watt, J.M. & Breyer-Brandwijk, M.G. 1962.** *The Medicinal and Poisonous Plants of Southern and Eastern Africa*, 2nd edition. Livingstone, London.
3. **Hutchings, A., Scott, A.H., Lewis, G. & Cunningham, A.B. 1996.** *Zulu Medicinal Plants. An Inventory*. University of Natal Press, Pietermaritzburg.
4. **Van Wyk, B-E., Van Oudtshoorn, B. & Gericke, N. 2000.** *Medicinal Plants of South Africa*, 2nd edition. Briza Publications, Pretoria.
5. **Pohl, T., Koorbanally, C., Crouch, N.R., & Mulholland, D.A. 2001.** Bufadienolides from *Drimia robusta* and *Urginea altissima* (Hyacinthaceae). *Phytochemistry* 58: 557-561.
6. **Vahrmeijer, J. 1981.** *Poisonous Plants of Southern Africa That Cause Stock Losses*. Tafelberg Publishers, Cape Town.
7. **Kellerman, T.S., Coetzer, J.A.W. & Naudé, T.W. 1988.** *Plant Poisonings and Mycotoxicoses of Livestock in Southern Africa*. Oxford University Press, Cape Town.

Drimia robusta

Flowers of *Drimia robusta*

Ornithoglossum viride

ECHIUM VULGARE

Boraginaceae

---

blue echium, blueweed (English); blou-echium (Afrikaans)

DESCRIPTION *E. vulgare* is a biennial herb with erect flowering branches sprouting from a basal rosette of leaves. The stems and leaves are covered with bristly hairs that have bulbous bases. The attractive blue flowers occur in one-sided clusters. A second species is *E. plantagineum* (= *E. lycopsis*), known as Patterson's curse or *pers-echium*. This plant is similar to blue echium but the basal leaves are broader and distinctly stalked, the flowers are purple (not blue) and two of the stamens protrude from the flower (five stamens protrude beyond the rim of the flower in *E. vulgare*)[1]. A well-known relative of *Echium* is comfrey (*Symphytum officinale*), a hairy perennial often grown in herb gardens.

TYPE OF TOXIN Pyrrolizidine alkaloid.

IMPORTANCE Teas containing echium and comfrey are toxic and should not be used by humans, as chronic consumption may lead to liver damage. Although stock losses due to *E. plantagineum* are known in Australia[2], poisoning is rare, probably because the extreme hairiness makes the plants unpalatable. They are nevertheless potentially dangerous and may cause liver damage in animals. The bristly hairs of the plants are also known to cause extreme skin irritation in humans.

POISONOUS INGREDIENTS *Echium* species and *Symphytum officinale* contain several pyrrolizidine alkaloids. Heliosupine is particularly common and occurs in both *E. vulgare* and *S. officinale*[3]. *E. vulgare* also contains a benzofuran, lithospermic acid. *E. plantagineum* is known to produce echimidine, echiumine and heliotrine[2], while *Symphytum* has lasiocarpine, heliosupine, echimidine, lithospermic acid, symphytine, intermedine, symlandine and uplandicine as major compounds[3,4].

PHARMACOLOGICAL EFFECTS Pyrrolizidine alkaloids are known for their cumulative effect and the fact that they cause veno-occlusive disease of the liver (the so-called Budd-Chiari syndrome), with thrombosis of the hepatic vein, leading to cirrhosis of the liver. These compounds are also known to be carcinogenic. Children are more susceptible than adults[5].

DISTRIBUTION *E. vulgare* is widely distributed in the summer rainfall region of South Africa, from the Eastern Cape Province northwards to Mpumalanga. *E. plantagineum* occurs mainly in the Western Cape Province, where it is an abundant and troublesome weed. The distribution areas of both species are shown in the map.

E. plantagineum   E. vulgare

Heliosupine

1. **Henderson, L. 2001.** *Alien Weeds and Invasive Plants.* Plant Protection Research Institute Handbook no. 12, Agricultural Research Council, Pretoria.
2. **Cheeke, P.R. 1989.** Pyrrolizidine alkaloid toxicity and metabolism in laboratory animals and livestock. In Cheeke, P.R. (ed.), *Toxicants of Plant Origin. Vol. 1. Alkaloids.* CRC Press, Boca Raton, Florida.
3. **Harborne, J.B., Baxter, H. & Moss, G.P. (eds) 1997.** *Dictionary of Plant Toxins.* John Wiley & Sons, Chichester.
4. **Couet, C.E., Crews, C. & Hanley, A.B. 1996.** Analysis, separation and bioassay of pyrrolizidine alkaloids from comfrey (*Symphytum officinale*). *Nat. Toxins* 4: 163-167.
5. **Mattocks, A.R. 1986.** The Chemistry and Toxicology of Pyrrolizidine Alkaloids. Academic Press, London.

Echium vulgare

Flowers of *Echium vulgare*

Echium plantagineum

Flowers of *Echium plantagineum*

ENCEPHALARTOS LONGIFOLIUS

Zamiaceae

---

cycads (English); broodbome, wilde dadels (Afrikaans)

DESCRIPTION Cycads are distinctive palm-like trees with thick, sturdy stems and very large, frond-like leaves[1]. The female cones are much larger than the male and at maturity they contain numerous brightly coloured, fleshy seeds, resembling dates. The seeds have a fleshy outer layer surrounding the actual seed kernel or endosperm (technically the female gametophyte)[1]. *E. longifolius* is one of the most commonly encountered cycads and has enormous female cones[1]. A close relative of cycads is *Stangeria eriopus*, a fern-like plant with short, thick, underground stems[2].

TYPE OF TOXIN Azoxy compound.

IMPORTANCE The seed kernels are highly toxic and human fatalities have been recorded[3,4]. While the pulp around the seeds is generally considered non-toxic[3,4] it may well contain low levels of toxin. A well-known case of human poisoning occurred during the Anglo-Boer War of 1899–1902, when General Jan Smuts and his commando ate seeds of *E. longifolius*[4]. Only some men were poisoned, and it is likely that those who only ate the fleshy part of the seeds and avoided the kernels were not affected[4]. The stems of *Stangeria eriopus* and *Encephalartos* species are commonly used as traditional medicine[4] and there is a risk of acute or chronic poisoning.

POISONOUS INGREDIENTS The toxicity of cycads is due to the presence of cycasin and macrozamin, two toxic glycosides of methylazoxymethanol[5-7]. These compounds are known from the seed kernels of both *Encephalartos* and *Stangeria* but cycasin was also shown to be present in *Stangeria* at levels of 0,17% in fresh and 0,21% in dried stem material[8]. The emetic use of the stems, however, was ascribed to the presence of high levels of sodium sulphate[8]. Neurotoxic amino acids are known from *Cycas* species but their presence in *Encephalartos* and *Stangeria* has not yet been demonstrated.

PHARMACOLOGICAL EFFECTS The azoxy compounds cycasin and macrozamin are known to cause severe liver damage in humans and animals and are also carcinogenic.

DISTRIBUTION *E. longifolius* occurs mainly in the Eastern Cape Province, but the genus is well represented in the eastern and northern parts of South Africa[1]. *S. eriopus* is restricted to sand dunes along the Eastern Cape and KwaZulu-Natal coastline[1].

Cycasin: R=H
Macrozamin: R=

1. **Goode, D. 1989**. *Cycads of Africa*. Struik-Winchester, Cape Town.
2. **Dyer, R.A. 1966**. Stangeriaceae. *Flora of Southern Africa* 1: 1-3.
3. **Steyn, D.G. 1949**. *Die Vergiftiging van Mens en Dier*. Van Schaik, Pretoria.
4. **Watt, J.M. & Breyer-Brandwijk, M.G. 1962**. *The Medicinal and Poisonous Plants of Southern and Eastern Africa*, 2nd edition. Livingstone, London.
5. **Altenkirk, B. 1974**. Occurrence of macrozamin in the seeds of *Encephalartos transvenosus* and *E. lanatus*. Lloydia 37: 636-637.
6. **Louw, W.K.A. & Oelofson, W. 1975**. Carcinogenic and neurotoxic components in the cycad *Encephalartos altensteinii* Lehm. (family Zamiaceae). *Toxicon* 13:447-452.
7. **Moretti, A., Sabato, S. & Gigliano, G.S. 1983**. Taxonomic significance of methylazoxymethanol glycosides in the cycads. *Phytochemistry* 22: 115-117.
8. **Osborne, R., Grove, A., Oh, P., Mabry, T.J. Ng, J.C. & Seawright, A.A. 1994**. The magical and medicinal usage of *Stangeria eriopus* in South Africa. *J. Ethnopharmacol*. 43: 67-72.

Cones of *Encephalartos longifolius*

Encephalartos longifolius

Seeds of *Encephalartos villosus*

Seeds of *Stangeria eriopus*

EQUISETUM RAMOSISSIMUM
Equisetaceae

horsetail, mare's tail (English); perdestert, bewerasiegras, drilgras, dronkgras, litjiesgras (Afrikaans); isikhumukele (Zulu); mohlakaphotwane (Sotho)

DESCRIPTION The plant is a fern relative with numerous black, subterranean stems and erect, green, ribbed aerial stems of up to 2 m in height[1]. Up to 14 small scale-leaves encircle the stems at each node, where up to 14 side branches may occur. The scale-leaves are fused for most of their length and usually turn black with age. The spore-bearing parts of the plant are found in small, oblong cones. Since there is only one species of this distinctive plant in southern Africa, it is unlikely to be confused with other plants.

TYPE OF TOXIN Macrocyclic alkaloid.

IMPORTANCE *Equisetum* species are known to cause livestock losses in many parts of the world where they grow[2-4]. Horses and mules appear to be most susceptible. In South Africa, only a few cases of poisoning have been reported.

POISONOUS INGREDIENTS *E. ramosissimum* and other species such as *E. palustre*, *E. arvense* and *E. silvaticum* contain the alkaloid palustrine, which is said to be the toxic compound[5]. However, these plants also contain the enzyme thiaminase, which breaks down thiamine (better known as vitamin B_1)[6,7]. Ruminants are less severely affected because thiamine is made in the rumen, but other animals, particularly horses, might suffer from severe thiamine deficiency. Thiaminase is known to be one of the toxic principles in *Pteridium aquilinum* and some other plants[7].

PHARMACOLOGICAL EFFECTS Symptoms of *Equisetum* poisoning in horses include excitability, reeling gait, falling over and eventually death from exhaustion[5]. The condition is known as equisetosis, shivers, blind staggers or stomach staggers (*dronksiekte, drilsiekte* or *bewerasiesiekte* in Afrikaans)[2-4]. If the poisoning is due to thiaminase and the resultant thiamine deficiency, then animals are successfully treated with injections of thiamine hydrochloride[6].

DISTRIBUTION *E. ramosissimum* is widely distributed over the eastern half of South Africa[1] and is usually found near water, where it may form large colonies.

Palustrine

Thiamine (Vitamin B_1)

1. **Schelpe, E.A.C.L.E. & Anthony, N.C. 1986.** Pteridophyta. *Flora of Southern Africa*. p. 29. Botanical Research Institute, Pretoria.
2. **Steyn, D.G. 1949.** *Die Vergiftiging van Mens en Dier.* Van Schaik, Pretoria.
3. **Watt, J.M. & Breyer-Brandwijk, M.G. 1962.** *The Medicinal and Poisonous Plants of Southern and Eastern Africa*, 2nd edition. Livingstone, London.
4. **Vahrmeijer, J. 1981.** *Poisonous Plants of Southern Africa That Cause Stock Losses.* Tafelberg Publishers, Cape Town.
5. **Harborne, J.B., Baxter, H. & Moss, G.P. (eds) 1997.** *Dictionary of Plant Toxins.* John Wiley & Sons, Chichester.
6. **Henderson, J.A., Evans, E.V. & McIntosh, R.A. 1952.** The antithiamine action of *Equisetum*. *J. Am. Vet. Med. Assoc.* 120: 375-378.
7. **Meyer, P. 1989.** Thiaminase activities and thiamine content of *Pteridium aquilinum*, *Equisetum ramosissimum*, *Malva parviflora*, *Pennisetum clandestinum* and *Medicago sativa*. *Onderstepoort J. Vet. Res.* 56: 145-146.

Equisetum ramosissimum

Stems of *Equisetum ramosissimum*

Cones of *Equisetum ramosissimum*

ERYTHRINA CAFFRA

Fabaceae

---

coast coral tree (English); kuskoraalboom (Afrikaans)

DESCRIPTION *E. caffra* is a medium-sized tree with thick stems that are covered with numerous prickles[1,2]. The leaves are compound and each comprises three pointed, more or less thorny leaflets. Attractive orange-red flowers are produced in August and September, followed by distinctive cylindrical pods that are strongly constricted between the seeds. The bright red seeds with their contrasting dark spots are widely known as lucky beans. *E. caffra* is closely related to *E. lysistemon*. It may be distinguished by the uppermost petal of the flower being broader, shorter and strongly curved backwards, so that the stamens are visible. In *E. lysistemon*, the standard petal is narrow and less curved, so that each flower is more tubular in shape[1,2].

TYPE OF TOXIN Isoquinoline alkaloid.

IMPORTANCE *Erythrina* species are not generally considered to be very toxic because the poisonous alkaloids they contain are unlikely to be lethal if taken by mouth. The seed has a highly resistant seed coat that has to be damaged otherwise the seeds will not be digested. The bark, whole stems or rarely the leaves or roots of *E. caffra* and *E. lysistemon* are commonly used in traditional medicine[3,4]. They are mainly applied as a topical application for sores, wounds and arthritis, or to relieve earache or

toothache, and accidental poisoning may occur. All parts of the cultivated South America species, *E. crista-galli* (cockspur coral tree) are known to be very poisonous.

POISONOUS INGREDIENTS A large number of tetracyclic isoquinoline alkaloids are known from several *Erythrina* species, e.g. erythraline and erysotrine. *Erythrina* alkaloids are known to be highly toxic[6]. A potent trypsin inhibitor is known from *E. caffra* seeds[7] and it is likely that toxic proteins and lectins[8] are present in this and other species.

PHARMACOLOGICAL EFFECTS Several *Erythrina* alkaloids, such as erysotrine, are known to have curare-like neuromuscular blocking effects[5]. The general term curare is used for substances that have a paralysing effect on skeletal muscles but is generally not toxic when ingested. These characteristics make them ideal dart and arrow poisons, because the muscle relaxing action allows the prey animals (monkeys and parrots) to be easily recovered and the meat can be safely consumed.

DISTRIBUTION *E. caffra* is strictly a coastal species, confined to the Eastern Cape and KwaZulu-Natal coast[1,2]. Several other *Erythrina* species, both indigenous and exotic, are cultivated in gardens.

Erythraline

Erysotrine

1. **Hennesy, E.F. 1991.** Erythrineae (Fabaceae) in southern Africa. *Bothalia* 21: 1-17.
2. **Coates Palgrave, K. 1977.** *Trees of Southern Africa.* Struik, Cape Town.
3. **Hutchings, A., Scott, A.H., Lewis, G. & Cunningham, A.B. 1996.** *Zulu Medicinal Plants. An Inventory.* University of Natal Press, Pietermaritzburg.
4. **Van Wyk, B-E., Van Oudtshoorn, B. & Gericke, N. 2000.** *Medicinal Plants of South Africa,* 2nd edition. Briza Publications, Pretoria.
5. **Harborne, J.B., Baxter, H. & Moss, G.P. (eds) 1997.** *Dictionary of Plant Toxins.* John Wiley & Sons, Chichester.
6. **Bruneton, J. 1999.** *Toxic Plants Dangerous to Humans and Animals.* Intercept, Hampshire.
7. **Joubert, F.J. 1982.** Purification and properties of the proteinase inhibitors form *Erythrina caffra* (coast Erythrina) seed. *Int. J. Biochem.* 14: 187-193.
8. **Ashford, D., Dwek, A.K., Welply, J.K., Amatayakul, S., Homans, S.W., Lis, H., Taylor, G.N., Sharon, N. & Rademacher, T.W. 1987.** The β1->2-D-xylose and α1->3-L-fucose substituted N-linked oligosaccharides from *Erythrina crista-gallii* lectin. *Eur. J. Biochem.* 166: 311-320.

Erythrina caffra

Seeds of *Erythrina caffra*

Erythrina lysistemon

Erythrina crista-galli

ERYTHROPHLEUM LASIANTHUM

Fabaceae

Swazi ordeal tree (English); umkhwangu (Zulu); Swazi-oordeelboom (Afrikaans)

DESCRIPTION *E. lasianthum* is a medium-sized tree with compound leaves and greenish-yellow flowers borne in elongated clusters. The fruit are large, flat pods of about 120 mm long and 35 mm wide. This species is distinguished from the closely related *E. suaveolens* (previously known as *E. guineense*) by hairy stamens and from *E. africanum* by the narrow leaflet tips and the many-seeded pods that split mostly along one suture. The pods are up to five-seeded in *E. africanum* and split along both sutures[1,2].

TYPE OF TOXIN Diterpenoid alkaloid.

IMPORTANCE *Erythrophleum* species have been widely used in Africa as part of the notorious trial by ordeal ritual[3,4]. If the accused vomits after taking the pounded bark mixed with water, he or she is deemed innocent, but if not, then death will almost certainly follow. An overdose is likely to induce vomiting (the controlling power of the person who prepares the mixture is clear). Similarly, a person confident of being innocent is likely to gulp the poison down and thus increase the chance of vomiting, while a guilty one may sip more hesitantly and be poisoned. Powdered bark of *E. lasianthum* is a popular Zulu traditional remedy for fever,

headache and other pains but has also been used in homicide[3].

POISONOUS INGREDIENTS *Erythrophleum* species contain various diterpenoid alkaloids such as cassaine and erythrophleine (also known as norcassamidide)[5-7]. The two main seed alkaloids of *E. lasianthum* have been identified[7] as 3ß-hydroxynorerythrosuamine and a glycoside thereof. The seeds are said to be more poisonous than the bark[8]. A mere 0,5 g of the bean is sufficient to kill a rabbit, while 60 g of bark and leaves may kill a sheep[8].

PHARMACOLOGICAL EFFECTS *Erythrophleum* alkaloids (including the two main seed alkaloids of *E. lasianthum*) are highly toxic[7-9] and have powerful cardiotonic activity similar to that of digitalis[7,9].

DISTRIBUTION *E. lasianthum* has a very limited distribution in the extreme northern part of KwaZulu-Natal and parts of the adjoining Swaziland and Mozambique[1,2]. *E. suaveolens* and *E. africanum* are widely distributed in Africa but do not occur in South Africa.

Cassaine

Erythrophleine

1. **Ross, J.H. 1977.** Caesalpinioideae. *Flora of Southern Africa* 16(2). Botanical Research Institute, Pretoria.
2. **Coates Palgrave, K. 1977.** *Trees of Southern Africa*. Struik, Cape Town.
3. **Watt, J.M. & Breyer-Brandwijk, M.G. 1962.** *The Medicinal and Poisonous Plants of Southern and Eastern Africa*, 2nd edition. Livingstone, London.
4. **Verdcourt, B. & Trump, E.C. 1969.** *Common Poisonous Plants of East Africa*. Collins, London.
5. **Merck 1989.** *The Merck Index*. 11th edition. Merck, Rahway.
6. **Jansson, S. & Cronlund, A. 1976.** Alkaloids from the bark of *Erythrophleum africanum*. *Acta Pharm. Suec.* 13: 51-54.
7. **Verotta, L., Aburjai, T., Rogers, C.B., Dorigo, P., Maragno, I., Fraccarollo, D., Santostasi, G., Gaion, R.M. & Carpenedo, F. 1995.** Chemical and pharmacological characterization of *Erythrophleum lasianthum* alkaloids. *Planta Med.* 61: 271-274.
8. **Steyn, D.G. 1949.** *Die Vergiftiging van Mens en Dier*. Van Schaik, Pretoria.
9. **Cronlund A. & Sandberg, F. 1976.** Cardiotonic effect and toxicity of *Erythrophleum* alkaloids. *Acta Pharm Suec.* 13: 35-42.

Fruit of *Erythrophleum lasianthum*

Flowers of *Erythrophleum lasianthum*

Erythrophleum africanum

Erythrophleum suaveolens

EUPHORBIA INGENS
Euphorbiaceae

---

candelabra tree (English); gewone naboom (Afrikaans)

DESCRIPTION This attractive succulent tree has numerous, robust, erect stems sprouting low down from a sturdy trunk[1]. The four-angled stems have pairs of small thorns along their ribs. Small, red, fleshy flowers are formed on the stems and they mature into three-lobed capsules. *E. tirucalli* (rubber euphorbia) may reach 5 m or more in height and differs from *E. ingens* in the much more sparser and slender stems. *E. mauritanica* (*melkbos* or *gifmelkbos* in Afrikaans) is a densely branched, rounded shrub of up to 2 m in height, easily recognised by the characteristic growth form, leafy stem tips and small yellow flowers[1]. The latex of *E. virosa* is an ingredient of arrow poisons in Namibia and Angola.

TYPE OF TOXIN Diterpenoid.

IMPORTANCE *Euphorbia* species contain irritant and toxic latex and several of them have been implicated in both human and livestock poisoning[2-6]. *E. ingens* is extremely toxic and the latex may cause temporary or even permanent blindness[2,3]. The latex causes severe injuries of the face, eyes, tongues and mouths of animals that come into accidental contact with it. *E. tirucalli* latex is also known to burn and inflame the eyes and mucus membranes. *E. mauritanica* is poisonous to animals and leads to occasional stock losses[5,6]. It is interesting to note that *noors* honey, made from the nectar of *Euphorbia* species such as *E. ingens* and *E. ledienii,* is not suitable for human use as it causes intense burning of the mouth and throat[3].

POISONOUS INGREDIENTS The irritant compounds are known to be diterpenoids[6]. In *E. ingens*, various esters of ingenol occur as the main irritant principles[6]. Several phorbol-related compounds, including esters of 4-deoxyphorbol and ingenol, have been found in *E. tirucalli*[6]. The well-known poinsettia (*E. pulcherrima*) is often considered to be toxic but it seems that people and animals can tolerate quite large amounts of the latex of this species without serious effect[7].

PHARMACOLOGICAL EFFECTS Irritant diterpenes cause injury and blindness but the exact cause of poisoning after ingesting the plants is poorly understood. *E. mauritanica*, for example, may cause a fatal nervous disorder in sheep characterised by muscle tremors, foaming at the mouth, bloat, diarrhoea and fever[4,5].

DISTRIBUTION *E. ingens* (see map) and *E. tirucalli* occur in the north-eastern parts of South Africa, while *E. mauritanica* is an exceptionally common plant of the western parts and the dry interior[4,5].

Ingenol

1. **White, A., Dyer, R.A. & Sloane, B.L. 1941.** *The Succulent Euphorbieae (Southern Africa).* Vols. 1 & 2. Abbey Garden, Pasadena.
2. **Watt, J.M. & Breyer-Brandwijk, M.G. 1962.** *The Medicinal and Poisonous Plants of Southern and Eastern Africa,* 2nd edition. Livingstone, London.
3. **Steyn, D.G. 1949.** *Die Vergiftiging van Mens en Dier.* Van Schaik, Pretoria.
4. **Vahrmeijer, J. 1981.** *Poisonous Plants of Southern Africa That Cause Stock Losses.* Tafelberg Publishers, Cape Town.
5. **Kellerman, T.S., Coetzer, J.A.W. & Naudé, T.W. 1988.** *Plant Poisonings and Mycotoxicoses of Livestock in Southern Africa.* Oxford University Press, Cape Town.
6. **Evans, F.J. & Taylor, S.E. 1983.** Pro-inflammatory, tumour-promoting and anti-tumour diterpenes of the plant families Euphorbiaceae and Thymelaeaceae. *Fortschr. Chem. Org. Naturst.* 44: 1-99.
7. **Bruneton, J. 1999.** *Toxic Plants Dangerous to Humans and Animals.* Intercept, Hampshire.

Euphorbia ingens

Euphorbia tirucalli

Euphorbia mauritanica

Euphorbia virosa

FADOGIA HOMBLEI

Rubiaceae

---

wild date (English); wildedadel, bosluisbessie (Afrikaans)

DESCRIPTION The plant is a perennial herb or shrublet with numerous erect stems of up to 50 cm high, arising from the thick, woody rhizome below the ground. Above-ground parts die back in winter. The leaves are very characteristic – they are borne in groups of three to five at each node; the upper surfaces are bright shiny and dark green, while the lower surfaces are silvery white due to the presence of a dense layer of white hairs. Small yellow, fragrant flowers are produced in clusters at the nodes, followed by round, green fruit that turn black when they ripen. These fruits are edible and resemble engorged ticks, hence the Afrikaans vernacular name, *bosluisbessie*[1]. The leaves of the mobola plum or *grysappel* (*Parinari curatellifolia*) are very similar to those of the wild date, but *grysappel* is usually a much smaller plant, with clusters of leaves seemingly arising directly from the ground. This distinctive growth form, in turn, makes it similar to other poisonous plants such as *gifblaar* (*Dichapetalum cymosum*, p. 88) and *gousiektebossie* (*Pachystigma pygmaeum*, p. 164) but both these species lack the characteristic silvery white hairs on the lower surfaces of the leaves. A key has been developed to identify the various dwarf shrublets that could be mistaken for *gifblaar* or *gousiekte*[2,3]. *F. homblei* was previously known as *F. fragrans* and *F. monticola*.

TYPE OF TOXIN Amine. The structure has not yet been published[4].

IMPORTANCE The fruits are edible and no cases of human poisoning are known, but the plant is potentially lethal to farm animals. *F. homblei* is closely related to *gousiekte* (*Pachystigma* species) and causes the same condition in stock[2,3]. Outbreaks have been reported from the Waterberg and Groblersdal regions in South Africa[2], where the plants are locally abundant. Animals are usually affected in the early summer, when grazing is scarce[2]. Various factors are known to influence the outbreak of *gousiekte*, including climatic conditions, variation in susceptibility amongst animals and variation in toxicity of the plants[3].

POISONOUS INGREDIENTS *Fadogia* has the same toxic substance (known to be a polyamine)[4] as is found in other *gousiekte*-inducing shrublets (*Pachystigma* and *Pavetta*)[5].

PHARMACOLOGICAL EFFECTS Animals characteristically drop dead without showing any warning signs, often after exercise. The condition is ascribed to acute heart failure and recovery is rare (for clinical signs of *gousiekte* see *Pachystigma pygmaeum*, p. 164). It is interesting that death occurs several weeks after ingestion of the toxic plant material.

DISTRIBUTION Wild date occurs in the northern parts of South Africa (see map).

1. **Smith, C.A. 1966.** *Common names of South African plants.* Botanical Survey Memoir No. 35. Department of Agricultural Technical Services, Pretoria.
2. **Vahrmeijer, J. 1981.** *Poisonous Plants of Southern Africa That Cause Stock Losses.* Tafelberg Publishers, Cape Town.
3. **Kellerman, T.S., Coetzer, J.A.W. & Naudé, T.W. 1988.** *Plant Poisonings and Mycotoxicoses of Livestock in Southern Africa.* Oxford University Press, Cape Town.
4. **Vleggaar, R. 2002.** Personal communication.
5. **Fourie, N., Erasmus, G.L., Schultz, R.A. & Prozesky, L. 1995.** Isolation of the toxin responsible for gousiekte, a plant-induced cardiomyopathy of ruminants in southern Africa. *Onderstepoort J. Vet. Res.* 62: 77-87.

Characteristic growth form of *Fadogia homblei*

Fadogia homblei

Flowers of *Fadogia homblei*

The non-toxic *Parinari curatellifolia*

FICUS SALICIFOLIA

Moraceae

---

wonderboom fig (English); wonderboomvy (Afrikaans)

DESCRIPTION *F. salicifolia* is a large shrub or tree of up to 9 m in height. All parts exude milky latex. The leaves have rounded to heart-shaped bases. Small figs of up to 8 mm long are borne on short stalks of about 2 mm long[1]. They are red with white spots when ripe. *F. salicifolia* is usually a medium-sized tree of up to 9 m in height, but the famous 'wonderboom fig' near Pretoria is a 1 000-year-old complex of 74 trees with a massive crown, covering an area of 2 233 square metres[2]. *F. salicifolia* is closely related to *F. cordata* (the Namaqua fig) and is sometimes known as *F. cordata* subsp. *salicifolia*. The Namaqua fig has stalkless, yellowish figs and occurs mainly in Namaqualand and Namibia[1]. *F. salicifolia* is also similar to *F. ingens* (red-leaved fig) but the latter has larger figs (9-12 mm long) and the spring flush of leaves are characteristically bright red[1].

TYPE OF TOXIN Furanocoumarin.

IMPORTANCE The leaves of *F. salicifolia* and *F. ingens* contain a furanocoumarin and are known to be phototoxic to cattle[3]. Several other *Ficus* species (see *F. carica*, p. 238), and indeed many other plants such as rue (*Ruta graveolens*), lemons (*Citrus limon*),

lime (*C. aurantiifolia*), bergamot (*C. aurantium* subsp. *bergiama*), lace flower (*Ammi majus*) and *Psoralea* species may all cause dermatitis[4]. Both *F. ingens* and *F. salicifolia* are also known to cause neurotoxicity in cattle, but this condition appears to be unrelated to the phototoxicity[5].

POISONOUS INGREDIENTS The compound in *F. salicifolia* has been identified as aviprin (oxypeucedanum hydrate)[3].

PHARMACOLOGICAL EFFECTS When exposed to bare skin or even when ingested, furano-coumarins cause dermatitis, but only in the presence of sunlight. This phenomenon has been used in medicine since ancient times to get rid of the signs of vitiligo and nowadays as a photo-chemotherapeutic treatment against psoriasis and other skin disorders, known as PUVA therapy[4].

DISTRIBUTION *F. salicifolia* occurs in the northeastern parts of South Africa (see map) and has a distribution area that overlaps to a large extent with that of *F. ingens*.

Aviprin

1. Van Wyk, A.E., Van Wyk, P. & Van Wyk, B-E. 2000. *Photographic Guide to Trees of Southern Africa*. Briza Publications, Pretoria.
2. Esterhuyse, N., Von Breitenbach, J. & Söhnge, H. 2001. *Remarkable Trees of South Africa*. Briza Publications, Pretoria.
3. Myburgh, J.G., Van Heerden, F.R., Picard, J.A., Van der Merwe, D., Krusbersky, N., Meyer, R., Van Greunen, J.V. & Van Wyk, A.E. 2002. Phototoxicity of leaf material collected from *Ficus cordata* subsp. *salicifolia* and *F. ingens* var. *ingens* in the Pretoria area. *Onderstepoort J. Vet. Res.*(in press).
4. Bruneton, J. 1999. *Toxic Plants Dangerous to Humans and Animals*. Intercept, Hampshire.
5. Myburgh, J.G., Fourie N., Van der Lugt, J.J., Kellerman, T.S., Cornelius, S.T. & Ward, C. 1994. A nervous disorder in cattle caused by the plants *Ficus ingens* var. *ingens* and *Ficus cordata* subsp. *salicifolia*. *Onderstepoort J. Vet. Res.* 61: 171-176.

Ficus salicifolia

Ficus salicifolia

Ficus ingens

GALENIA AFRICANA

Aizoaceae

---

kraalbos, geelbos, perdebos (Afrikaans)

DESCRIPTION *Kraalbos* is a dense rounded shrub of about 1 m in height[1]. Young, actively growing tips are slightly sticky and aromatic. The small, narrow, oblong leaves are somewhat grooved on their upper surfaces and turn from bright green to yellow with age. Minute, yellowish green flowers are borne on the branch tips. It is easy to recognise the plants by their dense rounded shape and the distinctive yellow colour of the mature foliage.

TYPE OF TOXIN Unknown.

IMPORTANCE *Galenia africana* contains an unknown toxin that causes a disease known as *waterpens* or water belly in sheep and sometimes in goats[2,3,4]. The disease occurs mainly in the dry western and southern parts of the Karoo. Animals would not normally browse on the plant, but during severe drought they are sometimes forced to feed on it. Ewes appear to be more susceptible, and only a small part of the total flock is usually affected[3]. *G. africana* is also used in traditional medicine, mainly in the western parts of the Karoo[4,5]. Leaves are chewed or a leaf infusion is taken in the morning and evening to relieve toothache[4,5]. Excessive use may cause burning or blistering of the mouth[4,5]. It is also used externally as a dressing, alone or in mixtures, to treat inflammation, wounds and lesions[4].

POISONOUS INGREDIENTS No information seems to be available on the chemical compounds of *Galenia* species. Feeding experiments with *G. pubescens* in America has shown that this species contains toxic levels of nitrate and oxalate[6]. It is unlikely, however, that these substances alone are responsible for the distinctive symptoms seen in South Africa.

PHARMACOLOGICAL EFFECTS The plant causes severe ascites in sheep and goats, so that the abdomen of poisoned animals becomes distended as fluid accumulates in the abdominal cavity (hence *waterpens* or water belly)[2,3]. The condition is also associated with heart failure and liver damage but is as yet poorly understood[7].

DISTRIBUTION *G. africana* is an exceptionally common plant and is found in large numbers in disturbed places such as kraals, overgrazed lands and road verges[1,2,3]. The natural distribution area extends over most of the western half of the Cape and the plant is particularly common in the western and southern parts of the Karoo.

1. **Adamson, R.S. 1956**. The South African species of Aizoaceae. III. *Galenia* L. *Jl S. Afr. Bot.* 22: 87-127.
2. **Vahrmeijer, J. 1981.** *Poisonous Plants of Southern Africa That Cause Stock Losses.* Tafelberg Publishers, Cape Town.
3. **Kellerman, T.S., Coetzer, J.A.W. & Naudé, T.W. 1988.** *Plant Poisonings and Mycotoxicoses of Livestock in Southern Africa.* Oxford University Press, Cape Town.
4. **Watt, J.M. & Breyer-Brandwijk, M.G. 1962.** *The Medicinal and Poisonous Plants of Southern and Eastern Africa,* 2nd edition. Livingstone, London.
5. **Van Wyk, B-E. & Gericke, N. 2000.** *People's Plants. A Guide to Useful Plants of Southern Africa.* Briza Publications, Pretoria.
6. **Williams, M.C. 1979.** Toxicological investigations on *Galenia pubescens. Weed Sci.* 27: 506-508.
7. **Van der Lugt, J.J., Schultz, R.A., Fourie, N., Hon, L.J., Jordaan, P. & Labuschagne, L. 1992.** *Galenia africana* L. poisoning in sheep and goats: hepatic and cardiac changes. *Onderstepoort J. Vet. Res.* 59: 323-333.

Galenia africana

Leaves and flowers of *Galenia africana*

GEIGERIA ORNATIVA

Asteraceae

---

vermeerbos, vomeerbos, misbeksiektebos (Afrikaans)

DESCRIPTION *G. ornativa* (previously known as *G. africana* or *G. passerinoides*)[1] is an annual or short-lived perennial with characteristic tufts of slender, sparsely hairy leaves and small, yellow flower heads borne half hidden amongst the leaves. A second species, *G. aspera*, is more toxic but less abundant than *G. ornativa*. It is a rounded shrublet with smaller leaves and larger flowers than *G. ornativa*. A third species is *G. burkei*, a branched shrublet with narrow leaves.

TYPE OF TOXIN Sesquiterpenoid lactone.

IMPORTANCE *Vermeersiekte* (vomiting disease) is one of the most important causes of sheep losses in South Africa[2-4]. In 1929 to 1930, approximately half a million sheep died in the Griqualand West region of the Northern Cape Province[2]. The plant is actually palatable and nutritious when it is only part of the diet but becomes a problem when large quantities are ingested[2-4]. This usually happens in degraded veld where *Geigeria* has become dominant at the expense of grasses. *G. aspera* is about ten times more toxic than *G. ornativa* but only causes localised outbreaks of the disease[4]. *G. burkei* subsp. *burkei* var. *hirtella* is also known to cause stock losses[5]. Poisoned animals typically regurgitate the ruminal contents through the nose and mouth so that the lips are stained green. *Geigeria* poisoning mainly affects sheep and goats, rarely cattle. The animals usually recover if they are removed from the poisonous grazing at an early stage of intoxication[4].

POISONOUS INGREDIENTS The toxicity of *G. aspera* is ascribed to vermeeric acid, which readily converts to its corresponding lactone, vermeerin[6]. Apart from vermeerin, several other sesquiter-penoid lactones are known from *Geigeria* species[4-7], such as geigerin, geigerinin, griesenin and dihydrogriesenin. So far only vermeeric acid has been definitely shown to cause *vermeersiekte*[7], but the other compounds (particularly those with an α,β- double bond in the lactone ring) are also known to be toxic to laboratory animals[4].

PHARMACOLOGICAL EFFECTS In addition to the typical regurgitation, *Geigeria* poisoning results in cough, diarrhoea or sometimes bloat, followed by stiffness and paralysis[4]. Death may be caused by choking, respiratory paralysis, exhaustion from vomiting and purgation, heart failure or very often pneumonia[4]. Feeding experiments showed that 10 to 15 g of vermeeric acid are lethal to sheep[7].

DISTRIBUTION *G. ornativa* occurs in the dry interior of South Africa (mainly in the Northern Cape Province, see map) while *G. aspera* is restricted to the high-lying summer rainfall region.

Vermeerin

1. **Wild, H. 1980**. Compositae of the *Flora Zambesiaca* area, 12 – Inulae (continued). *Kirkia* 12: 53-66.
2. **Steyn, D.G. 1949**. *Die Vergiftiging van Mens en Dier*. Van Schaik, Pretoria.
3. **Vahrmeijer, J. 1981**. *Poisonous Plants of Southern Africa That Cause Stock Losses*. Tafelberg Publishers, Cape Town.
4. **Kellerman, T.S., Coetzer, J.A.W. & Naudé, T.W. 1988**. *Plant Poisonings and Mycotoxicoses of Livestock in Southern Africa*. Oxford University Press, Cape Town.
5. **Botha, C.J., Gous, T.A., Penrith, M-L., Naude, T.W., Labuschagne, L. & Retief, E. 1997**. Vermeersiekte caused by *Geigeria burkei* Harv. subsp. *burkei* var. *hirtella* Merxm. in the Northern Province of South Africa. *J. S. Afr. Vet. Ass.* 68: 97-101.
6. **Anderson, L.A.P., De Kock W.T. & Pachler, K.G.R. 1967**. The structure of vermeerin, a sesquiterpenoid dilactone from *Geigeria africana* Gries. *Tetrahedron* 23: 4135-4160.
7. **Rimington, C., Roets, G.C.S. & Steyn, D.G. 1936**. Chemical studies upon the vermeerbos, *Geigeria aspera* Harv. II. Isolation of the active principle vermeeric acid. *Onderstepoort J. Vet. Sci.* 7: 507-520.

Geigeria ornativa

Flower heads of *Geigeria ornativa*

Geigeria burkei

GLORIOSA SUPERBA

Colchicaceae

---

flame lily (English); vlamlelie (Afrikaans)

DESCRIPTION The flame lily is a bulbous plant with branched, finger-like rhizomes that are pure white when young, becoming brown with age. The erect stems bear pointed, dark green, glossy leaves, each equipped with a tendril by means of which it clings onto other plants. The attractive flowers are borne on long stalks and have six erect petals ranging in colour from yellow to bright red[1]. The fruits are capsules that split open to release several bright orange seeds. Various colour forms of *G. superba* have been known as *G. simplex* and *G. virescens*, but all of them are now considered to belong to a single species[1,2].

TYPE OF TOXIN Alkaloid.

IMPORTANCE The rhizomes and seeds are highly toxic and have caused numerous human deaths in Africa[3,4], India and Sri Lanka[5]. The flame lily has been implicated in deaths due to accidental ingestion, overdose of traditional medicine, suicide and homicide. Stock losses are rare[6]. The plant has been grown in Sri Lanka and in South Africa as a commercial source of colchicine, which is extracted from the rhizome or seeds. In Europe, the bulb or seeds of autumn crocus (*Colchicum autumnale*) have been used since early times to treat acute attacks of gout[7,8]. It is the original source of colchicine, and is known to have caused 16 fatalities in Europe over a period of 30 years[7].

POISONOUS INGREDIENTS The main toxic compound in the rhizomes and seeds is colchicine, a well-known phenethylisoquinoline alkaloid with anticancer activity.

PHARMACOLOGICAL EFFECTS The toxic dose of colchicine in humans is 10 mg, while more than 40 mg is invariably fatal within three days of ingestion[8]. Symptoms include numbness of the mouth, nausea, vomiting, abdominal pain, gastroenteritis, diarrhoea with blood, partial to complete hair loss, respiratory failure, rapid weak pulse, renal failure and convulsions[3,8]. The mechanism of anticancer action of colchicine is well known. It acts as a spindle poison by binding to tubulin, the protein that forms the spindle (microtubules) during metaphase, thus preventing cell division[8]. The compound is too toxic, however, to be used in cancer treatment.

DISTRIBUTION The plant is widely distributed in the north-eastern parts of South Africa and further north to East Africa and India.

Colchicine

1. **Baker, J.G. 1897**. Liliaceae. *Flora Capensis* 6: 525-526.
2. **Field, D.V. 1971**. The identity of *Gloriosa simplex*. *Kew Bull.* 25: 243-245.
3. **Watt, J.M. & Breyer-Brandwijk, M.G. 1962**. *The Medicinal and Poisonous Plants of Southern and Eastern Africa*, 2nd edition. Livingstone, London.
4. **Verdcourt, B. & Trump, E.C. 1969**. *Common Poisonous Plants of East Africa*. Collins, London.
5. **Aleem, H.M.A. 1988**. *Gloriosa superba* poisoning. *J. Assoc. Physicians India* 40: 541-542.
6. **Steyn, D.G. 1949**. *Die Vergiftiging van Mens en Dier*. Van Schaik, Pretoria.
7. **Harborne, J.B., Baxter, H. & Moss, G.P. (eds) 1997**. *Dictionary of Plant Toxins*. John Wiley & Sons, Chichester.
8. **Bruneton, J. 1999**. *Toxic Plants Dangerous to Humans and Animals*. Intercept, Hampshire.

Gloriosa superba – orange form

Gloriosa superba – red form

Colchicum autumnale

GNIDIA KRAUSSIANA
Thymelaeaceae

---
yellow heads (English); harige gifbossie (Afrikaans)

DESCRIPTION *Gnidia* species (previously known as *Arthrosolen* and *Lasiosiphon* species) are erect shrublets with small leaves arranged along thin stems. Small, tubular, yellow flowers are arranged in sparse to dense heads. In *G. kraussiana*, the flowering stalks are leafless below the heads and the stems and leaves are hairy. *G. burchellii (harpuisbos)* is a woody shrub with leaves congested towards the branch ends. *Gnidia polycephala (Januariebos)* has numerous, erect branches that are leafless except when young, and few-flowered, hairy heads, each with a few large, papery bracts below the flowers.

TYPE OF TOXIN Diterpenoid.

IMPORTANCE Numerous fatalities in both humans and livestock are caused by *G. kraussiana* in various parts of Africa, including South Africa[1,2]. It is a traditional medicine and an overdose may be fatal. The plant has been used as a fish poison and arrow poison[3]. *G. burchellii, G. polycephala* and other species cause livestock losses in South Africa[4,5]. Related plants such as *Englerodaphne ovalifolia* and *Peddiea africana* are also known to be toxic.

POISONOUS INGREDIENTS *Gnidia* species contain toxic and irritant diterpenoids. Daphnane type esters are found in *D. kraussiana*, such as kraussianin and gnidilatin[6]. *G. burchellii* has been the source of 12-hydroxydaphnetoxin[7], and other *Gnidia* species produce several 12-esters of 12-hydroxydaphnetoxin, such as gnidicin and gniditrin[8].

PHARMACOLOGICAL EFFECTS *Gnidia* poisoning in livestock results in severe diarrhoea, weakness, fever and a rapid, weak pulse[1,4,5]. When large quantities are ingested, death may be sudden, without any obvious symptoms[5]. In humans, powdered material of *Gnidia* species causes irritation of the nose and throat, coughing and sneezing, followed by headache and nausea[1]. *Gnidia* diterpenoids have antitumour and antileukaemic activity[8].

DISTRIBUTION *G. kraussiana* occurs in the northern and eastern parts of South Africa (see map), *G. polycephala* mainly in Limpopo Province and *G. burchellii* in most parts except the central interior[4,5].

Kraussianin

12-Hydroxydaphnetoxin

1. **Watt, J.M. & Breyer-Brandwijk, M.G. 1962.** *The Medicinal and Poisonous Plants of Southern and Eastern Africa,* 2nd edition. Livingstone, London.
2. **Verdcourt, B. & Trump, E.C. 1969.** *Common Poisonous Plants of East Africa.* Collins, London.
3. **Neuwinger, H.D. 1996.** *African Ethnobotany: Poisons and Drugs: Chemistry, Pharmacology, Toxicology.* Chapman & Hall, Germany.
4. **Vahrmeijer, J. 1981.** *Poisonous Plants of Southern Africa That Cause Stock Losses.* Tafelberg Publishers, Cape Town.
5. **Kellerman, T.S., Coetzer, J.A.W. & Naudé, T.W. 1988.** *Plant Poisonings and Mycotoxicoses of Livestock in Southern Africa.* Oxford University Press, Cape Town.
6. **Borris, R.P. & Cordell, G.A. 1984.** Studies of the Thymelaeaceae. II. Antineoplastic principles of *Gnidia kraussiana*. *J. Nat. Prod.* 47: 270-278.
7. **Coetzer, J. & Pieterse, M.J. 1971.** The isolation of 12-hydroxydaphnetoxin, a degradation product of a constituent of *Lasiosiphon burchellii. J. S. Afr. Chem. Inst.* 24: 241-243.
8. **Harborne, J.B., Baxter, H. & Moss, G.P. (eds) 1997.** *Dictionary of Plant Toxins.* John Wiley & Sons, Chichester.

Gnidia kraussiana

Gnidia burchellii

Gnidia polycephala

Characteristic fruits of *Gnidia polycephala*

HELICHRYSUM ARGYROSPHAERUM

Asteraceae

---

wild everlasting (English); sewejaartjie, poprosie (Afrikaans)

DESCRIPTION The plant is an annual herb with trailing branches growing flat on the ground[1]. All parts are covered with grey, woolly hairs. The small, rounded flower heads are single and occur on the branch tips. They are surrounded by white or pinkish, papery scale leaves. At maturity, the tiny yellow florets are visible in the middle of each flower head.

TYPE OF TOXIN Unknown.

IMPORTANCE *H. argyrosphaerum* is not toxic to humans but has caused outbreaks of livestock poisoning in Namibia[2,3]. Despite the presence of the plant over large parts of South Africa, no cases of poisoning seem to have been recorded[2]. The poison mainly affects sheep, rarely cattle. The plant appears to be most toxic in the flowering stage and relatively large quantities have to be ingested over a long period before symptoms appear in sheep[2]. *H. cephaloideum* is known to be poisonous to sheep and causes paralysis of the alimentary tract[4]. Several *Helichrysum* species are used in South Africa as traditional medicine[5] but are not known to cause human poisoning.

POISONOUS INGREDIENTS The toxic compound is not known. Since there are some similarities with *Geigeria* poisoning[2], it may be speculated that sesquiterpenoid lactones or some other terpenoids may be responsible for the symptoms seen in sheep and cattle.

PHARMACOLOGICAL EFFECTS The symptoms of poisoning in sheep include weakness, blindness, paresis and paralysis[2]. There are marked lesions in the eye and nervous tissues[2,6]. Cattle show stiffness of the hindquarters or paralysis, but not blindness[2]. These symptoms are similar to those found in *vermeersiekte* (vomiting disease) caused by *Geigeria* species[2].

DISTRIBUTION *H. argyrosphaerum* occurs in sandy places and grows as a weed in disturbed areas. It is widely distributed over the northern and eastern parts of South Africa[1].

1. **Hilliard, O.M. 1983.** Asteraceae (Compositae) – Inuleae: Gnaphaliinae. *Flora of Southern Africa* 33,7,2: 61-310.
2. **Kellerman, T.S., Coetzer, J.A.W. & Naudé, T.W. 1988.** *Plant Poisonings and Mycotoxicoses of Livestock in Southern Africa.* Oxford University Press, Cape Town.
3. **Von Koenen, E. 1996.** *Heil-, Gift- u Essbare Pflanzen in Namibia.* Klaus Hess Verlag, Göttingen.
4. **Steyn, D.G. 1949.** *Die Vergiftiging van Mens en Dier.* Van Schaik, Pretoria.
5. **Watt, J.M. & Breyer-Brandwijk, M.G. 1962.** *The Medicinal and Poisonous Plants of Southern and Eastern Africa,* 2nd edition. Livingstone, London.
6. **Van der Lugt, J.J., Olivier, J. & Jordaan, P. 1996.** Status spongiosis, optic neuropathy, and retinal regeneration in *Helichrysum argyrosphaerum* poisoning in sheep and a goat. *Vet. Pathol.* 33: 495-502.

Helichrysum argyrosphaerum

Flower heads of *Helichrysum argyrosphaerum*

HOMERIA PALLIDA

Iridaceae

---

yellow tulp (English); geeltulp (Afrikaans)

DESCRIPTION *H. pallida* is a bulbous plant with a single, long, strap-shaped, leathery leaf[1]. Up to 10 star-shaped flowers are borne in a single inflorescence. They are yellow or rarely orange and have numerous small dark-coloured speckles towards the middle[1]. All the petals (tepals) are more or less similar in size, shape and colour, unlike most species of *Moraea*, where the three outer ones are markedly different from the inner ones. The three erect, petaloid style branches are characteristic. *Homeria* species are soon to be included in the genus *Moraea*[2]. *H. pallida* is the best known toxic species, and now also includes *H. glauca* (Natal yellow tulp)[1]. The latter was previously considered to be distinct. *H. miniata* (red *tulp* or *rooitulp*) usually has pinkish flowers, several leaves on each plant and a distinct star-shaped yellow marking in the middle of the flower[1].

TYPE OF TOXIN Cardiac glycoside (bufadienolide).

IMPORTANCE Poisoning by *Homeria* and *Moraea* species is known as *tulp* poisoning in both Afrikaans and English[3-5]. This type of poisoning is a serious problem in South Africa and sporadically causes severe losses of cattle, sheep, goats and donkeys[4]. Horses usually manage to avoid the plants. The toxicity is not lost on drying, so that hay contaminated with *tulp* remains poisonous[4]. Animals do not normally ingest the plants and are usually only poisoned when they are introduced into new pastures or when grazing becomes scarce. No human fatalities seem to have been reported[6]. *Tulp* poisoning is similar to *slangkop* poisoning (caused by *Urginea* and *Ornithoglossum*) but the latter slows the heart rate, while it is quickened in the case of *Homeria* species[3].

POISONOUS INGREDIENTS *Homeria* species are now known to contain heart glycosides (bufadienolides). *H. pallida* (previously *H. glauca*) has yielded two bufadienolides – the major compound was identified as 1α,2α-epoxyscillirosidin[7].

PHARMACOLOGICAL EFFECTS *Homeria* species are extremely toxic. About 700 g of flowering plants of *H. pallida* may kill a sheep within two hours[6]. When injected into test animals, the LD_{50} of 1α,2α-epoxyscillirosidin was less than 0,2 mg/kg for guinea-pigs and 3,6 mg/kg for mice[5]. The symptoms of poisoning in stock animals are typical for heart glycosides. Animals become apathetic and hold their heads down, and they may also show abnormal heartbeat, bloat, diarrhoea, and partial paralysis of the hindquarters[5].

DISTRIBUTION *H. pallida* is widely distributed (see map), while *H. miniata* is found only in the extreme west, from Cape Town to Namaqualand[1].

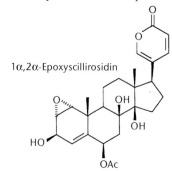

1α,2α-Epoxyscillirosidin

1. **Goldblatt, P. 1987.** Systematics and biology of *Homeria* (Iridaceae). *Ann. Missouri Bot. Gard.* 74: 542-569.
2. **Goldblatt, P. & Manning, J.C. 2000.** Iridaceae. In O.A. Leistner (ed.), Seed Plants of Southern Africa: Families and Genera. *Strelitzia* 10: 623-638. National Botanical Institute, Pretoria.
3. **Steyn, D.G. 1949.** *Die Vergiftiging van Mens en Dier.* Van Schaik, Pretoria.
4. **Vahrmeijer, J. 1981.** *Poisonous Plants of Southern Africa That Cause Stock Losses.* Tafelberg Publishers, Cape Town.
5. **Kellerman, T.S., Coetzer, J.A.W. & Naudé, T.W.1988.** *Plant Poisonings and Mycotoxicoses of Livestock in Southern Africa.* Oxford University Press, Cape Town.
6. **Watt, J.M. & Breyer-Brandwijk, M.G. 1962.** *The Medicinal and Poisonous Plants of Southern and Eastern Africa*, 2nd edition. Livingstone, London.
7. **Enslin, P.R., Naudé, T.W., Potgieter, T.J. & Van Wyk, A.J. 1966.** 1α,2α-Epoxyscillirosidin, the main toxic principle of *Homeria glauca* (Wood & Evans) N.E. Br. *Tetrahedron* 22: 3213-3220.

Homeria pallida

Homeria miniata

HYAENANCHE GLOBOSA

Euphorbiaceae

---

hyena poison (English); wolwegifboom, gifboom, boesmangif (Afrikaans)

DESCRIPTION The single species of *Hyaenanche* is a shrub or small rounded tree of up to 5 m in height, with dark green, leathery leaves arranged in fours at each node[1,2]. Male and female trees both have inconspicuous, reddish flowers without petals. The male flowers are borne in many-flowered clusters and the female flowers single or in twos or threes. The fruits are large, rounded capsules with three or four segments that split open at maturity to reveal six shiny black seeds[1,2]. The plant was previously known as *Toxicodendron capense* or *T. globosum*[1,2].

TYPE OF TOXIN Sesquiterpenoid lactone.

IMPORTANCE *Hyaenanche* is the Greek word for hyena poison, and was chosen because the fruits were used in former times to poison carcasses in order to destroy hyenas and other vermin[3-5]. The San people used the powdered seeds as arrow poison[3-5]. There are no recent reports of human or livestock poisoning.

POISONOUS INGREDIENTS The plant contains several toxic sesquiterpene lactones such as tutin, mellitoxin, urushiol III and isodihydro-hyaenanchine. Tutin (previously known as hyaenanchine) appears to be the major compound[6,7] but there are no recent studies.

PHARMACOLOGICAL EFFECTS The fruit and seeds of *H. globosa* (and possibly other parts) are extremely toxic. Ten grams of dry rind from an immature fruit produced, within a few minutes, convulsions and death in a rabbit[8]. The main toxic compound, tutin, is known to cause convulsions, delirium and coma in humans[9].

DISTRIBUTION *H. globosa* is a narrow endemic and is restricted to a single, flat-topped mountain near Van Rhynsdorp in southern Namaqualand. This mountain is known as the *Gifberg* ('Poison Mountain') because of the presence of these red trees[2,3].

Tutin

1. **Phillips, E.P. 1941.** *Toxicodendron globosum. Flowering Plants of Africa* 21: t. 837
2. **Coates Palgrave, K. 1977.** *Trees of Southern Africa.* Struik, Cape Town.
3. **Van Wyk, B-E. & Gericke, N. 2000.** *People's Plants. A Guide to Useful Plants of Southern Africa.* Briza Publications, Pretoria.
4. **Watt, J.M. & Breyer-Brandwijk, M.G. 1962.** *The Medicinal and Poisonous Plants of Southern and Eastern Africa*, 2nd edition. Livingstone, London.
5. **Neuwinger, H.D. 1996.** *African Ethnobotany: Poisons and Drugs: Chemistry, Pharmacology, Toxicology.* Chapman & Hall, Germany.
6. **Corbella, A., Jommi, G. & Scolastico, C. 1966.** Structural correlation between capensin and tutin. *Tetrahedron Lett.* 1966: 4819–4823.
7. **Harborne, J.B., Baxter, H. & Moss, G.P. (eds) 1997.** *Dictionary of Plant Toxins.* John Wiley & Sons, Chichester.
8. **Steyn, D.G. 1949.** *Die Vergiftiging van Mens en Dier.* Van Schaik, Pretoria.
9. **Merck 1989.** *The Merck Index.* 11th edition. Merck, Rahway.

Hyaenanche globosa

Leaves of *Hyaenanche globosa*

Fruits of *Hyaenanche globosa*

HYPERICUM AETHIOPICUM

Clusiaceae

St John's wort (English); Johanneskruid, seeroogbossie, vlieëbossie (Afrikaans)

DESCRIPTION *H. aethiopicum* is a small shrublet with erect, unbranched stems arising from a woody rootstock below the ground. The leaves are small, oval in shape, stalkless and arise in opposite pairs along the stems. Small, yellow flowers are borne in clusters at the branch tips. The leaves and calyx lobes have numerous small, black gland dots. Two subspecies have been described that differ in their distribution areas – subsp. *aethiopicum* has stalked glands, while subsp. *sonderi* has stalkless (sessile) glands[1]. *H. aethiopicum* is similar to the exotic *H. perforatum* (the original St John's wort)[1,2] that is well known as a herbal remedy for the treatment of depression. Another potentially harmful species is *H. revolutum* (known as curry bush or *kerriebos*), an indigenous woody shrub or small tree with large yellow flowers that has become a popular garden plant[1].

TYPE OF TOXIN Bianthraquinone.

IMPORTANCE *Hypericum* species cause primary photosensitivity in domestic animals[3-5]. The toxic principle is a photodynamic agent, hypericin, which reacts with sunlight to cause severe tissue damage. Only unpigmented parts of the animal are affected, so that dark-coloured animals are not at risk. *Hypericum* poisoning (hypericism) in South Africa is very rare[5], but a few incidences of primary photosensitivity have been attributed to *H. aethiopicum* and *H. revolutum*. *H. perforatum* frequently causes hypericism in other parts of the

world[6]. Despite its common occurrence in the Cape, no local cases of poisoning are known[5].

POISONOUS INGREDIENTS The photosensitivity caused by *Hypericum* species is ascribed to bianthraquinones (naphthodianthrones), of which hypericin is the major compound in *H. perforatum* and possibly also in the indigenous species.

PHARMACOLOGICAL EFFECTS The first obvious symptom is that the animals tend to avoid sunlight[3-5]. The facial tissues become swollen (hence the Afrikaans name *dikkop* for the syndrome) and later the skin turns leathery and parchment-like, so that the lips and eyelids become immobilised[5]. The condition may also be caused by the exotic buckwheat (*Fagopyrum esculentum*). Further symptoms of hypericum poisoning include loss of appetite, peeling of the skin, hair loss, convulsions and coma[3-5].

DISTRIBUTION *H. aethiopicum* subsp. *aethiopicum* occurs along the Cape coastal region, while the subsp. *sonderi* is widely distributed in the eastern grassland areas of South Africa (see map)[1]. *Hypericum revolutum* grows naturally from the Eastern Cape Province northwards to Limpopo Province[1]. *Hypericum perforatum* is an exotic (European) plant, accidentally introduced in 1942 as an impurity in vetch seed[2]. It has become a weed in the Western Cape Province and thousands of hectares have become infested.

Hypericin

1. **Killick, D.J.B. & Robson, N.K.B. 1976.** Clusiaceae. *Flora of Southern Africa* 22: 14-20.
2. **Henderson, M. & Anderson, J.G. 1966.** *Common Weeds in South Africa. Memoirs of the Botanical Survey of South Africa* 37.
3. **Watt, J.M. & Breyer-Brandwijk, M.G. 1962.** *The Medicinal and Poisonous Plants of Southern and Eastern Africa*, 2nd edition. Livingstone, London.
4. **Vahrmeijer, J. 1981.** *Poisonous Plants of Southern Africa That Cause Stock Losses.* Tafelberg Publishers, Cape Town.
5. **Kellerman, T.S., Coetzer, J.A.W. & Naudé, T.W. 1988.** *Plant Poisonings and Mycotoxicoses of Livestock in Southern Africa.* Oxford University Press, Cape Town.
6. **Harborne, J.B., Baxter, H. & Moss, G.P. (eds) 1997.** *Dictionary of Plant Toxins.* John Wiley & Sons, Chichester.

Hypericum aethiopicum

Flowers of *Hypericum aethiopicum*

Hypericum revolutum

Hypericum perforatum

JATROPHA CURCAS

Euphorbiaceae

---

purging nut (English); mathlapametse (Tswana); purgeerboontjie (Afrikaans)

DESCRIPTION *J. curcas* is a shrub or small tree of up to 6 m in height[1]. The leaves are heart-shaped and usually have five large lobes but are sometimes three-lobed or seven-lobed. The small male and female flowers are greenish-yellow and hairy. The fruit capsules are three-lobed, egg-shaped and dark brown or black at maturity. Each fruit contains three large black seeds (nuts) of about 20 mm long. *J. multifida* is a popular exotic garden plant. It is a shrub or small tree with cream-coloured flowers and leaves that resemble those of cassava (*Manihot esculenta*).

TYPE OF TOXIN Lectin.

IMPORTANCE *J. curcas* is a common cause of human poisoning in South Africa[2-4]. It is a popular Tswana traditional medicine, and extracts of the leaves, seeds or bark are taken as a purgative[3]. Two seeds are said to be strongly purgative[2], while larger numbers may cause severe diarrhoea, abdominal pain and vomiting[2-4]. The nuts are tasty and commonly cause acute poisoning in children[4], but recovery is usually rapid after treatment. The symptoms in animals are diarrhoea, laboured breathing, dehydration and loss of condition[5], but

there are so far no reports for South Africa. In contrast, leaves of *J. multifida* have caused stock losses.

POISONOUS INGREDIENTS The seeds of *J. curcas* (and *J. multifida*) contain curcin, a lectin (toxic protein or toxalbumin)[2-4]. Curcin is not fat-soluble, so that it does not occur in the seed oil. The purgative activity of the seed oil is ascribed to irritant diterpenoids[6] of the tiglian (phorbol) type, such as curcusone A and curcusone C, and also to curcanoleic acid, which is similar to ricinoleic acid (in castor oil) and crotonoleic acid (in croton oil)[3,4]. The leaves of *J. multifida*, are strongly cyanogenic.

PHARMACOLOGICAL EFFECTS The toxicity and gastro-intestinal irritation of *J. curcas* is ascribed to curcin but it may also be partly due to diterpene esters[7], some of which have anticancer and tumour-promoting activity[8].

DISTRIBUTION *J. curcas* is a tropical American plant but has become naturalised in the northern and eastern parts of South Africa, as shown on the map[1].

Curcusone A

1. **Coates Palgrave, K. 1977.** *Trees of Southern Africa*. Struik, Cape Town.
2. **Watt, J.M. & Breyer-Brandwijk, M.G. 1962.** *The Medicinal and Poisonous Plants of Southern and Eastern Africa*, 2nd edition. Livingstone, London.
3. **Mampane, K.J., Joubert, P.H. & Hay, I.T. 1987.** *Jatropha curcas*: use as a traditional Tswana medicine and its role as a cause of acute poisoning. *Phytother. Res.* 1: 50-51.
4. **Joubert, P.H., Brown, J.M.M., Hay, I.T. & Sebata, P.D.H. 1984.** Acute poisoning with *Jatropha curcas* (purging nut tree) in children. *S. Afr. Med. J.* 65: 729-730.
5. **Kellerman, T.S., Coetzer, J.A.W. & Naudé, T.W. 1988.** *Plant Poisonings and Mycotoxicoses of Livestock in Southern Africa*. Oxford University Press, Cape Town.
6. **Adolf, W., Opferkuch, H.J. & Hecker, E. 1984.** Irritant phorbol derivatives from four *Jatropha* species. *Phytochemistry* 23: 129-132.
7. **Neuwinger, H.D. 1994.** *Afrikanische Arzneipflanzen und Jagdgifte*. Wissenschaftliche Verlagsgesellschaft, Stuttgart.
8. **Hirota, M., Suttajit, M., Suguri, H., Endo, Y., Shudo, K., Wongchai, V., Hecker, E. & Fujiki, H. 1988.** A new tumor promotor from the seed oil of *Jatropha curcas* L., an intramolecular diester of 12-deoxy-16-hydroxyphorbol. *Cancer Res.* 48: 5800-5804.

Leaves of *Jatropha curcas*

Fruit of *Jatropha curcas*

Seeds (nuts) of *Jatropha curcas*

Jatropha multifida

KALANCHOE ROTUNDIFOLIA

Crassulaceae

---

nentabos, plakkie (Afrikaans)

DESCRIPTION *K. rotundifolia* is a succulent perennial herb with erect, unbranched stems and rounded to oblong fleshy leaves arranged in opposite pairs[1,2]. The tubular, orange or red flowers are borne in many-flowered clusters on a long stalk. *Kalanchoe* species can easily be distinguished from other genera (i.e. other *plakkies*) by the four petals and four fruit segments – *Cotyledon* and *Tylecodon* species invariably have five[1,2]. Another common toxic *Kalanchoe* is *K. lanceolata*, an erect annual or short-lived perennial with bright green, oblong, succulent leaves and yellow to orange flowers[1-3]. *K. thyrsiflora* is also known to be poisonous.

TYPE OF TOXIN Cardiac glycoside (bufadienolide).

IMPORTANCE *Kalanchoe* species are known to be toxic to livestock and cause the well-known poisoning syndrome known as *nenta* or *krimpsiekte*[2,3]. Several *Kalanchoe* species have been implicated in localised outbreaks, but other members of the Crassulaceae, particularly *Tylecodon* and *Cotyledon*, are better known for causing *krimpsiekte* under field conditions. Goats are mostly affected, followed by sheep, cattle, and to a lesser extent horses[3]. People and dogs can be poisoned by eating meat (even cooked meat) of a sheep or goat that has died from *krimpsiekte*[3,4]. *Krimpsiekte* occurs mainly in spring and summer, usually during droughts when grazing becomes scarce. Flowers are said to be more poisonous than leaves[3,4].

POISONOUS INGREDIENTS Three bufa-dienolides have been found in *K. lanceolata*, namely lanceotoxin A, lanceotoxin B and hellebrigenin[5,6].

PHARMACOLOGICAL EFFECTS Acute poisoning results in symptoms similar to those of other bufadienolides, while chronic and cumulative poisoning produce symptoms of *krimpsiekte* (see *Cotyledon orbiculata*, p. 76). Only 300 g of *K. rotundifolia* flowers are sufficient to kill a sheep within 36 hours[7]. Lanceotoxins A and B are highly poisonous – the LD_{50} when administered subcutaneously to guinea-pigs was 0,2 and 0,1 mg/kg respectively[5].

DISTRIBUTION *K. rotundifolia* is widely distributed in the eastern parts of South Africa (see map), while *K. lanceolata* is found north of the Free State only[1-3].

Lanceotoxin A:
R=

Lanceotoxin B:
R=

1. **Tölken, H.R. 1985.** Crassulaceae. *Flora of Southern Africa* 14: 61-71.
2. **Vahrmeijer, J. 1981.** *Poisonous Plants of Southern Africa That Cause Stock Losses.* Tafelberg Publishers, Cape Town.
3. **Kellerman, T.S., Coetzer, J.A.W. & Naudé, T.W. 1988.** *Plant Poisonings and Mycotoxicoses of Livestock in Southern Africa.* Oxford University Press, Cape Town.
4. **Steyn, D.G. 1949.** *Die Vergiftiging van Mens en Dier.* Van Schaik, Pretoria.
5. **Anderson, L.A.P., Schultz, R.A., Joubert, J.P.J., Prozesky, L., Kellerman, T.S., Erasmus, G.L. & Procos, J. 1983.** Krimpsiekte and acute cardiac glycoside poisoning in sheep caused by bufadienolides from the plant *Kalanchoe lanceolata* Forssk. *Onderstepoort J. Vet. Res.* 50: 295-300.
6. **Anderson, L.A.P., Steyn, P.S. & van Heerden, F.R. 1984.** The characterization of two novel bufadienolides, lanceotoxins A and B from *Kalanchoe lanceolata* (Forssk.) Pers. *J. Chem. Soc., Perkin Trans. I*, 1984: 1573-1575.
7. **Watt, J.M. & Breyer-Brandwijk, M.G. 1962.** *The Medicinal and Poisonous Plants of Southern and Eastern Africa*, 2nd edition. Livingstone, London.

Kalanchoe rotundifolia

Flowers of *Kalanchoe rotundifolia*

Kalanchoe thyrsiflora

Kalanchoe lanceolata

LANTANA CAMARA

Verbenaceae

lantana, tick-berry (English); gomdagga, wilderoosmaryn (Afrikaans)

DESCRIPTION *L. camara* is a weedy shrub or untidy climber with square stems and aromatic, dark green leaves that smell strongly when crushed[1]. The stems are covered with hairs and sharp, recurved prickles. Attractive flowers (usually pink and yellow, but sometimes orange, red, yellow or white) are borne in flat heads. The fruit (berry) is a cluster of one-seeded drupes that are at first glossy green but turn purplish black when they ripen[1].

TYPE OF TOXIN Triterpenoid.

IMPORTANCE The plant is one of the most common causes of livestock poisoning in South Africa[2-4], causing liver damage, jaundice and resultant photosensitivity, manifesting mainly as facial eczema. In Australia, the syndrome is known as pink nose[2]. This type of poisoning occurs almost exclusively in cattle[2-4]. Species of *Lippia* (see *L. rehmannii*, p. 140) are also known to be hepatotoxic and may cause similar outbreaks[2-4].

POISONOUS INGREDIENTS The toxins in the plant are oleanane type triterpenoids. Lantadene A and lantadene B are the main poisonous compounds[5-7].

PHARMACOLOGICAL EFFECTS The triterpenoids of *Lantana* are icterogenic and cause jaundice as a result of liver damage[3]. The characteristic swelling, yellowing and later peeling of unpigmented skin is due to the presence of phylloerythrin, a photodynamic porphyrin that reacts with sunlight and causes severe cell damage[3]. The compound is normally formed when chlorophyll is broken down by microorganisms in the rumen, but it now accumulates in the liver as a result of the damage caused by *Lantana* triterpenoids. In sheep, the oral toxicity of lantadene A is 60 mg/kg body-weight but when administered intravenously, only 2 mg/kg body-weight[8].

DISTRIBUTION *L. camara* is a noxious weed of tropical American origin that was originally imported as an ornamental garden shrub. Birds eat the berries and spread the seeds, so that the plant has escaped from gardens and is now widely distributed in South Africa[1].

Lantadene A

1. **Henderson, L. 2001.** *Alien Weeds and Invasive Plants.* Plant Protection Research Institute Handbook no. 12, Agricultural Research Council, Pretoria.
2. **Steyn, D.G. 1934.** *The Toxicology of Plants in South Africa.* Central News Agency, South Africa.
3. **Vahrmeijer, J. 1981.** *Poisonous Plants of Southern Africa That Cause Stock Losses.* Tafelberg Publishers, Cape Town.
4. **Kellerman, T.S., Coetzer, J.A.W. & Naudé, T.W. 1988.** *Plant Poisonings and Mycotoxicoses of Livestock in Southern Africa.* Oxford University Press, Cape Town.
5. **Louw, P.G.J. 1943.** Lantanin, the active principle of *Lantana camara* L. I. Isolation and preliminary results on the determination of its constitution. *Onderstepoort J. Vet. Res.* 18: 197-202.
6. **Louw, P.G.J. 1948.** Lantadene A, the active principle of *Lantana camara* L. II. Isolation of lantadene B and oxygen functions of lantadene A and lantadene B. *Onderstepoort J. Vet. Res.* 23: 233-238.
7. **Hart, N.K., Lamberton, J.A., Sioumis, A.A., & Suares, H. 1976.** New Triterpenes of *Lantana camara*. A comparative study of the constituents of several taxa. *Austr. J. Chem.* 29: 655-671.
8. **Harborne, J.B., Baxter, H. & Moss, G.P. (eds) 1997.** *Dictionary of Plant Toxins.* John Wiley & Sons, Chichester.

Flower heads of *Lantana camara*

Flowers and berries of *Lantana camara*

LASIOSPERMUM BIPINNATUM

Asteraceae

---

ganskweek (Afrikaans)

DESCRIPTION *L. bipinnatum* is an aromatic, creeping to erect perennial herb with soft, compound leaves that are feathery in appearance. Small heads of flowers are borne individually on long, slender stalks, well above the rest of the plant. Each head has numerous yellow disk florets in the middle and a single row of pure white ray florets around the edge.

TYPE OF TOXIN Sesquiterpenoid.

IMPORTANCE The plant is toxic to livestock and is known to cause liver damage and resultant photosensitivity in sheep and cattle[1-4]. Outbreaks have been reported mainly in the eastern Karoo and the Free State Province[1,4]. The plant is considered to be an important cause of poisoning in the Graaff-Reinet district[4]. *Ganskweek* is resistant to frost and it may become dominant in winter and early spring, before grasses have had a chance to recover[1]. Feeding experiments have confirmed that the plant causes hepatogenous photosensitivity in sheep[1-3].

POISONOUS INGREDIENTS The plant is said[1] to contain furanosesquiterpenoids similar to those isolated from the stock-poisoning Australian shrub *Myoporum deserti*. Examples of these compounds are dehydromyodesmone and dehydrongaione, the latter of which was experimentally shown to be hepatotoxic[5]. Two furanosesquiterpenoids have indeed been isolated from *L. radiatum*[6], namely lasiosperman and dehydrolasiosperman, and it is likely that *L. bipinnatum* have these or similar compounds.

PHARMACOLOGICAL EFFECTS *Ganskweek* is highly toxic – about 7 g/kg body-weight may be fatal to sheep[2]. Symptoms may appear within three days after the animals started ingesting the plant[1] and include photosensitivity, jaundice (icterus), colic, constipation and high temperature[1]. Lesions of the liver and lungs[7] are evident in poisoned sheep.

DISTRIBUTION The plant is widely distributed in South Africa but is particularly common in the eastern Karoo, Eastern Cape Province and the Free State Province.

Lasiosperman

1. **Kellerman, T.S., Coetzer, J.A.W. & Naudé, T.W. 1988.** *Plant Poisonings and Mycotoxicoses of Livestock in Southern Africa.* Oxford University Press, Cape Town.
2. **Adelaar, T.F., Terblanche, M., Smit, J.D., Naudé, T.W. & Codd, L.E. 1964.** A hitherto unknown poisonous plant: *Lasiospermum bipinnatum* (Thunb.) Druce. Preliminary communication. *J. S. Afr. Vet. Med. Ass.* 35: 11-16.
3. **Kellerman, T.S., Basson, P.A., Naudé, T.W., Van Rensburg, I.B.R. & Welman, W.G. 1973.** Photosensitivity in South Africa. I. A comparative study of *Asaemia axillaris* (Thunb.) Harv. ex Jackson and *Lasiospermum bipinnatum* (Thunb.) Druce poisoning in sheep. *Onderstepoort J. Vet. Res.* 40: 115-126.
4. **Thornton, D.J. 1977.** Ganskweek (*Lasiospermum bipinnatum*) poisoning in cattle. *J. S. Afr. Vet. Ass.* 48: 210-211.
5. **Harborne, J.B., Baxter, H. & Moss, G.P. (eds) 1997.** *Dictionary of Plant Toxins.* John Wiley & Sons, Chichester.
6. **Bornowski, H. 1971.** Die Struktur des Lasiospermans, ein neuer Typ von Furansesquiterpenen. *Tetrahedron* 27: 4101-4108.
7. **Williams, M.C. 1990.** The pathology of experimental *Lasiospermum bipinnatum* (Thunb.) Druce (Asteraceae) poisoning in sheep. I. Hepatic lesions; II. Pulmonary and miscellaneous lesions. *Onderstepoort J. Vet. Res.* 57: 249-261; 263-268.

Lasiospermum bipinnatum

Leaves of *Lasiospermum bipinnatum*

Flower heads of *Lasiospermum bipinnatum*

LEUCAENA LEUCOCEPHALA

Leguminosae

leucaena, giant wattle, giant leucaena, jumbie bean, lead tree (English); reusewattel (Afrikaans)

DESCRIPTION Giant wattle is a robust tree with hairy stems, large, compound leaves and large, globose, white or cream flower heads that are borne singly or in groups of two or three. The pods are oblong, flat and brown when ripe and are characteristically borne in clusters[1]. The stinkbean (*Paraserianthes lophantha*) is superficially similar, but the latter has oblong, bottlebrush-like flower clusters and the leaves emit a strong smell when crushed[1].

TYPE OF TOXIN Amino acid.

IMPORTANCE Giant wattle is grown as a multi-purpose plant in agroforestry for use as fodder and as a source of poles and firewood. It causes toxic effects when it forms more than 25% of the diet of animals[1] and may also cause poisoning when green pods, shoots and seeds are used as human food[2].

POISONOUS INGREDIENTS The toxicity of leucaena is caused by L-mimosine, a non-protein amino acid that occurs in concentrations of 2 to 5% (leaves) or up to 9% (seeds)[2]. A detoxification product of mimosine that is formed in ruminants,

3-hydroxy-4(1*H*)-pyridone, is also harmful[2]. The poisonous principle in stink bean (eaten in Java as djenkol bean) contains another amino acid, L-djenkolic acid, which may cause kidney malfunction if eaten in large quantities[2].

PHARMACOLOGICAL EFFECTS The characteristic symptom of mimosine poisoning is hair loss (alopecia) and animals may become completely bald[2]. Goitrogenic effects (thyroid impairment and goitre) are known to occur in ruminants or humans if 3-hydroxy-4(1*H*)-pyridone accumulates in the system[2]. L-djenkolic acid in stink bean may cause kidney malfunction in humans or animals when the acid crystallises from the urine in large quantities[2].

DISTRIBUTION *L. leucocephala* is indigenous to the extreme southern parts of North America[3]. It is sometimes grown as an ornamental tree in gardens despite the fact that it is a declared invader that has spread over large parts of KwaZulu-Natal and Mpumalanga Province[1]. *Paraserianthes* is an invader from Australia that is found mainly in the Western Cape Province and parts of the Eastern Cape Province[1].

L-Mimosine

L-Djenkolic acid

1. **Henderson, L. 2001.** *Alien Weeds and Invasive Plants.* Plant Protection Research Institute Handbook no. 12, Agricultural Research Council, Pretoria.
2. **Harborne, J.B., Baxter, H. & Moss, G.P. (eds) 1997.** *Dictionary of Plant Toxins.* John Wiley & Sons, Chichester.
3. **Griffiths, M. (ed.). 1994.** *Index of Garden Plants.* (The new Royal Horticultural Society Dictionary). Macmillan Press, London.

Leucaena leucocephala

Flower head and pods of *Leucaena leucocephala*   Pods of *Paraserianthes lophantha*

LIPPIA REHMANNII
Verbenaceae

---

laventelbossie (Afrikaans)

DESCRIPTION *L. rehmannii* is an aromatic, shrubby plant with erect branches sprouting from a woody base[1,2]. The elliptic leaves occur in opposite pairs along the stems. They are conspicuously veined, toothed along the margins and rough to the touch. Minute cream-coloured flowers are borne in short rounded heads that occur on long, unbranched stalks. This species is similar to *L. scaberrima* (*beukesbossie* in Afrikaans) but the latter has much larger bracts in the flower heads. Another well-known and very common species is *L. javanica* (fever tea or *koorsbossie*). It is similar to *L. scaberrima* but is a much taller plant and the bracts are shorter than the flowers, not longer than the flowers as in the latter[1].

TYPE OF TOXIN Triterpenoid.

IMPORTANCE *Lippia* species are known to cause liver damage and photosensitisation (*geeldikkop*) in livestock[2-5] but outbreaks are very rare[5]. *L. rehmannii, L. javanica* and *L. scaberrima* have been implicated in stock losses[2-5]. *L. javanica* and *L. scaberrima* are used in traditional medicine[4,6,7]. The leaves are rich in essential oils[7] and both species are used as a tea to treat coughs, colds, fever and bronchitis. Several other medicinal uses have been recorded[4,6]. In view of the known toxicity of *Lippia* species, the prolonged use of high doses of the plants is potentially harmful.

POISONOUS INGREDIENTS *L. rehmannii* contains rehmannic acid, better known as lantadene A (see *Lantana camara*, p. 134)[8]. The plant also yields icterogenin, another hepatotoxic triterpenoid.

PHARMACOLOGICAL EFFECTS *Lippia* triterpenoids are toxic and cause liver damage. The symptoms of intoxication and further details are given under *Lantana camara*.

DISTRIBUTION *L. rehmannii* occurs in the north-eastern parts of South Africa (see map). *L. javanica* has a similar distribution but the plant also occurs further south in KwaZulu-Natal and the Eastern Cape Province. *L. scaberrima* is abundant in the Northern Cape Province and the North West Province.

Lantadene A

1. **Pearson, H.H.W. 1912.** Verbenaceae. *Flora Capensis* 5(1): 192-197.
2. **Vahrmeijer, J. 1981.** *Poisonous Plants of Southern Africa That Cause Stock Losses.* Tafelberg Publishers, Cape Town.
3. **Steyn, D.G. 1949.** *Die Vergiftiging van Mens en Dier.* Van Schaik, Pretoria.
4. **Watt, J.M. & Breyer-Brandwijk, M.G. 1962.** *The Medicinal and Poisonous Plants of Southern and Eastern Africa*, 2nd edition. Livingstone, London.
5. **Kellerman, T.S., Coetzer, J.A.W. & Naudé, T.W. 1988.** *Plant Poisonings and Mycotoxicoses of Livestock in Southern Africa.* Oxford University Press, Cape Town.
6. **Van Wyk, B-E., Van Oudtshoorn, B. & Gericke, N. 2000.** *Medicinal Plants of South Africa*, 2nd edition. Briza Publications, Pretoria.
7. **Van Wyk, B-E. & Gericke, N. 2000.** *People's Plants. A Guide to Useful Plants of Southern Africa.* Briza Publications, Pretoria.
8. **Barton, D.H.R. & De Mayo, P. 1954.** Triterpenoids. Part XV. The constitution of icterogenin, a physiologically active triterpenoid. *Chem. Soc.* 1954: 887-900.

Lippia rehmannii

Flower heads of *Lippia rehmannii*

Lippia javanica

Lippia scaberrima

LOTONONIS LAXA

Fabaceae

---

wild lucerne (English); wildelusern (Afrikaans)

DESCRIPTION *L. laxa* is a creeping perennial herb with silver-hairy trifoliate leaves and a single stipule at the base of each leaf stalk[1]. The flowers are very small, yellow when young but sometimes turning to orange with age. The fruits are oblong hairy pods. *L. carnosa* is a sparse shrubby and practically hairless plant with narrow, fleshy leaves and bright blue flowers. *L. involucrata* is a hairy perennial herb with creeping annual branches radiating from a woody rootstock and clusters of bright yellow flowers. *L. fruticoides* is a robust, erect, annual with yellowish-green twigs that are branched in a zigzag pattern. It has narrowly oblong leaflets, clusters of a few, tiny yellow flowers and oblong, sharp-pointed pods[1].

TYPE OF TOXIN Cyanogenic glycoside.

IMPORTANCE Sporadic outbreaks of fatal poisoning of sheep due to *L. laxa*, *L. carnosa* and *L. involucrata* have been reported[2,3]. *L. fruticoides* is particularly toxic (it contains about 468 mg of cyanide per 100 g dry weight)[4] and has been implicated in sheep poisoning in the Middelburg and Beaufort West districts. Plants containing 20 mg cyanide per 100 g of dried material are usually considered poisonous, so that *L. fruticoides* is exceptionally toxic[4].

POISONOUS INGREDIENTS *Lotononis* species contain the well-known cyanogenic glucoside, prunasin, as well as malonyl esters of prunasin[4]. At least 60 of the 150 species in the genus are known to be cyanogenic[5], and most of them have very high levels of cyanogenic compounds. *L. involucrata* and several other species also contain senecionine and integerrimine[6], both hepatotoxic macrocyclic pyrrolizidine alkaloids.

PHARMACOLOGICAL EFFECTS Sheep that were killed by *L. laxa and L. involucrata* showed typical symptoms of hydrogen cyanide poisoning (*geilsiekte* in Afrikaans), some with severe diarrhoea[2]. Prussic acid (*blousuur* in Afrikaans) is present in plants as cyanogenic glycosides. When the plant material is damaged and cells are broken, hydrolysing enzymes are released that react with the glycosides (in this case prunasin) to form glucose and benzaldehyde. In the process, hydrogen cyanide (a lethal gas) is released.

DISTRIBUTION *L. laxa* is one of the most widespread species of *Lotononis* and occurs from the Eastern Cape Province northwards and eastwards (see map). *L. fruticoides* grows in the Eastern Karoo and *L. carnosa* mainly in the Eastern Cape Province.

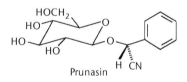

Prunasin

1. **Van Wyk, B-E. 1991.** A synopsis of the genus *Lotononis* (Fabaceae: Crotalarieae). *Contributions from the Bolus Herbarium* 14: 1-292.
2. **Steyn, D.G. 1949.** *Die Vergiftiging van Mens en Dier.* Van Schaik, Pretoria.
3. **Watt, J.M. & Breyer-Brandwijk, M.G. 1962.** *The Medicinal and Poisonous Plants of Southern and Eastern Africa*, 2nd edition. Livingstone, London.
4. **Lechtenberg, M., Nahrstedt, A., Brinker, A.M., Seigler, D.S. & Readel, K. 1999.** Prunasin 6'-malonate from *Lotononis fruticoides* and *Lotononis aff. falcata* (Fabaceae). *Biochem. Syst. Ecol.* 27: 607-612.
5. **Van Wyk, B.E. 1989.** The taxonomic significance of cyanogenesis in *Lotononis* and related genera. *Biochem. Syst. Ecol.* 17: 297-303.
6. **Van Wyk, B.E. & Verdoorn, G.H. 1989.** A chemotaxonomic survey of major alkaloids in *Lotononis* and *Buchenroedera*. *Biochem. Syst. Ecol.* 17: 385-389.

Lotononis laxa

Lotononis carnosa

Lotononis involucrata

MELIA AZEDARACH

Meliaceae

---

syringa tree, Persian lilac (English); seringboom (Afrikaans)

DESCRIPTION M. azedarach is a medium-sized to large tree with a spreading crown and smooth, reddish-brown bark[1,2]. The compound leaves are glossy green and turn yellow in autumn. Strongly scented flowers are produced in large, sparse clusters in spring and early summer. The fruit is a round, green, thinly fleshy berry that turns yellowish-brown and becomes wrinkled when it ripens. The berries often persist long after the leaves have fallen[1,2].

TYPE OF TOXIN Triterpenoid (limonoid).

IMPORTANCE Syringa berries (less often bark or leaves) are one of the most common causes of human poisoning in South Africa and numerous cases end up in hospitals each year[3,4]. Fortunately, the patients (usually infants and children) often recover after treatment, but fatalities have nevertheless been recorded[3]. Ruminants and chickens are occasionally poisoned, but pigs are quite sensitive[3,5-7]. Ripe berries are more poisonous than green berries or leaves[5-7]. It is interesting that only some trees and trees from some areas are toxic.

POISONOUS INGREDIENTS M. azedarach contains numerous limonoids, of which melinoon and melianol are the two major compounds. The toxicity, however, is linked mainly to four relatively minor compounds, namely the tetranor-triterpenoids[8], meliatoxins A_1, A_2, B_1 and B_2. Studies on the ripe fruits have confirmed that these meliatoxins are responsible for most but not all the symptoms of poisoning[8]. The concentration of meliatoxins in the ripe fruits was found to be about 0,5% of the dry weight, but some samples contained none of the toxins at all[8]. Meliatoxins are somewhat unstable and decompose in acid medium, a fact that may explain the known variability in toxicity of different trees[8].

PHARMACOLOGICAL EFFECTS The meliatoxins were found to have an LD_{50} for orally dosed pigs of about 6,4 mg/kg body-weight, while the figure is 16 mg/kg when injected into mice[8]. Symptoms of poisoning in pigs are vomiting, respiratory distress, convulsions, rapid and weak heartbeat, below normal body temperature and dilated pupils[3,5,6,8].

DISTRIBUTION The syringa tree is indigenous to Asia. An Indian cultivar was originally imported into South Africa[2] and it is now a troublesome weed over a large part of the country.

Meliatoxin A_1: R=MeCH$_2$CHMeCO
Meliatoxin A_2: R=Me$_2$CHCHO

1. **White, F. & Styles, B.T. 1986.** Meliaceae. *Flora of Southern Africa* 18: 49.
2. **Henderson, L. 2001.** *Alien Weeds and Invasive Plants.* Plant Protection Research Institute Handbook no. 12, Agricultural Research Council, Pretoria.
3. **Watt, J.M. & Breyer-Brandwijk, M.G. 1962.** *The Medicinal and Poisonous Plants of Southern and Eastern Africa*, 2nd edition. Livingstone, London.
4. **Munday, J. 1988.** *Poisonous Plants in South African Gardens and Parks.* Delta Books, Johannesburg.
5. **Steyn, D.G. 1949.** *Die Vergiftiging van Mens en Dier.* Van Schaik, Pretoria.
6. **Vahrmeijer, J. 1981.** *Poisonous Plants of Southern Africa That Cause Stock Losses.* Tafelberg Publishers, Cape Town.
7. **Kellerman, T.S., Coetzer, J.A.W. & Naudé, T.W. 1988.** *Plant Poisonings and Mycotoxicoses of Livestock in Southern Africa.* Oxford University Press, Cape Town.
8. **Oelrichs, P.B., Hill, M.W., Vallely, P.J., Macleod, J.K. & Molinsky, T.F. 1983.** Toxic tetranortriterpenes of the fruit of *Melia azdarach*. *Phytochemistry* 22: 531-534.

Melia azedarach

Flowers of *Melia azedarach*

Berries of *Melia azedarach*

MELIANTHUS COMOSUS
Melianthaceae

---

kruidjie-roer-my-niet (Afrikaans); ibonya (Zulu)

DESCRIPTION *M. comosus* is a much-branched shrub of up to 3 m in height, producing a strong, unpleasant smell when touched. The leaves have about five pairs of leaflets and are prominently toothed at the margins. Clusters of green and bright red flowers are followed by four-winged, papery and bladdery capsules[1]. Another common species is *M. major,* a more robust plant with large, greyish leaves and clusters of dark purplish-red flowers on purple flowering stalks borne at the tips of the branches.

TYPE OF TOXIN Cardiac glycoside (bufadienolide).

IMPORTANCE *Melianthus* species are very poisonous and have caused death in people and animals[2,3]. *M. comosus, M. major* and other species are popular in traditional medicine, mainly to treat sores, wounds, burns and rheumatism (external use relieves pain and promotes healing)[3,4]. Weak infusions are sometimes taken, but internal use is dangerous. Honey produced from the characteristic black nectar may also be toxic[3]. Livestock rarely ingest the plant because of the unpleasant smell,

but may be forced to do so during drought and scarcity of grazing[5,6]. The roots are said to be particularly toxic and parasitic mistletoes (such as *Tapinanthus* species) growing on the branches also become poisonous[6].

POISONOUS INGREDIENTS *M. comosus* roots contain at least six heart glycosides, including melianthugenin, melianthusigenin and hellebrigenin 3-acetate[7,8].

PHARMACOLOGICAL EFFECTS Symptoms of human poisoning are poorly recorded but ingestion of leaf or root infusions are known to cause foaming vomit and sometimes death[3]. Animals show signs of gastro-intestinal irritation, lack of appetite, diarrhoea, colic, bloat, cyanosis, apathy and a rapid, weak pulse[2]. About 500 g of leaves is fatal to a sheep and death may occur a few hours after ingestion[2].

DISTRIBUTION *Melianthus* species occur only in southern Africa. *M. comosus* is common in the dry interior (see map), while *M. major* is restricted to the Western Cape[1].

Melianthugenin

1. **Phillips, E.P. & Hofmeyr, J. 1927.** The genus *Melianthus.* Bothalia 2: 351-355.
2. **Steyn, D.G. 1949.** *Die Vergiftiging van Mens en Dier.* Van Schaik, Pretoria.
3. **Watt, J.M. & Breyer-Brandwijk, M.G. 1962.** *The Medicinal and Poisonous Plants of Southern and Eastern Africa*, 2nd edition. Livingstone, London.
4. **Van Wyk, B-E., Van Oudtshoorn, B. & Gericke, N. 2000.** *Medicinal Plants of South Africa*, 2nd edition. Briza Publications, Pretoria.
5. **Vahrmeijer, J. 1981.** *Poisonous Plants of Southern Africa That Cause Stock Losses.* Tafelberg Publishers, Cape Town.
6. **Kellerman, T.S., Coetzer, J.A.W. & Naudé, T.W. 1988.** *Plant Poisonings and Mycotoxicoses of Livestock in Southern Africa.* Oxford University Press, Cape Town.
7. **Anderson, L.A.P. & Koekemoer, J.M. 1968.** The chemistry of *Melianthus comosus* Vahl. Part II. The isolation of hellebrigenin 3-acetate and other unidentified bufadienolides from the rootbark of *Melianthus comosus* Vahl. *J. S. Afr. Chem. Inst.* 21: 155-158.
8. **Anderson, L.A.P. & Koekemoer, J.M. 1969.** The chemistry of *Melianthus comosus* Vahl. Part III. The constitution of melianthugenin and melianthusigenin, new bufadienolides from the rootbark. *J. S. Afr. Chem. Inst.* 22: 191-197.

Melianthus comosus

Flowers and fruits of *Melianthus comosus*

Flowers and fruits of *Melianthus major*

MELICA DECUMBENS

Poaceae

---

dronkgras (Afrikaans); staggers grass (English)

DESCRIPTION *M. decumbens* is an evergreen, densely tufted, short grass with unbranched culms and erect, coarse leaves. The spikelets are purplish, covered with soft hairs, and are mostly arranged to one side of the flowering stalk[1-3]. The Afrikaans common name *dronkgras* is sometimes also applied to the fern *Equisetum ramosissimum*, which causes symptoms (staggering and shivers) similar to that of *M. decumbens*.

TYPE OF TOXIN Unknown (cyanogenic glycoside?).

IMPORTANCE The plant has been known to be toxic to livestock since early times but affected animals usually recover[4,5]. Because the leaves are coarse and tough, animals seldom graze large quantities unless forced to do so by drought. Young cattle are mostly affected[6], but intoxication of horses, donkeys and to a lesser extent sheep has also been reported[3]. Several other grasses regularly cause poisoning in stock, such as *Lolium* species (ryegrass), *Cynodon dactylon* (kweek), *Paspalum dilatatum* (Dallis grass) and *Phalaris minor* (canary grass)[6]. These grasses respectively cause annual ryegrass toxicosis, *kweek* tremors, paspalum staggers and *phalaris* staggers[6]. Most of these conditions are due to mycotoxicoses, i.e. the toxins are not produced by the grass but by fungi such as ergot (*Claviceps*

species), *Aspergillus*, *Diplodia* and others[6]. Several grasses are known to be cyanogenic and cause poisoning due to the enzymatic release of prussic acid (hydrogen cyanide) from cyanogenic glycosides in the plants (see *Sorghum*, p. 198, and the list of cyanogenic plants on p. 265)[6].

POISONOUS INGREDIENTS Nothing appears to have been published on the chemical compounds of *M. decumbens*. The grass is known to be cyanogenic, but the symptoms of *Melica* poisoning do not appear to be consistent with prussic acid poisoning, so that the poisonous substance is suspected to be some neurotoxin[6].

PHARMACOLOGICAL EFFECTS As the English and Afrikaans common names suggest, *M. decumbens* causes staggering and loss of muscular co-ordination (ataxia) in animals. A young calf that was experimentally fed with large amounts of the grass showed swaying, unsteadiness, muscular tremors and tended to trip and fall without being able to rise[6].

DISTRIBUTION *M. decumbens* is restricted to South Africa and occurs mainly in the Eastern Cape, Northern Cape and Free State Provinces[1-3].

1. **Gibbs Russell, G.E. & Ellis, R.P. 1982.** The genus *Melica* L. (Poaceae) in southern Africa. *Bothalia* 14: 37-44.
2. **Gibbs Russell, G.E. *et al.* 1990.** *Grasses of Southern Africa. Memoirs of the Botanical Survey of South Africa* 58.
3. **Van Oudtshoorn, F. 1999.** *Guide to Grasses of Southern Africa.* Briza Publications, Pretoria.
4. **Steyn, D.G. 1949.** *Die Vergiftiging van Mens en Dier.* Van Schaik, Pretoria.
5. **Watt, J.M. & Breyer-Brandwijk, M.G. 1962.** *The Medicinal and Poisonous Plants of Southern and Eastern Africa*, 2nd edition. Livingstone, London.
6. **Kellerman, T.S., Coetzer, J.A.W. & Naudé, T.W. 1988.** *Plant Poisonings and Mycotoxicoses of Livestock in Southern Africa.* Oxford University Press, Cape Town.

Melica decumbens

Spikelets of *Melica decumbens*

Cynodon dactylon

Phalaris minor

MELILOTUS ALBA

Fabaceae

white sweet clover, Bokhara clover (English); witstinkklawer, bokhaarklawer (Afrikaans)

DESCRIPTION The plant is an erect annual herb, with leaflets that are characteristically toothed along the margins. Numerous small, white flowers are borne in dense clusters and the tiny, rounded pods are borne on slender, elongated stalks[1,2]. Two yellow-flowered species of *Melilotus* also occur in South Africa: *M. indica* (previously known as *M. parviflora*) and *M. officinalis*. Both these species are known as annual yellow sweet clover or stink clover, because the meat and milk of animals feeding on them become tainted[1,2].

TYPE OF TOXIN Coumarin.

IMPORTANCE *M. alba* is well known as a cause of stock poisoning but outbreaks have not yet been recorded in South Africa[3-5]. Cattle (particularly young cattle), pigs and rabbits are more susceptible than sheep or horses. The plant becomes poisonous only when it is spoilt, as happens when damp material is stored as hay. Human poisonings are rare.

POISONOUS INGREDIENTS The toxic substance is dicoumarol. It is not present in the plant, but is formed from *o*-coumaric acid via 4-hydroxycoumarin through microbial activity in decomposing hay or silage[5,6]. *O*-coumaric acid is a natural substance in the plant.

PHARMACOLOGICAL EFFECTS Dicoumarol is an anticoagulant factor that causes delay in the clotting of blood[7]. It suppresses the synthesis of prothrombin in the liver, by inhibiting the formation of vitamin K (the latter is required for the formation of prothrombin and other clotting factors)[5]. Symptoms appear suddenly in animals, but only when large quantities of material have been consumed for about a month. Most animals die within three days of the onset of bleeding, which manifests as haemorrhages and haematomas on exposed and internal parts of the body[5]. Successful treatment is possible with repeated doses of vitamin K and by blood transfusions[5]. Dicoumarol is similar to synthetic derivatives such as warfarin, which is well known as commercial rat poison[7]. Warfarin is also used medically as an anticoagulant to prevent blood clotting and thrombosis.

DISTRIBUTION *Melilotus* species are sometimes cultivated as a fodder crop but they have become troublesome weeds in most parts of South Africa and are often seen in disturbed places such as cultivated lands, roadsides and river banks[1,2].

Dicoumarol   Warfarin

1. **Gillett, J.B. 1971.** Leguminosae. Papilionoideae. *Flora of Tropical East Africa* 4: 1039.
2. **Henderson, M. & Anderson, J.G. 1966.** *Common Weeds in South Africa. Memoirs of the Botanical Survey of South Africa* 37.
3. **Steyn, D.G. 1949.** *Die Vergiftiging van Mens en Dier.* Van Schaik, Pretoria.
4. **Watt, J.M. & Breyer-Brandwijk, M.G. 1962.** *The Medicinal and Poisonous Plants of Southern and Eastern Africa*, 2nd edition. Livingstone, London.
5. **Kellerman, T.S., Coetzer, J.A.W. & Naudé, T.W. 1988.** *Plant Poisonings and Mycotoxicoses of Livestock in Southern Africa.* Oxford University Press, Cape Town.
6. **Merck 1989.** *The Merck Index.* 11th edition. Merck, Rahway.
7. **Harborne, J.B., Baxter, H. & Moss, G.P. (eds) 1997.** *Dictionary of Plant Toxins.* John Wiley & Sons, Chichester.

Melilotus alba

Melilotus alba

Melilotus indica

MORAEA POLYSTACHYA

Iridaceae

---

blue tulp, Karoo blue tulp (English); bloutulp, Karoobloutulp (Afrikaans)

DESCRIPTION This bulbous plant has three to five long, strap-shaped, flat leaves and attractive, blue flowers borne on a branched flowering stem. The outer lobes (tepals) of the flower are each marked with a bright yellow spot, while the inner tepals are unmarked and erect. Together with its close relative, *M. venenata*, it can be distinguished from other blue-flowered species by the larger size of the flowers[1]. The poisonous *M. polyanthos* (also known as blue tulp) differs in the '*Homeria*-like' flowers – the inner and outer tepals are all similarly marked and spreading. *Homeria* (see p. 124) will soon be included in *Moraea*. Other species reported to be toxic[3,4] are *M. huttonii* (formerly *M. rivularis*), *M. spathulata* (= *M. spathacea*), *M. unguiculata* (=*M. tenuis*), *M. stricta* (=*M. trita*), *M. graminicola* and *M. carsonii*.

TYPE OF TOXIN Cardiac glycoside (bufadienolide).

IMPORTANCE *Moraea* species are important causes of tulp poisoning, mostly in cattle[2,3,4]. Stock losses usually occur during the winter months, when the leaves emerge from the bulbs at a time when other grazing is scarce. Newly introduced or hungry animals are especially at risk. Drying does not destroy the toxins, so that contaminated hay may also cause fatalities[3]. A few cases of fatal human poisoning have been reported[3], where rural children ate the corms of poisonous species instead of edible ones, such as *M. fugax*.

POISONOUS INGREDIENTS Three heart glycosides have been isolated from *M. polystachya* and *M. graminicola*[5,6], of which 16β-formyloxy-bovogenin A was the main compound.

PHARMACOLOGICAL EFFECTS *M. polystachya* is extremely poisonous – less than 2 g/kg body-weight of dried flowering plant are sufficient to kill sheep and cattle within one or two days[5]. Symptoms, typical of cardiac glycosides, include bloat, nervousness, immobility, and a weak heart[4]. Treatment with activated charcoal can be effective[7].

DISTRIBUTION *M. polystachya* is widely distributed in the central interior of South Africa and northwards into Namibia. It often forms dense stands, especially in overgrazed areas. Several other poisonous species occur in the western and eastern parts of South Africa.

16β-Formyloxybovogenin A

---

1. **Goldblatt, P. 1986**. *The Moraeas of Southern Africa. Annals of Kirstenbosch Botanical Gardens* 14.
2. **Vahrmeijer, J. 1981**. *Poisonous Plants of Southern Africa That Cause Stock Losses*. Tafelberg Publishers, Cape Town. (note: the photographs of '*M. polyanthos*' on page 57 are actually *M. polystachya*).
3. **Steyn, D.G. 1949**. *Die Vergiftiging van Mens en Dier*. Van Schaik, Pretoria.
4. **Kellerman, T.S., Coetzer, J.A.W. & Naudé, T.W.1988**. *Plant Poisonings and Mycotoxicoses of Livestock in Southern Africa*. Oxford University Press, Cape Town.
5. **Van Wyk, A.J. & Enslin, P.R. 1968**. Bufadienolides of *Moraea polystacha* Ker and *M. graminicola* Oberm. *J. S. Afr. Chem. Inst.* 21: 33-38.
6. **Van Wyk, A.J. 1972**. A new bufadienolide of *Moraea polystacha* Ker and *M. graminicola* Oberm. *J. S. Afr. Chem. Inst.* 25: 82-84.
7. **Joubert, J.P. & Schulze, R.A. 1982**. The minimal dose of activated charcoal in the treatment of sheep poisoned with the cardiac glycoside containing plant *Moraea polystachya* (Thunb.) Ker-Gawl. *J. S. Afr. Vet. Assoc.* 53: 265-266.

Moraea polystachya

Flowers of *Moraea polystachya*

Moraea graminicola

Flower of *Moraea polyanthos*

MUNDULEA SERICEA

Fabaceae

---

cork bush (English); kurkbos (Afrikaans)

DESCRIPTION The well-known cork bush is a shrub or small tree with silvery leaves and a thick, corky bark. Flowers are typically pea-like and vary from deep to pale purple or rarely white, and the pods are flat, narrow and covered with velvety hairs.

TYPE OF TOXIN Rotenoid.

IMPORTANCE The bark, leaves, roots and seeds are widely used as fish poison, insecticide and traditional medicine[1]. It is a Zulu emetic for treating human poisoning[2]. The plant is widely known as a source of very effective fish and insect poison in South Africa and is known to kill fish (not merely stun them) and even crocodiles[1]. Although the bark is not generally considered to be very poisonous to humans when taken by mouth, there are some reports suggesting that it may be quite toxic[1,3].

POISONOUS INGREDIENTS *Mundulea* and related plants such as *Derris*, *Neorautanenia* and *Tephrosia* are sources of rotenoids – well known as fish and insect poisons[4,5]. Examples are rotenone (obtained mainly from the roots of *Derris elliptica*) and tephrosin (present in leaves of *Tephrosia vogelii*)[4-6].

Early studies suggested that rotenone is present in *Mundulea sericea* bark[1], but there may be regional variation and these reports need confirmation. Other rotenoids, including deguelin and tephrosin, were definitely found in the bark[7].

PHARMACOLOGICAL EFFECTS Rotenone and tephrosin are not thought to be very poisonous when taken by mouth (*Mundulea* leaves are safely browsed by cattle and game), but can be dangerous if inhaled or injected[4-6]. Rotenone is quite toxic when injected (LD_{50} of 2,8 mg/kg body-weight in mice) and has been used as an arrow poison and for committing suicide[4]. When taken by mouth, it is a powerful emetic, also in dogs[3]. This may explain the traditional use of *Mundulea* bark in treating poisoning and explain why it is generally not considered to be toxic to humans.

DISTRIBUTION *Mundulea sericea* is widely distributed in Africa, India, Sri Lanka and Madagascar[4,8]. In South Africa, it is exceptionally common in the north-eastern region (see map). *Tephrosia vogelii* is sometimes cultivated in South Africa.

Rotenone

Deguelin: R=H
Tephrosin: R=OH

1. **Watt, J.M. & Breyer-Brandwijk, M.G. 1962.** *The Medicinal and Poisonous Plants of Southern and Eastern Africa*, 2nd edition. Livingstone, London.
2. **Van Wyk, B-E. & Gericke, N. 2000.** *People's Plants. A Guide to Useful Plants of Southern Africa.* Briza Publications, Pretoria.
3. **Steyn, D.G. 1949.** *Die Vergiftiging van Mens en Dier.* Van Schaik, Pretoria.
4. **Southon, I.W. (1994).** *Phytochemical Dictionary of the Leguminosae.* Chapman & Hall, London.
5. **Merck 1989.** *The Merck Index.* 11th edition. Merck, Rahway.
6. **Harborne, J.B., Baxter, H. & Moss, G.P. (eds) 1997.** *Dictionary of Plant Toxins.* John Wiley & Sons, Chichester.
7. **Luyengi, L., Lee, I-K., Mar, W. Fong, H.S. Pezzuto, J.M. & Kinghorn, A.D. 1994.** Rotenoids and chalcones from *Mundulea sericea* that inhibit phorbol ester-induced ornithine decarboxylase activity. *Phytochemistry* 36: 1523-1526.
8. **Verdcourt, B. 1971.** Leguminosae. Papilionoideae. *Flora of Tropical East Africa* 3(1): 15.

Mundulea sericea

Flowers of *Mundulea sericea*

Neorautanenia amboensis

Tephrosia vogelii

NERIUM OLEANDER

Apocynaceae

oleander (English); selonsroos (Afrikaans)

DESCRIPTION Oleander is a robust, woody shrub of up to 6 m high. The leaves are oblong, with a prominent, white midrib and numerous parallel lateral veins (fragments are easily identified). The attractive flowers can be single and pink (in the invading form of the species) and single or double, and variously coloured – pink, white, purple or yellow – in garden cultivars[1]. When the long, narrow, seed capsules burst open, they release numerous small, brown seeds with long, reddish-brown hairs. Oleander should not be confused with yellow oleander (*Thevetia peruviana*) – see under exotic garden plants (p. 259).

TYPE OF TOXIN Cardiac glycoside (cardenolide).

IMPORTANCE All parts of the plant are known to be extremely poisonous. The leaves are fibrous and very bitter, so it is unlikely that children will consume more than a tiny amount. Eating meat skewered on the stems or inhaling the smoke from burning wood and leaves can lead to intoxication[2]. Human fatalities have occurred after drinking extracts or ingesting about 15 leaves (estimated at 4 g)[2]. Poisoning of livestock and domestic animals occurs sporadically, also in South Africa, but it is not considered a serious problem[3,4]. Small stock or domestic animals exposed to gardens, hedge clippings or stagnant water into which flowers or leaves had fallen may be at risk. A case is known where 30 lambs were killed[5]. The lethal dose in sheep is reported to be 1–5 g dry leaf (this is about 3–15 g fresh leaves) and in horses and cattle about 15–30 g dry leaves[4].

POISONOUS INGREDIENTS Oleander leaves and seeds contain more than 30 different cardiac glycosides, of which oleandrin is the main compound. Oleandrin was formerly used as a cardiac tonic and diuretic. Extracts are still used in homeopathy.

PHARMACOLOGICAL EFFECTS Symptoms include nausea, vomiting, weakness, confusion and visual disturbances, followed by a slowing and weakening of the heartbeat to 30 or 40 beats per minute. In fatal cases, bradycardia, atrio-ventricular block and fibrillation are typical[2].

DISTRIBUTION *N. oleander* occurs naturally in a large area, stretching from the Mediterranean region to Western China. It adapts well to drought and is nowadays a very popular garden shrub in many parts of the world. It is particularly well suited to Mediterranean climates. In South Africa, the plant has become an invader that spreads along watercourses, particularly in the drier interior of the Western Cape Province.

Oleandrin

1. **Pagen, F.J.J. 1987.** Series of revisions of Apocynaceae part XX. Oleanders: *Nerium* L. and the oleander cultivars. *Agricultural University of Wageningen Papers* 87(2): 1-53.
2. **Bruneton, J. 1999.** *Toxic Plants Dangerous to Humans and Animals.* Intercept, Hampshire.
3. **Vahrmeijer, J. 1981.** *Poisonous Plants of Southern Africa That Cause Stock Losses.* Tafelberg Publishers, Cape Town.
4. **Kellerman, T.S., Coetzer, J.A.W. & Naudé, T.W. 1988.** *Plant Poisonings and Mycotoxicoses of Livestock in Southern Africa.* Oxford University Press, Cape Town.
5. **Steyn, D.G. 1949.** *Die Vergiftiging van Mens en Dier.* Van Schaik, Pretoria.

Nerium oleander

Nerium oleander – pink form

Nerium oleander – white form

Nerium oleander – red form

NICOTIANA GLAUCA

Solanaceae

---

wild tobacco, tree tobacco (English); wildetabak, jan twak (Afrikaans)

DESCRIPTION Wild tobacco is a lax, erect shrub or small tree with drooping branches and bluish-green, somewhat fleshy, stalked leaves. Tubular, yellow flowers are borne in large numbers at the branch ends. The fruit capsule with its numerous small, brown seeds develops within the persistent calyx[1]. The related *Nicotiana tabacum* is a leafy herb that is commonly cultivated as commercial tobacco.

TYPE OF TOXIN Pyridine alkaloid.

IMPORTANCE In recent years, there have been several tragic cases of human poisoning in South Africa[2]. Young plants of *N. glauca* are sometimes mistaken for other plants used as traditional cooked spinach (known as *marog*). Despite sporadic incidences of fatal livestock poisoning, including ostriches[3], and teratogenic defects in sheep, the plant is not considered to be a serious risk because it is hardly ever grazed[4]. Tobacco (from *N. tabacum*) is highly toxic but accidental fatalities are rare. Harvesters may suffer from 'green tobacco sickness' and the use of protective clothing is recommended when handling tobacco[5].

POISONOUS INGREDIENTS In South Africa, all above-ground parts of the plant contain high levels of anabasine as practically the only alkaloid present[2]. Plants in other parts of the world are said to also contain nicotine.

PHARMACOLOGICAL EFFECTS The symptoms of anabasine and nicotine poisoning are similar and appear rapidly. They include nausea, weakness, headaches, salivation, convulsions, confusion, difficulty in breathing and hypertension. In extreme cases, paralysis of the respiratory muscles leads to rapid death[5]. Nicotine is the addictive component of tobacco, and has tranquilising properties. The fatal dose in humans is about 50 mg[6]. Nicotine (or powdered tobacco leaf) is very poisonous to most insects and is widely used as an insecticide.

DISTRIBUTION Both *Nicotiana* species occur naturally in South America. Wild tobacco comes from Argentina and was accidentally introduced to Namibia during the German occupation early in the twentieth century, and from there to South Africa. It is drought tolerant and has become a common weed of roadsides, dry riverbeds, cultivated fields and other disturbed places in most parts of South Africa[1].

Nicotine

Anabasine

1. **Henderson, L. 2001.** *Alien Weeds and Invasive Plants.* Plant Protection Research Institute Handbook no. 12, Agricultural Research Council, Pretoria.
2. **Steenkamp, P.A., Govender, L., Van Heerden, F.R. & Van Wyk, B-E. 2002.** Accidental fatal poisoning by *Nicotiana glauca*. A method for the forensic identification of anabasine by high performance liquid chromatography / photodiode array / mass spectrometry. *Forensic Sci.* (in press).
3. **Watt, J.M. & Breyer-Brandwijk, M.G. 1962.** *The Medicinal and Poisonous Plants of Southern and Eastern Africa*, 2nd edition. Livingstone, London.
4. **Kellerman, T.S., Coetzer, J.A.W. & Naudé, T.W. 1988.** *Plant Poisonings and Mycotoxicoses of Livestock in Southern Africa.* Oxford University Press, Cape Town.
5. **Bruneton, J. 1999.** *Toxic Plants Dangerous to Humans and Animals.* Intercept, Hampshire.
6. **Harborne, J.B., Baxter, H. & Moss, G.P. (eds) 1997.** *Dictionary of Plant Toxins.* John Wiley & Sons, Chichester.

Nicotiana glauca

Leaves and flowers of *Nicotiana glauca*

Nicotiana tabacum

ORNITHOGALUM THYRSOIDES

Hyacinthaceae

---

chinkerinchee, star-of-Bethlehem (English); tjienkerientjee, witviooltjie (Afrikaans)

DESCRIPTION *O. thyrsoides* is an attractive bulbous plant with a basal rosette of strap-shaped leaves, a single, erect, flowering stalk and multi-flowered clusters of attractive, star-shaped, white flowers. It is commonly sold as a cut flower. Also well known is *O. saundersiae*, easily distinguished by the conspicuous black ovaries in the middle of the cream-coloured flowers[1]. Other species known to be poisonous include *O. conicum*, *O. ornithogaloides*, *O. prasinum*, *O. tenellum*[2], and the recently described miniature species, *O. toxicarium*[3]. The common names chinkerinchee and *viooltjie* refer to the squeaky sound that is generated when flower stalks are rubbed against each other.

TYPE OF TOXIN Steroid glycoside.

IMPORTANCE *Ornithogalum* species are amongst the most poisonous plants in South Africa. People (especially children) can be poisoned from accidental ingestion of garden plants or cut flowers. Animals may be at risk from bulbs and leaves in garden waste, or from leaves inadvertently included in hay or fresh fodder. Dense natural stands of the plants may also lead to sporadic outbreaks of chinkerinchee poisoning[2,4]. The fatal doses in

animals are often measured in mg/kg rather than the usual g/kg body-weight[2]. Even though *O. toxicarium* is such a small plant, it killed nearly 3 000 small livestock in one season[3].

POISONOUS INGREDIENTS The toxic compound in *O. thyrsoides* was identified as prasinoside G, a steroid glycoside[5]. Similar compounds occur in *O. prasinum*[5] and *O. saundersiae*[6]. Some species, including *O. toxicarium*, also contain cardiac glycosides[3,7].

PHARMACOLOGICAL EFFECTS Chinkerinchee poisoning typically results in severe diarrhoea that may last up to three weeks[2]. Death usually occurs within a few days, preceded by abdominal pain and convulsions. Temporary or permanent blindness is highly characteristic, but this symptom occurs only in cattle[2].

DISTRIBUTION *O. thyrsoides* is restricted to the Western and Eastern Cape Provinces (see map) and often forms dense stands in vleis. *O. saundersiae* occurs in the north-eastern parts of South Africa, while *O. prasinum* and *O. toxicarium* are found in the dry central interior[1-3].

Prasinoside G

1. **Obermeyer, A.A. 1978.** *Ornithogalum*: a revision of the southern African species. *Bothalia* 12: 323-376.
2. **Kellerman, T.S., Coetzer, J.A.W. & Naudé, T.W. 1988.** *Plant Poisonings and Mycotoxicoses of Livestock in Southern Africa*. Oxford University Press, Cape Town.
3. **Archer, C. & Archer, R.H. 1999.** A new species of *Ornithogalum* subgenus *Urophyllon* (Hyacinthaceae) from central South Africa and southern Namibia. *S. Afr. J. Bot.* 65: 431-433.
4. **Vahrmeijer, J. 1981.** *Poisonous Plants of Southern Africa That Cause Stock Losses*. Tafelberg Publishers, Cape Town.
5. **Van der Westhuizen, D. 1996.** Structural Studies on the Toxic Principle of *Ornithogalum thyroides*. M.Sc. Thesis. University of Pretoria.
6. **Mimaki, Y., Kuroda, M., Sashida, Y., Hirano, T., Oka, K., Dobashi, A., Koshino, H. & Uzawa, J. 1996.** Three novel rearranged cholestane glycosides from *Ornithogalum saundersiae* bulbs and their cytostatic activities on leukemia HL-60 and MOLT-4 cells. *Tetrahedron Lett.* 37: 1245-1248.
7. **Harborne, J.B., Baxter, H. & Moss, G.P. (eds) 1997.** *Dictionary of Plant Toxins*. John Wiley & Sons, Chichester.

Ornithogalum thyrsoides

Ornithogalum conicum

Ornithogalum saundersiae

Ornithogalum prasinum

Ornithogalum toxicarium

OXALIS PES-CAPRAE

Oxalidaceae

---

sorrel, yellow sorrel (English); suring, geelsuring (Afrikaans)

DESCRIPTION Sorrels are perennial herbs emerging from fleshy roots, corms or rhizomes[1,2]. The leaves have long, slender stalks and are divided into three leaflets that display sleeping motions – they characteristically droop or fold at night. The attractive, funnel-shaped flowers have five petals – yellow in *O. pes-caprae*, pink or purple in *O. latifolia*, and variously coloured in others. There are 500 species in total, of which about 270 occur in southern Africa. The name sorrel also applies to various *Rumex* species.

TYPE OF TOXIN Oxalic acid.

IMPORTANCE *Oxalis* and other plants containing soluble oxalic acid are not really poisonous but they can lead to human and animal fatalities if excessive amounts are consumed[3-5]. High levels occur also in rhubarbs (*Rheum* species) and sorrels (*Rumex* species), both of the family Polygonaceae. Other known sources are *vygies* (e.g. *Mesembryanthemum, Psilocaulon*, Mesembryanthemaceae), true spinach (*Spinacia oleracea*, Chenopodiaceae), *marog* (*Amaranthus*, Amaranthaceae), prickly pear (*Opuntia*, Cactaceae)[5] and *spekboom* (*Portulacaria afra*, Portulacaceae). Plants must contain more than 10% oxalic acid on a dry weight basis to be potentially harmful to humans or animals[5]. A few people have died in Europe as a result of excessive consumption of rhubarb or sorrel leaves (as dessert or as soup)[3]. In South Africa (as in many other parts of the world), outbreaks of oxalate poisoning have been reported, resulting from pastures infested with *Oxalis* or *Rumex* species[4,5]. Under field conditions, sheep are mostly affected, but cattle and horses may suffer from degenerative conditions of the bones after prolonged exposure to low levels of oxalates[5].

POISONOUS INGREDIENTS Soluble oxalates occur in plants as sodium, potassium and ammonium salts. They readily form insoluble salts with calcium and magnesium.

PHARMACOLOGICAL EFFECTS Abdominal pain and vomiting are typical, followed by other disorders which result from paralysis of the nervous system[3]. Sodium oxalate and other soluble oxalates can crystallise in various tissues as insoluble calcium oxalate, and are capable of precipitating blood calcium. The lethal dose of oxalic acid is 10–15 g in adults, 5–10 g in children[3].

DISTRIBUTION *O. pes-caprae* occurs mainly in the Western Cape Province of South Africa and has become a troublesome weed in many parts of the world[2]. A Mexican species, *O. latifolia*, is mostly found in the eastern parts of South Africa, where it is a common weed in gardens and cultivated lands[2].

Calcium oxalate

1. **Salter, T.M. 1944.** The genus *Oxalis* in South Africa. *Jl S. Afr. Bot. Suppl.* 1: 1-355.
2. **Henderson, M. & Anderson, J.G. 1966.** *Common Weeds in South Africa. Memoirs of the Botanical Survey of South Africa* 37.
3. **Bruneton, J. 1999.** *Toxic Plants Dangerous to Humans and Animals.* Intercept, Hampshire.
4. **Vahrmeijer, J. 1981.** *Poisonous Plants of Southern Africa That Cause Stock Losses.* Tafelberg Publishers, Cape Town.
5. **Kellerman, T.S., Coetzer, J.A.W. & Naudé, T.W. 1988.** *Plant Poisonings and Mycotoxicoses of Livestock in Southern Africa.* Oxford University Press, Cape Town.

Oxalis pes-caprae

Flowers of *Oxalis pes-caprae*

Oxalis latifolia

PACHYSTIGMA PYGMAEUM

Rubiaceae

hairy gousiektebossie (English); harige gousiektebossie (Afrikaans)

DESCRIPTION This is a dwarf shrublet with small, leafy branchlets arising from a woody rhizome below the ground. Leaves are borne in opposite pairs and are yellowish-green, with a layer of soft hairs on the surface. The small, star-shaped flowers are borne in clusters at ground level and are yellowish-green in colour[1]. A closely related species, *P. thamnus*, is almost identical to *P. pygmaeum* in all details except that the leaves are completely hairless[1] (hence the vernacular name smooth *gousiektebossie*). Other members of the Rubiaceae known to cause *gousiekte* in animals include *Fadogia homblei* (wild date, see p. 110), *Pavetta harborii* (*tonnabossie*) and *P. schumanniana* (poisonous bride's bush or *gousiekte* tree)[2,3]. Both *Pavetta* species have clusters of tubular flowers with protruding styles, followed by small, black, fleshy fruits. Characteristic opaque spots caused by bacteria are visible in both species when the leaves are held up to the light. *Pavetta harborii* is a small shrub with stalkless leaves, while *P. schumanniana* is a large shrub or small tree with stalked leaves. *Pygmaeothamnus zeyheri* has the same characteristic growth form as *Pachystigma* and is often confused with it. This species is not known to be poisonous. For this reason, a photograph of the former is also included here.

TYPE OF TOXIN Amine.

IMPORTANCE *Gousiekte* is a fatal heart disease of domestic ruminants caused by various plants of the coffee family (Rubiaceae)[2,3]. Death typically occurs after a long latent period of four to eight weeks after the plants were eaten[3]. A single dose can occasionally be fatal, but relatively large quantities of plant material have to be ingested. The lethal dose of *Pachystigma pygmaeum* for sheep is about 175 g of fresh leaves per kg body-weight[3].

POISONOUS INGREDIENTS *P. pygmaeum* contains the same toxic polyamine[4] as is found in other known *gousiekte*-inducing members of the Rubiaceae[5].

PHARMACOLOGICAL EFFECTS Animals show various clinical signs related to heart failure[6].

DISTRIBUTION *P. pygmaeum* occurs over large parts of the grasslands of South Africa. It is more common than *P. thamnus*, but the latter is particularly abundant in southern Mpumalanga and the adjoining northern parts of KwaZulu-Natal[2,3]. *Pavetta harborii* is limited to the extreme north-western parts of South Africa, west and north of the Waterberg, and across the border in the Machudi area of Botswana. *P. schumanniana* is widely distributed in the north-eastern parts of South Africa[2,3].

1. **Boshoff, S. 1987.** 'n Hersiening van die Genus *Pachystigma* Hochst. (Rubiaceae) in Suidelike Afrika. Unpublished M.Sc. thesis, University of Pretoria.
2. **Vahrmeijer, J. 1981.** *Poisonous Plants of Southern Africa That Cause Stock Losses.* Tafelberg Publishers, Cape Town.
3. **Kellerman, T.S., Coetzer, J.A.W. & Naudé, T.W. 1988.** *Plant Poisonings and Mycotoxicoses of Livestock in Southern Africa.* Oxford University Press, Cape Town.
4. **Vleggaar, R. 2002.** Personal communication.
5. **Fourie, N., Erasmus, G.L., Schultz, R.A. & Prozesky, L. 1995.** Isolation of the toxin responsible for gousiekte, a plant-induced cardiomyopathy of ruminants in southern Africa. *Onderstepoort J. Vet. Res.* 62: 77-87.
6. **Hay, L., Pipedi, M., Schutte, P.J., Turner, M.L. & Smith, K.A. 2001.** The effect of *Pavetta harborii* extracts on cardiac function in rats. *S. A. J. Sci.* 97: 481-494.

Pachystigma pygmaeum

Pygmaeothamnus zeyheri

Flowers of *Pachystigma pygmaeum*

Pavetta schumanniana

PEDDIEA AFRICANA

Thymelaeaceae

---

poison olive (English); gifolyf (Afrikaans)

DESCRIPTION The poison olive is a shade-loving shrub or small tree from evergreen forests. The bark is sometimes used as rope because it is tough and fibrous. Leaves are glossy green, clustered towards the branch tips and are borne on very short stalks. Attractive yellowish-green, tubular flowers occur in rounded clusters, followed by oval berries that turn black and shiny when they ripen.

TYPE OF TOXIN Diterpenoid.

IMPORTANCE Despite the fact that the plant is used in traditional medicine and also for homicide[2], surprisingly little is known about the toxicity. When used as a poison in Zimbabwe, an infusion of the whole plant is given orally[3]. *Peddiea* species are also known to contain skin irritant compounds that are responsible for severe allergic reactions in some people.

POISONOUS INGREDIENTS A diterpene of the daphnane type, known as *Peddiea* factor A_1, has been isolated from roots of the plant[4]. *P. volkensii* contains two structurally similar diterpenes[4]. The related *P. fischeri* is a source of several quinones and coumarins, some of which have anticancer effects[5]. See also *Gnidia* species (p. 120) where similar daphnane type diterpenes are found.

PHARMACOLOGICAL EFFECTS None known. It is assumed that the toxicity is due to diterpenoids, but no details are available other than the stated skin irritant effects.

DISTRIBUTION *P. africana* is distributed along the South African coastal region and further north to Mpumalanga, Limpopo Province and Zimbabwe[1]. It is usually found as a shrub on the forest margin.

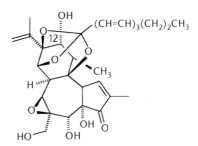

Peddiea factor A_1

1. **Van Wyk, B. & Van Wyk, P.** *Field Guide to Trees of Southern Africa*, p. 222. Struik Publishers, Cape Town.
2. **Watt, J.M. & Breyer-Brandwijk, M.G. 1962.** *The Medicinal and Poisonous Plants of Southern and Eastern Africa*, 2nd edition. Livingstone, London.
3. **Gelfand, M., Mavi, S., Drummond, R.B. & Ndemera, B. 1985.** *The Traditional Medical Practitioner in Zimbabwe.* Mambo Press, Gweru, Zimbabwe.
4. **Adolph, W., Dossaji, S.F., Seip, E.H. & Hecker, E., 1985.** Skin irritant diterpene orthoesters of the daphnane type from *Peddiea africana* and *P. volkensii. Phytochemistry* 24: 2047-2049.
5. **Handa, S.S., Kinghorn, A.D., Cordell, G.A. & Farnsworth, N.R. 1983.** Plant anticancer agents. XXVI. Constituents of *Peddiea fischeri. J. Nat. Prod.* 46: 248-250.

Flowers of *Peddiea africana*

Fruits of *Peddiea africana*

PEUCEDANUM GALBANUM

Apiaceae

---

blister bush (English); bergseldery (Afrikaans)

DESCRIPTION This plant is a robust, erect shrub of about 2 m in height with a strong, resinous smell. The large leaves are divided into numerous diamond-shaped leaflets with serrated edges. Small, yellow flowers are arranged in characteristic groups (umbels) and are followed by dry, flat, winged fruit. The large size and distinctive shape of the leaflets make it easy to distinguish this species from various other members of the family.

TYPE OF TOXIN Furanocoumarin.

IMPORTANCE The name blister bush is derived from the fact that contact with the plant results in blistering of the skin. Hiking guides for Table Mountain and other Cape mountains include cautionary notes[1] and experienced mountaineers know that contact with bare skin should be avoided. The plant is unlikely to be very toxic, as infusions and tinctures have been used in the Cape to treat bladder and kidney problems, as well as obesity in men[2,3].

POISONOUS INGREDIENTS The skin blistering effect (vesiculation) is ascribed to linear furanocoumarins, of which psoralen, xanthotoxin and bergapten are the major ones found in *P. galbanum*[1,4]. The essential oil contains large quantities of *p*-cymene[4], a monoterpenoid with known poisonous properties.

PHARMACOLOGICAL EFFECTS Accidental skin contact with toxic furanocoumarins results in itching and blistering, about 40 to 50 hours after exposure[1]. Sunlight is required for the blistering effect to develop so affected parts should be kept away from the sun. The blisters heal slowly and leave dark patches on the skin for several weeks[1]. Bergapten is commercially available for oral use in photochemotherapy – this technique is used to treat skin diseases, including psoriasis[5]. *p*-Cymene occurs in the essential oils of cumin seeds (*Cuminum cymicum*) and thyme (*Thymus vulgaris*) and is toxic to mammals[6]. The oral LD_{50} in rats is reported to be 4,75 mg/kg body-weight. It may be used as a local painkiller to treat rheumatism[6].

DISTRIBUTION *P. galbanum* occurs only in fynbos areas of the Western Cape Province, where it grows at medium to high altitudes[3] – it is, for example, common on top of Table Mountain. Plants usually prefer partially shaded, moist places.

Psoralen

Xanthotoxin

Bergapten

p-Cymene

1. **Finkelstein, N., Albrecht, C.F. & Van Jaarsveld, P.P. 1993.** Isolation and structure elucidation of xanthotoxin, a phototoxic furanocoumarin from *Peucedanum galbanum*. *S. Afr. J. Bot.* 59: 81-84.
2. **Watt, J.M. & Breyer-Brandwijk, M.G. 1962.** *The Medicinal and Poisonous Plants of Southern and Eastern Africa*, 2nd edition. Livingstone, London.
3. **Van Wyk, B-E., Van Oudtshoorn, B. & Gericke, N. 2000.** *Medicinal Plants of South Africa*, 2nd edition. Briza Publications, Pretoria.
4. **Campbell, W.E., Mathee, S. & Wewers, F. 1993.** Phytochemical studies on the blister bush, *Peucedanum galbanum*. *Planta Med.* 60: 586-587.
5. **Bruneton, J. 1999.** *Toxic Plants Dangerous to Humans and Animals*. Intercept, Hampshire.
6. **Harborne, J.B., Baxter, H. & Moss, G.P. (eds) 1997.** *Dictionary of Plant Toxins*. John Wiley & Sons, Chichester.

Peucedanum galbanum

PHYTOLACCA DIOICA

Phytolaccaceae

---

belhambra tree, pokeberry tree, bella sombra (English);
belhambraboom, bobbejaandruifboom (Afrikaans)

DESCRIPTION The belhambra tree can easily be recognised by the massive trunk, simple, somewhat fleshy leaves borne on pinkish stalks, pendulous clusters of white flowers and black, ribbed berries. Several herbaceous species are also found in South Africa, including *P. americana* (pokeweed – it has dark purple to black berries), *P. octandra* (known as inkberry or *inkbessie* in South Africa – it has black berries) and *P. dodecandra* (known as *endod* in Ethiopia – it has orange to red berries)[1].

TYPE OF TOXIN Triterpenoid (and lectin?).

IMPORTANCE *Phytolacca* species have attractive, fleshy berries that are known to have caused human and animal poisoning[2-4]. The fruits, leaves and roots are all thought to be poisonous but there seems to be considerable variation[4].

POISONOUS INGREDIENTS The toxic substances are thought to be triterpenoid saponins, as the plants are well known for the high levels that accumulate in leaves, roots and berries. The saponins of *P. dioica* are not known, but *P. americana* contains phytolaccagenin, while *P. dodecandra* has oleanoglycotoxin-A and lemmatoxin[5]. It is possible that the toxicity is also due to lectins, as a compound similar to ricin (the lethal lectin in *Ricinus communis* seeds) is found in the leaves and seeds of *Phytolacca* species[4].

PHARMACOLOGICAL EFFECTS The leaves, roots and fruits of *Phytolacca* species are known to have cause animal deaths[2,3] and are potentially lethal to humans[4]. A lectin or lectins may be responsible[4]. Saponins from *Phytolacca* (especially oleano-glycotoxin-A) are highly toxic to snails and are used to combat bilharzia in Africa[5].

DISTRIBUTION The belhambra tree was introduced to South Africa from South America and the weedy *P. americana* from North America and *P. octandra* from tropical America. *P. dodecandra* is indigenous to Africa and South Africa[1].

Oleanoglycotoxin A

---

1. **Stannard 1988**. Phytolaccaceae. *Flora Zambesiaca* 9(1): 163-167.
2. **Steyn, D.G. 1949**. *Die Vergiftiging van Mens en Dier*. Van Schaik, Pretoria.
3. **Storie, G.J., McKenzie, R.A. and Fraser, I.R. 1992**. Suspected packalacca (*Phytolacca dioica*) poisoning of cattle and chickens. *Austr. Vet. J.* 69: 21-22.
4. **Bruneton, J. 1999**. *Toxic Plants Dangerous to Humans and Animals*. Intercept, Hampshire.
5. **Harborne, J.B., Baxter, H. & Moss, G.P. (eds) 1997**. *Dictionary of Plant Toxins*. John Wiley & Sons, Chichester.

Flowers of *Phytolacca dioica*

Berries of *Phytolacca dioica*

Phytolacca octandra

Phytolacca americana

PTERIDIUM AQUILINUM

Dennstaedtiaceae

---

bracken fern (English); adelaarsvaring (Afrikaans); ukozani (Zulu)

DESCRIPTION Bracken is a fern with numerous firm-textured leaves arising from branched, underground, perennial stems. The stems and leaf stalks are covered with reddish brown hairs. Young leaves are characteristically coiled like watch-springs before they unfold. The mature leaves are finely dissected, glossy dark green and smooth. Masses of brown, powdery spores are produced on the lower side, along the edges of the leaf[1].

TYPE OF TOXIN Sesquiterpenoid.

IMPORTANCE Bracken poses a threat to animal and human health[2]. In Japan and other parts of the world, large amounts of young bracken ferns are eaten as food. Processing of the fronds by cooking remove much but not all of the toxic and carcinogenic substances[2]. In areas where cattle are exposed to the plant, sufficient quantities may be passed into the milk to cause concern about the safety of dairy products[2]. In animals, bracken is responsible for thiamine deficiency, as well as acute haemorrhage syndrome, bovine enzootic haematuria and 'bright blindness', resulting in significant stock losses[2-4]. Fortunately, cattle and sheep rarely graze on bracken in South Africa, so that outbreaks of poisoning are not as common here as in other parts of the world.

POISONOUS INGREDIENTS A sesquiterpenoid, ptaquiloside, is the main toxin, together with the enzyme thiaminase[2]. A cyanide-producing glycoside, prunasin, is also present[5].

PHARMACOLOGICAL EFFECTS Ptaquiloside is a carcinogenic and mutagenic norsesquiterpene that has been linked with high incidences of certain forms of cancer in areas where young bracken fronds are consumed as human food[2]. Ptaquiloside destroys bone marrow and thereby reduces the production of blood platelets and white blood cells. The lack of blood platelets leads to internal bleeding, while the lack of white blood cells makes the animal susceptible to infectious diseases[2-4]. Thiaminase destroys vitamin B_1 (also known as thiamine). As a result, non-ruminants such as horses and pigs may develop serious vitamin B_1 deficiencies (nervous symptoms, lack of co-ordination). Ruminants (cattle, sheep, goats) have the ability to produce their own thiamine in the rumen[3,4].

DISTRIBUTION Bracken is one of the most cosmopolitan of all plants. In South Africa, it occurs over the entire southern and eastern part of the country. It is common in moist regions and at high altitudes, where it often forms dense stands, particularly after fire.

Prunasin

Ptaquiloside

1. Jacobsen, W.B.G. 1983. *The Ferns and Fern Allies of Southern Africa*. Butterworths, Pretoria.
2. Fenwick, G.R. 1988. Bracken (*Pteridium aquilinum*) – toxic effects and toxic constituents. *J. Sci. Food Agric.* 46: 147-173.
3. Kellerman, T.S., Coetzer, J.A.W. & Naudé, T.W. 1988. *Plant Poisonings and Mycotoxicoses of Livestock in Southern Africa*. Oxford University Press, Cape Town.
4. Vahrmeijer, J. 1981. *Poisonous Plants of Southern Africa That Cause Stock Losses*. Tafelberg Publishers, Cape Town.
5. Kofod, H. & Eyjolfsson, R. 1966. The isolation of the cyanogenic glycoside prunasin from *Pteridium aquilinum* (L.) Kühn. *Tetrahedron Lett.* 1966: 1289-1291.

Pteridium aquilinum emerging after fire

Pteridium aquilinum

Frond of *Pteridium aquilinum*

PTERONIA PALLENS

Asteraceae

Scholtz bush (English); Scholtz-bossie, armoedbossie, gombossie, witbossie (Afrikaans)

DESCRIPTION *P. pallens* is a woody shrub of about 50 cm high. The white branches and bright green, thick, needle-shaped leaves are useful field characteristics, as are the sticky, shiny flower heads (hence the name *gombossie* – *gom* is the Afrikaans word for glue). A tuft of small, bright yellow flowers are present in each flower head, followed by seeds with fluffy seed hairs (pappus) that aid in wind dispersal[1-3]. Several Karoo bushes similar to Scholtz bush have been implicated in stock losses from time to time[2-4]. Examples are *springbokbos* (*Hertia pallens*) and the related *ertjiebos* (*H. cluytiifolia*), as well as *geelbergdraaibos* or *perdebos* (*Pegolettia retrofracta*) and *Nolletia gariepina* (previously known as *Felicia gariepina*).

TYPE OF TOXIN Unknown.

IMPORTANCE Scholtz bush (and the other bushes listed above) sporadically cause acute liver poisoning of sheep in parts of the Karoo[2-4]. Losses usually occur during drought periods when livestock (mostly sheep or goats) are forced to graze on the plant or when animals are newly introduced into areas where Scholtz bush is common. Scholtz bush and *springbokbos* are known to be variable in their toxicity – plants from some farms appear to be harmless and quite palatable, while others can be lethal[4]. In some cases, only about 500 g of dry material of both Scholtz bush and *springbokbos* are sufficient to kill a sheep in 30 hours[4].

POISONOUS INGREDIENTS Scholtz bush and *springbokbos* contain an unknown liver poison.

PHARMACOLOGICAL EFFECTS Little is known about the effects of Scholtz bush except that it results in chronic or acute liver damage[2-5]. Symptoms include heavy breathing, fast and weak pulse, general weakness, apathy (hence the common name *domsiekte* in some parts of the Karoo) and jaundice[2-4]. Scholtz bush and other species listed above cause extensive necrosis of the liver, often accompanied by damage to the lungs and kidneys[3,5].

DISTRIBUTION *Pteronia pallens* occurs is the western and southern parts of the Karoo (see map, area on left), where it is usually found in lime-rich soils on flat areas. *Hertia pallens* is widely distributed in the dry central part of South Africa (see map, area on right).

Pteronia pallens   Hertia pallens

1. **Hutchinson, J. & Phillips, E.P. 1917.** A revision of the genus *Pteronia* (Compositae). *Ann. S. Afr. Mus.* 9: 277-329.
2. **Vahrmeijer, J. 1981.** *Poisonous Plants of Southern Africa That Cause Stock Losses.* Tafelberg Publishers, Cape Town.
3. **Kellerman, T.S., Coetzer, J.A.W. & Naudé, T.W. 1988.** *Plant Poisonings and Mycotoxicoses of Livestock in Southern Africa.* Oxford University Press, Cape Town.
4. **Steyn, D.G. 1949.** *Die Vergiftiging van Mens en Dier.* Van Schaik, Pretoria.
5. **Prozesky, L., Kellerman, T.S. & Welman, W.G. 1986.** An ovine hepatotoxicosis by the plant *Pteronia pallens* (Asteraceae). *Onderstepoort J. Vet. Res.* 53: 9-12.

Pteronia pallens

Hertia pallens

Hertia cluytiifolia

RANUNCULUS MULTIFIDUS

Ranunculaceae

---

buttercup (English); botterblom, kankerblare (Afrikaans); uxhaphozi (Zulu)

DESCRIPTION This buttercup is a perennial herb of up to 50 cm in height with numerous usually hairy leaves emerging from underground stems. The leaves are borne on slender stalks and are pinnately to bipinnately divided into numerous feathery or wedge-shaped segments. Attractive, glossy, bright yellow flowers are borne at the branch ends. The plant is easily recognised by the numerous small structures (free carpels) in the middle of the flower – these are characteristic for the family, and develop into a compound fruit – a cluster of tiny nutlets. The green sepals and yellow petals distinguish *Ranunculus* species from *Knowltonia* species, which have no petals, only coloured sepals[1,2].

TYPE OF TOXIN Lactone.

IMPORTANCE *R. multifidus* is known to be poisonous to humans and animals. It is also widely used in traditional medicine[3]. Occasional stock losses, mainly sheep, have been reported in South Africa despite the fact that the plant is highly unpalatable[4,5]. There are about 250 species of *Ranunculus* all over the world and heavy stock losses have been reported from North America[6]. Like many other members of the family (e.g. *Knowltonia*

bracteata – known as *brandblare* – or *Clematis* species), buttercups cause blistering of the skin. Leaf poultices of these plants are widely used in traditional medicine to treat wounds, external cancers and rheumatism[3]. *Knowltonia bracteata* is believed to be poisonous and has been implicated in a human fatality[3].

POISONOUS INGREDIENTS *Ranunculus* species and other members of the family contain a bitter tasting glycoside, ranunculin. When fresh plants are eaten or bruised, this compound is enzymatically converted to protoanemonin, a toxic oil with an acrid taste that causes blistering of human skin. Protoanemonin is toxic and responsible for livestock losses[6].

PHARMACOLOGICAL EFFECTS Protoanemonin is well known as an irritant vesicant oil that causes blistering of human skin. It is highly toxic – the lethal dose in sheep fed on a North American plant that contains ranunculin was 11 g wet weight per kg body-weight[6].

DISTRIBUTION *R. multifidus* is widely distributed from the Western Cape Province northwards to the summer rainfall regions of South Africa.

Ranunculin

1. **Dreyer, L.L. & Jordaan, M. 2000**. Ranunculaceae. In O.A. Leistner (ed.), Seed Plants of Southern Africa: Families and Genera. *Strelitzia* 10: 463-464. National Botanical Institute, Pretoria.
2. **Rasmussen, H. 1979**. The genus *Knowltonia* (Ranunculaceae). *Opera Botanica* 53: 1-39.
3. **Watt, J.M. & Breyer-Brandwijk, M.G. 1962**. *The Medicinal and Poisonous Plants of Southern and Eastern Africa*, 2nd edition. Livingstone, London.
4. **Steyn, D.G. 1949**. *Die Vergiftiging van Mens en Dier*. Van Schaik, Pretoria.
5. **Kellerman, T.S., Coetzer, J.A.W. & Naudé, T.W. 1988**. *Plant Poisonings and Mycotoxicoses of Livestock in Southern Africa*. Oxford University Press, Cape Town.
6. **Nachman, R.J. & Olsen, J.D. 1983**. Ranunculin: a toxic constituent of the poisonous range plant bur buttercup (*Ceratocephalus testiculatus*) *Agric. Food. Chem.* 31: 1358-1360.

Ranunculus multifidus

Flowers of *Ranunculus multifidus*

Knowltonia bracteata

RAUVOLFIA CAFFRA

Apocynaceae

quinine tree (English); kinaboom (Afrikaans); umhlambamanzi (Zulu)

DESCRIPTION *R. caffra* is a large tree of up to 20 m in height, with a wide, spreading crown and attractive, glossy, green leaves arranged in groups of three to five along the branches. Small, white, waxy flowers occur in many-flowered clusters. The berries are rounded or egg-shaped, often dotted with white spots, at first bright green but becoming black and wrinkled when they ripen[1,2].

TYPE OF TOXIN Indole alkaloid.

IMPORTANCE *R. caffra* is a popular traditional medicine and incorrect use may lead to human poisoning[3,4]. The bark is said to be bitter and may produce severe purgation and abdominal pain[3]. In South Africa, the plant does not appear to be particularly dangerous, but in Tanzania, 70 deaths per year have been reported[5].

POISONOUS INGREDIENTS Complex mixtures of alkaloids have been isolated from the leaves, root bark and stem bark[5]. Of interest is the presence of reserpine and ajmalicine, as well as ajmaline (0,16%) in root bark[5].

PHARMACOLOGICAL EFFECTS Reserpine was formerly widely used as medication to lower blood pressure but it causes depression as a side-effect[6]. Ajmalicine increases blood flow to the brain and is an ingredient of products used to treat senility and sensory problems. Ajmaline is known to be toxic and is no longer used commercially[6].

DISTRIBUTION *R. caffra* occurs naturally in the southern and eastern parts of South Africa and further north into east Africa. It is mainly found in coastal forests.

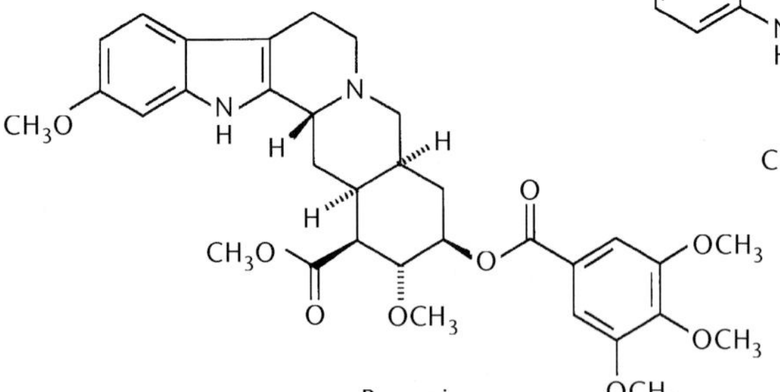

Reserpine

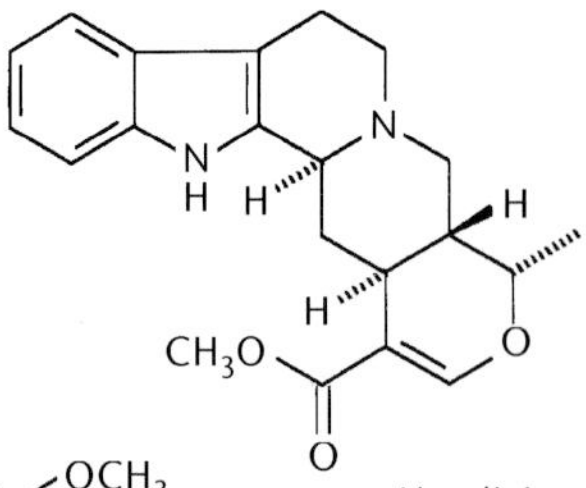

Ajmalicine

1. **Codd, L.E. 1963.** Apocynaceae. *Flora of Southern Africa* 26: 244-296.
2. **Van Dilst, F.J.H. & Leeuwenberg, A.J.M. 1991.** *Rauvolfia* L. in Africa and Madagascar. Series of revisions of Apocynaceae XXXIII. *Bull. Jard. Bot. Nat. Belg.* 61: 21-69.
3. **Watt, J.M. & Breyer-Brandwijk, M.G. 1962.** *The Medicinal and Poisonous Plants of Southern and Eastern Africa*, 2nd edition. Livingstone, London.
4. **Hutchings, A., Scott, A.H., Lewis, G. & Cunningham, A.B. 1996.** *Zulu Medicinal Plants. An Inventory.* University of Natal Press, Pietermaritzburg.
5. **Madati, P.J., Kayani, M.J., Pazi, H.A. & Nyamgenda, A.F. 1977.** Alkaloids of *Rauvolfia caffra* Sond. I. Phytochemical and toxicological studies. *Planta Med.* 32: 258-267.
6. **Bruneton, J. 1999.** *Pharmacognosy, Phytochemistry, Medicinal Plants.* Intercept, Hampshire.

Rauvolfia caffra

Flowers of *Rauvolfia caffra*

Fruits of *Rauvolfia caffra*

RICINUS COMMUNIS

Euphorbiaceae

castor oil plant (English); kasterolieboom (Afrikaans);
mokhura (Northern Sotho); umhlakuva (Xhosa, Zulu)

DESCRIPTION The castor oil plant is a large shrub or small tree of up to 4 m in height, with large, hand-shaped leaves on long, stout leaf stalks[1]. Female flowers are borne above the male flowers at the tips of the branches. The fruits are three-lobed, three-seeded capsules, with soft spines on their surfaces. The glossy seeds of about 10 mm long are irregularly mottled with silver, brown and black. At the tip of the seed is a hard, white aril[1]. Castor oil is grown commercially on a large scale for the seed oil, which is mainly an industrial product, used as a lubricant and as starting material in the manufacturing of polymers and various other products.

TYPE OF TOXIN Lectin; also a piperidine alkaloid.

IMPORTANCE The seeds of the castor oil plant are extremely poisonous. Only one or two seeds may cause fatal poisoning in humans[2,3]. The oil is not toxic in moderate doses. Punctured seeds are used in necklaces and are attractive to children, so that accidental poisoning may occur. Animals are usually not poisoned under field conditions but by the accidental inclusion of castor seed cake in stock rations[4,5]. Leaves are almost never browsed but at least one case of poisoning in cattle has been reported[3].

POISONOUS INGREDIENTS Two toxins are present in the seed (but not in the seed oil, because the compounds are not oil-soluble) – ricinine (an alkaloid) and ricin (a mixture of four lectins)[3].

PHARMACOLOGICAL EFFECTS Ricin is one of the most toxic substances known to man. A single seed may contain a lethal dose (about 0,25 mg) of ricin[3]. Surprisingly, very few deaths have been reported and this could perhaps be ascribed to slow absorption of the toxin or its instability in the digestive tract[6]. The alkaloid ricinine is highly toxic and is suspected to be a problem in rare cases when leaves are browsed by livestock[3].

DISTRIBUTION The plant is believed to be indigenous to north-eastern Africa and India but has become a weed in many parts of the world, including most parts of southern Africa[1]. It is sometimes grown as an ornamental plant.

Ricinine

1. **Henderson, M. & Anderson, J.G. 1966.** *Common Weeds in South Africa. Memoirs of the Botanical Survey of South Africa* 37.
2. **Watt, J.M. & Breyer-Brandwijk, M.G. 1962.** *The Medicinal and Poisonous Plants of Southern and Eastern Africa*, 2nd edition. Livingstone, London.
3. **Harborne, J.B., Baxter, H. & Moss, G.P. (eds) 1997.** *Dictionary of Plant Toxins.* John Wiley & Sons, Chichester.
4. **Vahrmeijer, J. 1981.** *Poisonous Plants of Southern Africa That Cause Stock Losses.* Tafelberg Publishers, Cape Town.
5. **Kellerman, T.S., Coetzer, J.A.W. & Naudé, T.W. 1988.** *Plant Poisonings and Mycotoxicoses of Livestock in Southern Africa.* Oxford University Press, Cape Town.
6. **Bruneton, J. 1999.** *Toxic Plants Dangerous to Humans and Animals.* Intercept, Hampshire.

Flowers of *Ricinus communis*

Fruits of *Ricinus communis*

Seeds of *Ricinus communis*

SALSOLA TUBERCULATIFORMIS
Chenopodiaceae

---

cauliflower saltwort (English); blomkoolbossie, blomkoolganna, koolganna (Afrikaans)

DESCRIPTION Cauliflower saltwort is a densely branched shrub up to 1 m in height. It is usually kept quite low by repeated grazing – this results in the dense 'cauliflower'-like appearance of the plants. The slender twigs bear minute, densely packed, silvery leaves. Inconspicuous pale pink flowers are borne along the branch tips. The small capsules each contain a single winged seed[1].

TYPE OF TOXIN Possibly acetophenones[2] or hydroxyphenyl aziridine derivatives[3].

IMPORTANCE *Salsola* species are generally regarded as excellent grazing and the plants often occur in large numbers. At least six different species are responsible for poisoning of sheep, which happens mainly during drought periods. Poisoning may affect from 3% to as high as 33%[4] of the total flock[4] and is characterised by the extension of the period of pregnancy, resulting in abnormally large lambs (a disease known as *grootlamsiekte*). Instead of a normal birth weight of 4 kg, some lambs may attain 12 kg[4,5]. As a result, both the ewe and the lamb may die. Ewes show no signs of illness except for an unusually large abdomen and smaller than usual udder[4,5]. Karakul sheep and Karakul-Persian crossbreeds are mainly affected[4].

POISONOUS INGREDIENTS There is still uncertainty about the toxic compounds, but they are thought to be labile acetophenones[2] (the more stable but still active 4-hydroxyacetophenone and 4-hydroxy-3-methoxyacetophenone have been identified from the plant) and / or hydroxyphenyl aziridine derivatives and / or their precursor[3]. One species of *Salsola* (*S. richteri*) is known to contain the isoquinoline alkaloid, (–)-salsoline[6].

PHARMACOLOGICAL EFFECTS The toxins in *Salsola* seem to interfere with the hormone balance and the level of progesterone and corticosterone, thereby disrupting the normal reproductive cycle in sheep[2,3]. Salsoline is known to be highly toxic when injected, but not when taken by mouth[6].

DISTRIBUTION *S. tuberculatiformis* is widely distributed in the dry western and central interior of southern Africa.

4-Hydroxyacetophenone   4-Hydroxyphenyl-*N*-methyl-aziridine

1. **Botschantzev, V. 1974.** A synopsis of *Salsola* (Chenopodiaceae) from South and South-West Africa. *Kew Bull.* 29: 597-614.
2. **Swart, P., Van der Merwe, K.J., Swart, A.C., Todres, P.C. and Hofmeyr, J-H. S. 1992.** Inhibition of cytochrome P-450$_{11\beta}$ by some naturally occurring acetophenones and plant extracts from the shrub *Salsola tuberculatiformis*. *Planta Med.* 59: 139-143.
3. **Louw, A. & Swart, P. 1999.** *Salsola tuberculatiformis* Botschantzev and an aziridine precursor analog mediate the *in vivo* increase in free corticosterone and decrease in corticosteroid-binding globulin in female Wistar rats. *Endocrinology* 140: 2044-2053.
4. **Kellerman, T.S., Coetzer, J.A.W. & Naudé, T.W. 1988.** *Plant Poisonings and Mycotoxicoses of Livestock in Southern Africa.* Oxford University Press, Cape Town.
5. **Vahrmeijer, J. 1981.** *Poisonous Plants of Southern Africa That Cause Stock Losses.* Tafelberg Publishers, Cape Town.
6. **Harborne, J.B., Baxter, H. & Moss, G.P. (eds) 1997.** *Dictionary of Plant Toxins.* John Wiley & Sons, Chichester.

Salsola tuberculatiformis

Woody branch of *Salsola tuberculatiformis*

Leaves and flowers of *Salsola tuberculatiformis*

SARCOSTEMMA VIMINALE
Asclepidaceae

---

melktou, spantoumelkbos (Afrikaans); mutungu (Venda)

DESCRIPTION *S. viminale* is a robust, leafless, succulent shrub or more usually a climber that may form dense masses in and over trees[1,2]. The stems are bright green or yellowish-green but turn reddish during drought. *Melktou* is easily recognised by the milky latex that oozes from broken stems, the small, yellow, star-shaped flowers, and the paired fruit capsules that resemble the horns of a goat. Another climber of the same family from Peru, the so-called mothcatcher (*Araujia sericifera*), also has milky latex in the stems. It has become a troublesome weed in gardens and can easily be distinguished by the large leaves, large, white flowers and pear-shaped fruits, which produce a multitude of seeds with fluffy seed hairs[3].

TYPE OF TOXIN Steroid glycoside.

IMPORTANCE *Sarcostemma* is used to a limited extent in traditional medicine[4], but it is not clear how toxic it is to humans. During times when grazing is scarce, animals may ingest sufficient material to be poisoned. Angora goats, horses and cattle are mostly affected[1,2]. Cattle and sheep in Australia are similarly poisoned by *Sarcostemma australis*[1]. Plants from different regions seem to differ greatly in toxicity – in some areas the plant can be grazed without any effect[1]. There is one report of fatal poisoning of cattle ascribed to *Araujia sericifera*[5].

POISONOUS INGREDIENTS The active principles[6] in *S. viminalis* have been identified as a steroid (pregnane) glycoside called sarcovimiside A, as well as two derivatives, sarcovimisides B and C. The aglycones of these compounds are shown here.

PHARMACOLOGICAL EFFECTS Poisoned animals display symptoms similar to cynanchosis (see *Cynanchum africanum*, p. 84) – hypersensitivity, seizures and paralysis[1].

DISTRIBUTION *S. viminale* is very widely distributed in South Africa and occurs in a wide variety of habitats.

Sarcovimiside A
(R=triglycoside)

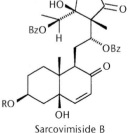

Sarcovimiside B

1. **Kellerman, T.S., Coetzer, J.A.W. & Naudé, T.W. 1988.** *Plant Poisonings and Mycotoxicoses of Livestock in Southern Africa.* Oxford University Press, Cape Town.
2. **Vahrmeijer, J. 1981.** *Poisonous Plants of Southern Africa That Cause Stock Losses.* Tafelberg Publishers, Cape Town.
3. **Henderson, M. & Anderson, J.G. 1966.** *Common Weeds in South Africa. Memoirs of the Botanical Survey of South Africa 37.*
4. **Watt, J.M. & Breyer-Brandwijk, M.G. 1962.** *The Medicinal and Poisonous Plants of Southern and Eastern Africa,* 2nd edition. Livingstone, London.
5. **Steyn, D.G. 1949.** *Die Vergiftiging van Mens en Dier.* Van Schaik, Pretoria.
6. **Vleggaar, R., Van Heerden, F.R., Anderson, L.A.P. & Erasmus, G.L. 1993.** Toxic constituents of the Asclepiadaceae. Structure elucidation of sarcovimiside A-C, pregnane glycosides of *Sarcostemma viminale*. *J. Chem. Soc.* 1993: 483-487.

Sarcostemma viminale completely covering a tree

Stems and flowers of *Sarcostemma viminale*

Araujia sericifera

SCADOXUS PUNICEUS

Amaryllidaceae

red paintbrush (English); rooikwas (Afrikaans); umphopo (Zulu)

DESCRIPTION This is an attractive bulbous plant of shady places. It has long, erect, strap-shaped leaves with wavy margins[1]. The attractive, orange-red flowers are borne in dense clusters on a long, thick, purple-spotted stalk. Leaves are usually formed after the flowering time[1]. The related *S. multiflorus* has a wider, open flower cluster. *Scadoxus* species were previously considered to be part of the genus *Haemanthus*. The latter includes *H. coccineus* (known as April's Fool because, in keeping with many other Amaryllidaceae, it flowers in autumn)[2].

TYPE OF TOXIN Isoquinoline alkaloid (Amaryllidaceae type).

IMPORTANCE *Scadoxus* species are widely used in traditional medicine and their inappropriate use may cause accidents and fatalities[3-6]. The same applies to the genus *Haemanthus*, of which *H. coccineus* is an old Cape antiseptic and diuretic[6]. Children and domestic animals may also be exposed to the plants when they are grown in gardens.

POISONOUS INGREDIENTS *Scadoxus* and *Haemanthus* species contain isoquinoline alkaloids (so-called Amaryllidaceae alkaloids). Haemanthamine and haemanthidine have been isolated from *S. puniceus*, while *H. coccineus* contains coccinine and an isomer, montanine[7].

PHARMACOLOGICAL EFFECTS Amaryllidaceae alkaloids are known to be very toxic. Montanine, for example, has an LD_{50} of 42 mg/kg body-weight in dogs when injected and is said to be a weak hypotensive and convulsive agent[7].

DISTRIBUTION *S. puniceus* occurs over a large part of the summer rainfall areas of South Africa[1] (see map) and has become a popular garden plant. The bright orange, globose flower heads are exceptionally beautiful. In nature, the plants are usually found in forests and other shady places. *H. coccineus* is found mainly in the fynbos region of the Western Cape Province, but also Namaqualand and the Eastern Cape Province[2].

Haemanthamine: R=H
Haemanthidine: R=OH

Montanine

1. **Friis, I. & Nordal, I. 1976.** Studies on the genus *Haemanthus* (Amaryllidaceae). IV. Division of the genus into *Haemanthus s. str.* and *Scadoxus* with notes on *Haemanthus s. str. Norw. J. Bot.* 23: 63-77.
2. **Snijman, D.A. 1984.** A revision of the genus *Haemanthus* (Amaryllidaceae). *Jl S. Afr. Bot. Suppl.* 12: 1-139.
3. **Watt, J.M. & Breyer-Brandwijk, M.G. 1962.** *The Medicinal and Poisonous Plants of Southern and Eastern Africa*, 2nd edition. Livingstone, London.
4. **Hutchings, A., Scott, A.H., Lewis, G. & Cunningham, A.B. 1996.** *Zulu Medicinal Plants. An Inventory.* University of Natal Press, Pietermaritzburg.
5. **Veale, D.J.H., Furman, K.I. & Oliver, D.W. 1992.** South African traditional medicines used during pregnancy and childbirth. *J. Ethnopharmacol.* 36: 341-346.
6. **Van Wyk, B-E., Van Oudtshoorn, B. & Gericke, N. 2000.** *Medicinal Plants of South Africa*, 2nd edition. Briza Publications, Pretoria.
7. **Harborne, J.B., Baxter, H. & Moss, G.P. (eds) 1997.** *Dictionary of Plant Toxins.* John Wiley & Sons, Chichester.

Scadoxus puniceus

Scadoxus multiflorus

Bulbs of *Scadoxus puniceus*

Haemanthus coccineus

SCILLA NATALENSIS

Hyacinthaceae

---

inguduza (Zulu); blouberglelie, blouslangkop (Afrikaans)

DESCRIPTION *S. natalensis* is an attractive bulbous plant with its papery bulb scales often visible above the ground. The leaves are relatively short and broad and have distinct veins on them[1]. Attractive clusters of small, blue flowers are produced on robust stalks in spring. A related genus is *Ledebourea*, characterised by purple spots on the leaves and stems[1].

TYPE OF TOXIN Cardiac glycoside (bufadienolide).

IMPORTANCE *S. natalensis* is an important traditional medicine[2-5] and may cause injury or perhaps even death if not used correctly. There are reports that some species of *Ledebouria* used in traditional medicine (e.g. *L. ovatifolia*) are poisonous[2] but others are edible[5]. *S. natalensis* is known to be toxic to animals but is not very important in livestock poisoning[6].

POISONOUS INGREDIENTS Typical symptoms of cardiac glycoside poisoning have been recorded for *S. natalensis* and *S. rigidifolia*, but the bufadienolide(s) in *S. natalensis* has not yet been isolated. A recent screening of bulbs of *S. natalensis*, using proscillaridin A as reference compound, suggested that the latter might be present[7].

PHARMACOLOGICAL EFFECTS In dosing trials on sheep, bulbs administered at 10–18 g fresh weight per kg body-weight caused death within 12 to 48 hours[6]. The symptoms were similar to those caused by cardiac glycosides[6].

DISTRIBUTION *S. natalensis* occurs over a wide area in the eastern parts of South Africa[1]. In recent years, this attractive bulbous plant has become a popular garden subject and is successfully cultivated on the highveld.

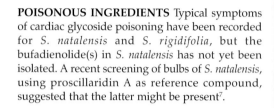

Proscillaridin A

1. **Jessop, J.P. 1970.** Studies in the bulbous Liliaceae: 1. *Scilla, Schizocarpus* and *Ledebouria*. *Jl S. Afr. Bot.* 36: 233-266.
2. **Watt, J.M. & Breyer-Brandwijk, M.G. 1962.** *The Medicinal and Poisonous Plants of Southern and Eastern Africa*, 2nd edition. Livingstone, London.
3. **Hutchings, A., Scott, A.H., Lewis, G. & Cunningham, A.B. 1996.** *Zulu Medicinal Plants. An Inventory*. University of Natal Press, Pietermaritzburg.
4. **Van Wyk, B-E., Van Oudtshoorn, B. & Gericke, N. 2000.** *Medicinal Plants of South Africa*, 2nd edition. Briza Publications, Pretoria.
5. **Van Wyk, B-E. & Gericke, N. 2000.** *People's Plants. A Guide to Useful Plants of Southern Africa*. Briza Publications, Pretoria.
6. **Kellerman, T.S., Coetzer, J.A.W. & Naudé, T.W. 1988.** *Plant Poisonings and Mycotoxicoses of Livestock in Southern Africa*. Oxford University Press, Cape Town.
7. **Sparg, S.G., Van Staden, J. & Jäger, A.K. 2002.** Pharmacological and phytochemical screening of two Hyacinthaceae species: *Scilla natalensis* and *Ledebouria ovatifolia*. *J. Ethnopharmacol.* (in press).

Scilla natalensis

Flowering plant of *Scilla natalensis*

Flowers of *Scilla natalensis*

Bulb of *Scilla natalensis*

SENECIO LATIFOLIUS

Asteraceae

---

ragwort, staggers bush, Molteno disease plant (English); gifbossie, dunsiektebossie (Afrikaans)

DESCRIPTION *Senecio* species are erect herbs with alternate leaves and groups of small, yellow flower heads. The green involucral bracts around each flower heads are in a single row in *Senecio* species, while they are in two or more rows in most other genera[1]. There are about 1 500 species of *Senecio* worldwide, with more than 300 in southern Africa. Many of them are poisonous but only a few have well-recorded track records of causing poisoning in southern Africa. These are, amongst others, *S. latifolius* (including *S. sceleratus*), *S. retrorsus*, *S. isatideus* and *S. burchellii*[2]. The species are often difficult to identify because their flowers and inflorescences are quite uniform in general appearance. They differ rather subtly in growth form and in the size, shape and colour (green or greyish-green) of the leaves.

TYPE OF TOXIN Pyrrolizidine alkaloid.

IMPORTANCE *Senecio* species are widely used in traditional medicine (and sometimes even as green spinach) and pose a threat to human health[2,3]. Contamination of wheat (bread poisoning) and other foods should also be considered. These plants cause one of the most serious of all livestock poisonings in South Africa, known as seneciosis[4,5].

POISONOUS INGREDIENTS A large number of macrocyclic pyrrolizidine alkaloids are known from *Senecio* species[6]. They are usually named after the species from which they were originally extracted: examples are sceleratine from *S. sceleratus* (now included in *S. latifolius*), retrorsine from *S. retrorsus* and isatidine from *S. isatideus*[5-7].

PHARMACOLOGICAL EFFECTS Pyrrolizidine alkaloids cause acute poisoning of humans and livestock or, more often, chronic poisoning that may go undetected for a long period. The latter is known as Molteno disease in cattle and *dunsiekte* in horses[4,5]. Damage to the liver (less often also the lungs and kidneys) is similar in humans and animals – necrosis and chemical lesions, ascribed to highly reactive pyrrole derivates that are formed inside the liver[6]. In humans, this damage causes veno-occlusive liver disease, a condition that may be more widespread in South Africa than is currently recognised[8].

DISTRIBUTION *Senecio* species of importance in poisoning are mostly found in the eastern parts of South Africa. The distribution area of *S. latifolius* (see map) overlaps to a large extent with that of most of the other poisonous species.

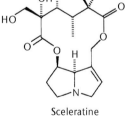

Retrorsine   Sceleratine

---

1. **Hilliard, O.M. 1977.** *Compositae in Natal.* University of Natal Press, Pietermaritzburg, pp. 387-502.
2. **Watt, J.M. & Breyer-Brandwijk, M.G. 1962.** *The Medicinal and Poisonous Plants of Southern and Eastern Africa,* 2nd edition. Livingstone, London.
3. **Hutchings, A., Scott, A.H., Lewis, G. & Cunningham, A.B. 1996.** *Zulu Medicinal Plants. An Inventory.* University of Natal Press, Pietermaritzburg.
4. **Vahrmeijer, J. 1981.** *Poisonous Plants of Southern Africa That Cause Stock Losses.* Tafelberg Publishers, Cape Town.
5. **Kellerman, T.S., Coetzer, J.A.W. & Naudé, T.W. 1988.** *Plant Poisonings and Mycotoxicoses of Livestock in Southern Africa.* Oxford University Press, Cape Town.
6. **Mattocks, A.R. 1986.** *Chemistry and Toxicology of Pyrrolizidine Alkaloids.* Academic Press, London.
7. **Stegelmeier, B. 1999.** Pyrrolizidine alkaloids – methodology & toxicity. *J. Nat. Toxins* 8: 95-116.
8. **Steenkamp, V., Stewart, M.J. & Zuckerman, M. 2000.** Clinical and analytical aspects of pyrrolizidine poisoning caused by South African traditional medicines. *Ther. Drug Monit.* 22: 302-306.

Senecio latifolius

Flower heads of *Senecio latifolius*

Senecio burchellii

SESBANIA PUNICEA

Fabaceae

---

red sesbania (English); rooisesbania (Afrikaans)

DESCRIPTION Sesbania is a sparsely branched shrub or small tree shrub with compound leaves borne mostly towards the branch ends. Attractive, bright orange to reddish flowers are borne in drooping clusters, followed by the characteristic pale brown, oblong, winged pods. Each of the latter contains several small, hard, greyish-brown bean-like seeds[1,2].

TYPE OF TOXIN Piperidine alkaloid.

IMPORTANCE The leaves, flowers and seeds of *S. punicea* are all known to be poisonous[3,4]. Poultry are mainly at risk, as the seeds are attractive but very toxic. Poisoning of fowls and pigeons has been reported[3], but there appear to be no records of other animals being harmed[4].

POISONOUS INGREDIENTS Sesbanimide A is the active compound in *Sesbania* seeds[5]. It co-occurs with related alkaloids (such as sesbanimides B and C)[6].

PHARMACOLOGICAL EFFECTS The fatal dose of seeds in fowls and turkey was found to be about 2,5 g/kg body-weight (about 20 to 70 seeds)[3,4]. The seeds are also lethal to sheep. As little as 0,1 mg/kg/day of ground seeds caused death within six days[3,4]. Small doses over an extended period result in a cumulative effect. Sesbanimide A is highly active and has antitumour properties[6], and it has been shown to be the main toxic substance in *Sesbania*[5].

DISTRIBUTION *S. punicea* was originally introduced from South and Central America (Brazil, Argentina and Mexico) as a popular garden plant, but it has escaped into natural veld and the seeds are now dispersed along rivers and into disturbed places. Over the last few decades the plant has become an aggressive invader and was declared a noxious weed in 1979[2]. A beetle from Argentina is proving to be effective as a biological control agent[2]. *S. punicea* is widely distributed in all parts of South Africa except for the dry central interior region.

Sesbanimide A

1. **Henderson, L. 2001.** *Alien Weeds and Invasive Plants.* Plant Protection Research Institute Handbook no. 12, Agricultural Research Council, Pretoria.
2. **Bromilow, C. 2001.** *Problem Plants of South Africa.* Briza Publications, Pretoria.
3. **Terblanche, M., De Klerk, W.A., Smit, J.D. & Adelaar, T.F. 1966.** A toxicological study of the plant *Sesbania punicea* Benth. *J. S. Afr. Vet. Med. Ass.* 37: 191-197.
4. **Kellerman, T.S., Coetzer, J.A.W. & Naudé, T.W.1988.** *Plant Poisonings and Mycotoxicoses of Livestock in Southern Africa.* Oxford University Press, Cape Town.
5. **Gorst-Allman, C.P., Steyn, P.S., Vleggaar, R. & Grobbelaar, N. 1984.** Structure elucidation of sesbanimide using high-field N.M.R. spectroscopy. *J. Chem. Soc., Perkin Trans. I*, 1984: 1311-1131.
6. **Harborne, J.B., Baxter, H. & Moss, G.P. (eds) 1997.** *Dictionary of Plant Toxins.* John Wiley & Sons, Chichester.

Sesbania punicea

Growth form of *Sesbania punicea*

Pods and seeds of *Sesbania punicea*

SMODINGIUM ARGUTUM

Anacardiaceae

African poison ivy, rainbow leaf (English); pynbos (Afrikaans)

DESCRIPTION *Smodingium* is a shrub or small tree with multiple branches, the tips of which tend to droop[1,2]. The leaves are trifoliate. Each of the three leaflets is narrowly lanceolate to oblong and hairless, with coarsely toothed margins. Small, white flowers are borne in large clusters on the branch ends. The fruits are small, flat, winged nuts. Trifoliate leaves are also characteristic of the related *karee* or *taaibos* plants (*Rhus* species) but the latter produce small, fleshy berries shaped like miniature mangoes. The spectacular yellow or red autumn colours make this a very attractive ornamental plant for indigenous gardens.

TYPE OF TOXIN Alkylphenol.

IMPORTANCE *Smodingium* contains highly irritating substances that may cause severe blistering of the skin[3]. Not all people seem to be affected, but allergic persons experience extreme pain and may have to receive medical attention. Since it is often planted in gardens, care should be taken to avoid places where people could accidentally come into contact with it. *Smodingium* is the South African equivalent of the North American 'poison ivy' (*Toxicodendron radicans*), 'poison oak' (*T. diversilobum*) and 'poison sumach' (*T. vernix*). These species are sometimes included in the genus *Rhus*. Along with cashew nut (*Anacardium occidentale*), all of these plants belong to the Anacardiaceae (cashew nut family) and all produce resins with skin-blistering

properties. The resin is quite stable and can be transferred from person to person through clothing and contaminated objects.

POISONOUS INGREDIENTS *Smodingium*, like 'poison ivy' and other members of the family Anacardiaceae, produce resins with alkylphenols[4]. The main compound in *Smodingium* is 3-(8,11-heptadecadienyl)catechol[4]. The North American plants ('poison ivy', 'poison oak') contain a resin called urushiol, to which more than 50% of Americans show allergic reactions[5]. Urushiol consists of a mixture of closely related compounds, one of which is illustrated below. Exposure is usually through skin contact, but firefighters who inhale the smoke and dust released by burning plant material may also be at risk[5]. Skin should be washed thoroughly with cold water and soap as soon as possible after contact.

PHARMACOLOGICAL EFFECTS Alkylphenols cause dermatitis through the ease with which they penetrate the upper skin layers[5]. Here they are oxidised to highly reactive quinones. The quinones react with proteins in the skin, causing severe immune reactions, including rashes and blistering[5].

DISTRIBUTION The natural distribution area is centred in KwaZulu-Natal and extends northwards into Mpumalanga[1,2]. *S. argutum* is commonly cultivated in gardens.

3-(8,11-Heptadecadienyl)catechol

Urushiol component

---

1. **Coates Palgrave, K. 1977.** *Trees of Southern Africa.* Struik, Cape Town.
2. **Van Wyk, B. & Van Wyk, P.** *Field Guide to Trees of Southern Africa.* Struik Publishers, Cape Town.
3. **Findlay, G.H. 1974.** *Smodingium* (African 'poison ivy') dermatitis. History, comparative plant chemistry and anatomy, clinical and histological features. *Br. J. Dermatol.* 90: 535-541.
4. **Gorst-Allman, C.P., Steyn, P.S., Heyl, T., Wells, M.J. & Fourie, D.M.C. 1987.** Plant dermatitis - isolation and chemical investigation of the major vesicant principle of *Smodingium argutum. S. Afr. J. Chem.* 40: 82-86.
5. **Bruneton, J. 1999.** *Toxic Plants Dangerous to Humans and Animals.* Intercept, Hampshire.

Smodingium argutum

Flowers of *Smodingium argutum*

Young leaves of *Smodingium argutum*

SOLANUM INCANUM

Solanaceae

---

thorn apple (English); bitterappel, gifappel, grysbitterappel (Afrikaans)

DESCRIPTION *S. incanum* is a robust herb with curved prickles on the stems, leaf stalks and upper surfaces of the broad, lobed leaves. The stems and lower leaf surfaces have a felt-like layer of white hairs. Pale purple to whitish flowers are borne in few-flowered clusters. The fruits are dark green and mottled at first but turn pale green and yellow as they ripen. *S. panduriforme* (poison apple or *gifappel*) is similar but the leaves are narrower and elliptic in shape and there are usually no thorns or prickles. Another cause of livestock poisoning is *S. kwebense* (*rooibessie* in Afrikaans), an erect shrubby plant of up to 2 m in height with hairy upper leaf surfaces and red berries[1-3]. The leaves and green fruits of *S. nigrum* (know as *msoba* or nastergal) are very toxic, while ripe fruits are edible and popular for making jam. Green fruits of alien invaders such as *S. mauritianum* (bugweed or *luisboom*), *S. elaeagnifolium* (*satansbos*) and *S. sisymbriifolium* (thorny bitter apple) are also poisonous.

TYPE OF TOXIN Steroid alkaloid.

IMPORTANCE The leaves and more specifically the green fruit of *S. incanum*, *S. nigrum* and *S. panduriforme* (and indeed many other exotic weeds such as *S. mauritinum*) are poisonous and potentially lethal to humans and livestock[1-3]. Children may be at risk, and also people who use the fruit incorrectly in traditional medicine[2]. *S. kwebense* causes *maldronksiekte* (literally 'mad drunk disease') in cattle[3].

POISONOUS INGREDIENTS Solasonine is the major alkaloid in fruits of *S. incanum*[4], while its aglycone, solasodine, is found as a major constituent in *S. nigrum*[4]. Solanidine and various glycosidic forms of it, such as α-solanine (see *S. tuberosum* under garden plants) may also be present. The toxic compound in *S. kwebense* is not known, but calystegines (polyhydroxynortropanes) in *S. dimidiatum* are linked to similar symptoms of poisoning in North America (known as 'crazy cow syndrome' in Texas)[5].

PHARMACOLOGICAL EFFECTS The symptoms of human poisoning include headache, salivation, nausea, vomiting, diarrhoea, fever and coma[1-3]. In severe cases death may occur through cardiac and respiratory arrest. In animals, salivation, vomiting, diarrhoea, bloat, rapid pulse and breathing, cramps and paralysis may occur[3]. *Maldronksiekte* is characterised by degeneration of the cerebellum through damage to the Purkinje cells, resulting in seizures[3].

DISTRIBUTION *S. incanum* occurs in the eastern half of the country (see map) while *S. nigrum* is found in all parts as a naturalised weed. *S. kwebense* is limited to the extreme northern parts[3].

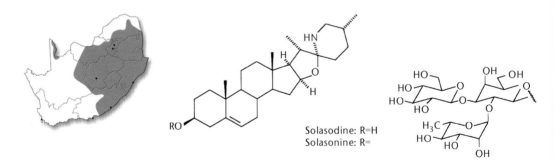

Solasodine: R=H
Solasonine: R=

1. **Steyn, D.G. 1949.** *Die Vergiftiging van Mens en Dier.* Van Schaik, Pretoria.
2. **Watt, J.M. & Breyer-Brandwijk, M.G. 1962.** *The Medicinal and Poisonous Plants of Southern and Eastern Africa,* 2nd edition. Livingstone, London.
3. **Kellerman, T.S., Coetzer, J.A.W. & Naudé, T.W. 1988.** *Plant Poisonings and Mycotoxicoses of Livestock in Southern Africa.* Oxford University Press, Cape Town.
4. **Harborne, J.B., Baxter, H. & Moss, G.P. (eds) 1997.** *Dictionary of Plant Toxins.* John Wiley & Sons, Chichester.
5. **Bruneton, J. 1999.** *Toxic Plants Dangerous to Humans and Animals.* Intercept, Hampshire.

Fruiting plant of *Solanum incanum*

Flowers and green fruits of *Solanum incanum*

Solanum mauritianum

Solanum nigrum

Solanum elaeagnifolium

SORGHUM BICOLOR

Poaceae

---

grain sorghum, millet (English); graansorghum (Afrikaans)

DESCRIPTION S. bicolor is a robust grass with broad, sheathing leaves that have prominent white midribs. The inflorescence is a much-branched, rounded panicle in S. bicolor subsp. bicolor (grain sorghum), a loose, open panicle in S. bicolor subsp. arundinaceum (common wild sorghum), and a compact panicle in S. bicolor subsp. drummondii (Sudan grass, previously known as S. sudanense)[1-3]. Common wild sorghum is easily confused with S. halepense (Johnson grass), a weed from the Mediterranean region, but the latter has thick, deep-rooted underground stems that are lacking in wild sorghum[2,3]. S. bicolor subsp. bicolor is a well-known and important grain crop in South Africa.

TYPE OF TOXIN Cyanogenic glycoside.

IMPORTANCE Sorghum species are all known to cause prussic acid (HCN, hydrogen cyanide) poisoning (geilsiekte or blousuurvergiftiging in Afrikaans)[4-6]. Young shoots and plants that were damaged by hail, frost, drought or herbicide application are particularly dangerous. The application of nitrogen fertilisers is thought to increase the risk. Several other grasses are known to occasionally cause hydrogen cyanide poisoning

when young and wilted, including Stipagrostis uniplumis (silky bushman grass), Chloris gayana (Rhodes grass), Themeda triandra (rooigras), Cynodon dactylon (quick grass, Bermuda grass, kweek) and even maize (Zea mais)[4-6].

POISONOUS INGREDIENTS All the species of Sorghum contain dhurrin, a hydrogen cyanide releasing (cyanogenic) glucoside[7]. Rapid ingestion of wilted plants may lead to death through excessive fermentation and bloat (opblaas)[4-6]. Dhurrin is known to vary from plant to plant, depending on genetic and environmental factors.

PHARMACOLOGICAL EFFECTS Damage to plant cells through wilting or digestion causes the cyanogenic glycosides to be mixed with hydrolyzing enzymes (the glycosides are compartmentalised separately from the enzymes in intact cells), causing a reaction that releases hydrogen cyanide (HCN), a lethal gas.

DISTRIBUTION Sorghum species are common in the interior and eastern parts of South Africa[2,3]. The map shows the distribution of common wild sorghum.

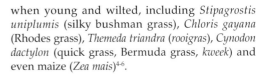

Dhurrin

1. **De Wet, J.M.J. 1978.** Systematics and evolution of Sorghum sect. Sorghum (Gramineae). Am. J. Bot. 65: 477-482.
2. **Gibbs Russell, G.E. et al. 1990.** Grasses of Southern Africa. Memoirs of the Botanical Survey of South Africa 58. National Botanical Institute, Pretoria.
3. **Van Oudtshoorn, F. 1999.** Guide to Grasses of Southern Africa. Briza Publications, Pretoria.
4. **Steyn, D.G. 1949.** Die Vergiftiging van Mens en Dier. Van Schaik, Pretoria.
5. **Watt, J.M. & Breyer-Brandwijk, M.G. 1962.** The Medicinal and Poisonous Plants of Southern and Eastern Africa, 2nd edition. Livingstone, London.
6. **Kellerman, T.S., Coetzer, J.A.W. & Naudé, T.W. 1988.** Plant Poisonings and Mycotoxicoses of Livestock in Southern Africa. Oxford University Press, Cape Town.
7. **Mao, C.-H., Blocher, J.P., Anderson, L. & Smith, D.C. 1965.** Cyanogenesis in Sorghum vulgare – I. An improved method for the isolation of dhurrin; Physical properties of dhurrin. Phytochemistry 4: 297-303.

Sorghum bicolor subsp. *arundinaceum*

Sorghum bicolor hybrid – cultivated fodder sorghum

Inflorescence of *Sorghum bicolor* subsp. *arundinaceum*

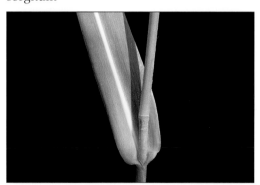

Leaf of *Sorghum bicolor* subsp. *arundinaceum*

Spikelet of *Sorghum bicolor* subsp. *arundinaceum*

SPIROSTACHYS AFRICANA

Euphorbiaceae

---

tamboti (English); tambotie (Afrikaans)

DESCRIPTION Tamboti is a medium-sized, deciduous tree with a rounded crown and dark grey or blackish, flaky bark. The leaves are elliptic in shape and turn yellow or red in autumn. The wood, stems and leaves contain poisonous milky latex. Two minute dark glands are visible where the leaf blade is attached to the stalk. The inconspicuous flowers are borne in dense, spike-like clusters. A few female flowers are found at the base of each spikelet – the rest are all male. The fruit is a small capsule that splits into three segments at maturity[1,2].

TYPE OF TOXIN Diterpene.

IMPORTANCE Stem bark, root bark and latex are used in traditional medicine as an emetic, purgative, painkiller, vermifuge and numerous other uses[3-5], but deaths have been recorded[3]. All parts of the tree, including the wood, contain an irritant latex that may cause inflammation and blistering of the skin, and severe damage or even blindness if accidentally applied to the eyes[3,5]. The wood is hard, heavy, durable and exceptionally beautiful, with a natural lustre and a characteristic spicy smell. Workers may be at risk from the highly irritant sawdust[3]. The poisonous latex makes the wood unsuitable for fuel, as the smoke is highly irritant, causing headache and a burning sensation in the lungs. It is said to taint and even poison food[3].

POISONOUS INGREDIENTS Latex from the wood of tamboti contains complex mixtures of diterpenes, such as stachenone[6], stachenol[7] and several other structurally related compounds (acid metabolites[8] and diosphenols[7]). It is not clear which of these are mainly responsible for the toxicity of the timber.

PHARMACOLOGICAL EFFECTS As is the case with other members of the family Euphorbiaceae (see *Euphorbia*, p. 108), the latex is highly irritant and causes blistering of skin and destruction of mucous membranes.

DISTRIBUTION Tamboti is fairly common in the warm bushveld regions of the north-eastern part of South Africa, from where it extends northwards into tropical Africa[1,2].

Stachenone   Stachenol

1. **Radcliffe-Smith, A. 1987.** Euphorbiaceae (Part 1). *Flora of Tropical East Africa*: 385-386.
2. **Coates Palgrave, K. 1977.** *Trees of Southern Africa.* Struik, Cape Town.
3. **Watt, J.M. & Breyer-Brandwijk, M.G. 1962.** *The Medicinal and Poisonous Plants of Southern and Eastern Africa,* 2nd edition. Livingstone, London.
4. **Neuwinger, H.D. 2000.** *African Traditional Medicine. A Dictionary of Plant Use and Application.* Medpharm Scientific Publishers, Stuttgart.
5. **Verdcourt, B. & Trump, E.C. 1969.** *Common Poisonous Plants of East Africa.* Collins, London.
6. **Baarschers, W.H., Horn, D.H.S. & Johnson, L.R.F. 1962.** The structure of some diterpenes from tambooti wood, *Spirostachys africana. J. Chem. Soc.* 1962: 4046-4055.
7. **Munkombwe, N.M., Maswabi, T. & Hughes, N.A. 1997.** Diosphenols from *Spirostachys africana. Phytochemistry* 45: 1217-1220.
8. **Munkombwe, N.M., Hughes, N.A. & Duri, Z.J. 1998.** Acid metabolites from *Spirostachys africana. Phytochemistry* 47: 1653-1655.

Spirostachys africana

Fruits of *Spirostachys africana*

Leaves and flowers of *Spirostachys africana*

Timber of *Spirostachys africana*

STROPHANTHUS SPECIOSUS

Apocynaceae

common poison rope (English); gewone giftou (Afrikaans)

DESCRIPTION The common poison rope is a shrub or woody climber of up to 10 m in height. The bright green, hairless leaves are mostly arranged in groups of three at each node. Attractive yellow and orange flowers with long, slender petals are borne on the branch ends, followed by forked capsules resembling the horns of an antelope. Another species, *S. kombe*, may be distinguished from all others in South Africa by the very large and hairy leaves[1,2]. A species from equatorial West Africa, *S. gratus*, is well known as a commercial source of ouabain, used as a heart tonic. This plant is a robust climber with attractive pink flowers[2].

TYPE OF TOXIN Cardiac glycoside (cardenolide).

IMPORTANCE *Strophanthus* species are traditionally used in Africa as arrow and spear poisons, both for hunting and for criminal purposes[3-6]. It is thought that *S. speciosus* was the source of poison in a homicide[4]. The use of arrow poison prepared from *S. kombe* seeds is well recorded in southern and eastern Africa – it is said to bring down large game within 100 metres[6]. All species are likely to be poisonous and are potentially dangerous to humans and animals, but very few cases of poisoning seem to have been recorded.

POISONOUS INGREDIENTS *Strophanthus* species contain complex mixtures of cardiac glycosides. Seeds of *S. kombe* were once the basis of a small industry in Malawi for the extraction of K-strophanthin, a mixture of heart glycosides used as a heart tonic in congestive heart failure[5]. Another commercial source is the seeds of the West African *S. gratus*, which yield the well-known cardiac glycoside, ouabain (strophanthin-G)[6]. Christyoside has been isolated from *S. speciosus*[6].

PHARMACOLOGICAL EFFECTS Cardiac glycosides increase the force and speed of contraction of the heart. An overdose affects not only the cardiovascular system, but also the gastrointestinal, respiratory and nervous systems (see heart glycosides, p. 28). The glycosides impart a very bitter taste to the plants, are usually poorly absorbed when taken orally and induce vomiting, so that lethal quantities are rarely ingested.

DISTRIBUTION *S. speciosus* is widely distributed in the eastern parts of South Africa and is sometimes grown in gardens. *S. kombe* is quite rare in South Africa (recorded from only a few localities in the extreme north-eastern parts) but the species is widely distributed in tropical Africa[1,2].

Strophanthidin   Christyoside

1. **Codd, L.E. 1963.** Apocynaceae. *Flora of Southern Africa* 26: 289-295.
2. **Beentje, H.J. 1982.** A monograph on *Strophanthus* DC. (Apocynaceae). *Mededelingen van de Landbouwhogeschool te Wageningen* 82(4): 1-191.
3. **De Villiers, H. 1949.** An arrow poison from Southern Africa. *S. Afr. Med. J.* 1949: 23 & 110.
4. **Watt, J.M. & Breyer-Brandwijk, M.G. 1962.** *The Medicinal and Poisonous Plants of Southern and Eastern Africa*, 2nd edition. Livingstone, London.
5. **Verdcourt, B. & Trump, E.C. 1969.** *Common Poisonous Plants of East Africa*. Collins, London.
6. **Neuwinger, H.D. 1996.** *African Ethnobotany: Poisons and Drugs: Chemistry, Pharmacology, Toxicology.* Chapman & Hall, Germany.

Strophanthus speciosus

Strophanthus kombe

STRYCHNOS SPINOSA

Strychnaceae (formerly Loganiaceae)

---

green monkey orange (English); groenklapper (Afrikaans)

DESCRIPTION *Strychnos* species are shrubs or small trees with simple leaves that characteristically have three to five main veins diverging from the base. *S. spinosa* has spiny branches, small clusters of greenish-yellow flowers arranged on the branch tips and large, woody, yellowish brown fruits that contain a bright orange, edible pulp[1,2]. It is similar to *S. madagascariensis* (black monkey orange) but the latter lacks spines and has the flowers densely clustered in the leaf axils[1,2]. It may also be confused with *S. cocculoides* (corky monkey orange) but this species has conspicuously corky bark and long hairs on the young twigs[1,2]. The nux vomica tree (*S. nux-vomica*) from southern Asia is famous as the original source of strychnine.

TYPE OF TOXIN Indole alkaloid.

IMPORTANCE The fruit pulp of *Strychnos* species is commonly used as food in southern Africa, while the seeds (at least those of *S. spinosa* and *S. madagascariensis*) are known to be extremely bitter and toxic[3,4]. Empty, dry fruits are sometimes decorated with beads and used as containers. The bark, leaves, fruit rind and leaves of *Strychnos* species (especially those of *S. henningsii*) are widely used in traditional medicine and are known to be

poisonous[3,5]. The use of *Strychnos* species for food and medicine therefore has some risk to humans, although very few cases of poisoning are known[4,5].

POISONOUS INGREDIENTS *Strychnos* species contain strychnine and numerous other, structurally related alkaloids, which have been used as rodent, arrow and ordeal poisons[6]. Extracts of the seeds of *S. nux-vomica* were formerly used as ingredients of invigorating bitter tonics[7]. Numerous alkaloids have also been isolated from *S. spinosa*, *S. madagascariensis* and *S. henningsii* but the main compounds, their toxicity and concentration in the various plant parts are not clear. 10-Hydroxyakagerine is an example from leaves of *S. spinosa*[8].

PHARMACOLOGICAL EFFECTS Strychnine and related alkaloids are extremely poisonous. The lethal dose of strychnine in adults is a mere 0,2 mg/kg body-weight[7]. It is sometimes used for criminal purposes and accidental deaths have been reported from China[7].

DISTRIBUTION *S. spinosa* is found along the eastern coast and also the northern bushveld region of South Africa[2]. Several other species have similar distribution patterns.

Strychnine   10-Hydroxyakagerine

1. Verdoorn, I.C. 1963. Loganiaceae. *Flora of Southern Africa* 26: 139-149.
2. Van Wyk, B. & Van Wyk, P. *Field Guide to Trees of Southern Africa*. Struik Publishers, Cape Town.
3. Watt, J.M. & Breyer-Brandwijk, M.G. 1962. *The Medicinal and Poisonous Plants of Southern and Eastern Africa*, 2nd edition. Livingstone, London.
4. Verdcourt, B. & Trump, E.C. 1969. *Common Poisonous Plants of East Africa*. Collins, London.
5. Van Wyk, B-E., Van Oudtshoorn, B. & Gericke, N. 2000. *Medicinal Plants of South Africa*, 2nd edition. Briza Publications, Pretoria.
6. Neuwinger, H.D. 1996. *African Ethnobotany: Poisons and Drugs: Chemistry, Pharmacology, Toxicology*. Chapman & Hall, Germany.
7. Bruneton, J. 1999. *Toxic Plants Dangerous to Humans and Animals*. Intercept, Hampshire.
8. Oguakwa, J.U., Galeffi, C., Nicoletti, M., Messana, I., Patamia, M. & Marini-Bettolo, G.B. 1980. On the alkaloids of *Strychnos*. XXXIV. The alkaloids of *Strychnos spinosa* Lam. *Gazz. Chim. Ital.* 110: 97-100.

Strychnos spinosa

Fruits of *Strychnos spinosa*

Strychnos madagascariensis

Strychnos spinosa fruit showing edible pulp

SYNADENIUM CUPULARE

Euphorbiaceae

---

dead-man's tree (English); muswoswo (Venda); umbulele (Zulu); gifboom (Afrikaans)

DESCRIPTION This succulent plant is a rounded, large shrub of up to 2 m in height. It has thick, fleshy, smooth stems and large, hairless, succulent leaves that are obovate in shape and ridged along the midrib below. All parts of the plant exude copious amounts of milky latex when broken. Inconspicuous flowers, each surrounded by bracts forming a cup-shaped structure (involucre), are borne in short clusters in the leaf axils[1]. This species is closely related to *S. grantii* from tropical Africa, but the latter is usually larger (up to 3 m in height) and has larger leaves that are often tinged with purple. Since *S. grantii* has been introduced to Europe and North America from east Africa as an attractive houseplant, this species is better known than *S. cupulare*, which is less frequently cultivated[1]. *Synadenium* may be confused with *Monadenium lugardii*, a superficially similar and equally poisonous plant. *Monadenium* is a small shrub of less than 1 m in height with tuberculate scars on the stems and much smaller leaves[1].

TYPE OF TOXIN Diterpene.

IMPORTANCE The milky latex of *S. cupulare* and *S. grantii* is highly irritant and may cause severe burning and itching of the skin, eyelids, nostrils and

lips that often last for several hours[2-4]. It is claimed that the plant releases an irritant vapour, and that the burning sensation is felt even if there was no direct skin contact[1]. The latex may cause permanent blindness by completely destroying the eye. Both plants have numerous uses in traditional medicine[2,3]. Domestic animals, adults and especially children may be at risk if *Synadenium* plants are cultivated in the house[4,5].

POISONOUS INGREDIENTS *S. grantii* contains several tigliane-type diterpene esters of the 4-deoxyphorbol type[6,7]. The main skin-irritant principle is 12-*O*-tigloyl-4-deoxyphorbol-13-isobutyrate[6]. It is likely that *S. cupulare* contains the same or similar compounds. Similar compounds are found in other members of the Euphorbiaceae.

PHARMACOLOGICAL EFFECTS The latex produces severe local reactions, including inflammation (erythema), oedema and blistering of the skin[4,5].

DISTRIBUTION *S. cupulare* occurs in the warm eastern parts of South Africa, while *S. grantii* is found in Mozambique, Zimbabwe and further north into tropical East Africa[1].

4-Deoxy-13-*O*-phenylacetyl-
12-*O*-tigloylphorbol
(Synadenium factor G$_1$)

---

1. **White, A., Dyer, R.A. & Sloane, B.L. 1941.** *The succulent Euphorbiaceae (Southern Africa)*. Vols. 1 & 2. Abbey Garden, Pasadena.
2. **Watt, J.M. & Breyer-Brandwijk, M.G. 1962.** *The Medicinal and Poisonous Plants of Southern and Eastern Africa*, 2nd edition. Livingstone, London.
3. **Verdcourt, B. & Trump, E.C. 1969.** *Common Poisonous Plants of East Africa*. Collins, London.
4. **Spoerke, D.G., Montanio, C.D. & Rumack, B.H. 1985.** Pediatric exposure to the houseplant *Synadenium grantii*. *Vet. Hum. Toxicol.* 28: 283-284.
5. **Bruneton, J. 1999.** *Toxic Plants Dangerous to Humans and Animals*. Intercept, Hampshire.
6. **Kinghorn, A.D. 1980.** Major skin-irritant principle from *Synadenium grantii*. *J Pharm. Sci.* 69: 1446-1447.
7. **Bagavathi, R., Sorg, B. & Hecker, E. 1988.** Tigliane-type diterpene esters from *Synadenium grantii*. *Planta Med.* 506-510.

Synadenium cupulare

Flowers of *Synadenium cupulare*

Leaves of *Synadenium cupulare* showing milky latex

Monadenium lugardii

THESIUM LINEATUM

Santalaceae

---

witstorm (Afrikaans)

DESCRIPTION *T. lineatum* is a seemingly leafless, semi-parasitic, woody shrub of up to 1 m in height, with fleshy, somewhat thorny, green stems. The small, green leaves fall early, leaving bare stems. Inconspicuous white flowers appear in summer, followed by distinctive round, white berries[1,2]. Another poisonous species is *T. namaquense* (poison bush or *gifbossie*), which can easily be distinguished by the smaller, more densely branched, less woody growth form and the minute, dark brown, persistent leaves along the twigs[1,2]. Of the many species of *Thesium*, only these two are known to be poisonous.

TYPE OF TOXIN Cardiac glycoside (bufadienolide).

IMPORTANCE *T. lineatum* and *T. namaquense* are known to be poisonous to livestock under certain conditions and sheep losses have been reported in the Beaufort West and Murraysburg districts[1,2]. Outbreaks of poisoning are unpredictable and it is possible that climatic factors, topography or population differences play a role. Affected animals (sheep, goats and cattle) may show symptoms such as rapid and laboured breathing and diarrhoea, but they usually die suddenly[1,2]. Symptoms typical of acute cardiac glycoside poisoning were reported[3].

POISONOUS INGREDIENTS The active principle of *T. lineatum* was isolated from the plant as a white crystalline substance and named thesiuside[3]. Its chemical structure was later elucidated[4], confirming that it is a cardiac glycoside of the bufadienolide type. The compound appears to be produced by the *Thesium* plants themselves and not by the host plants on which they grow as root parasites[3].

PHARMACOLOGICAL EFFECTS The symptoms of poisoning in livestock are typical for cardiac glycoside poisoning – rapid death, with diarrhoea and laboured breathing in surviving animals – but signs of kidney failure were also present[2].

DISTRIBUTION *T. lineatum* is widely distributed in the dry western parts of southern Africa (see map), from the southern and eastern parts of the Karoo northwards into Namibia[3]. *T. namaquense* has a more restricted distribution and is found mainly in the central parts of the Karoo[1,2].

Thesiuside

1. **Vahrmeijer, J. 1981.** *Poisonous Plants of Southern Africa That Cause Stock Losses.* Tafelberg Publishers, Cape Town.
2. **Kellerman, T.S., Coetzer, J.A.W. & Naudé, T.W. 1988.** *Plant Poisonings and Mycotoxicoses of Livestock in Southern Africa.* Oxford University Press, Cape Town.
3. **Anderson, L.A., Joubert, J.P., Schultz, R.A., Kellerman, T.S. & Pienaar, B.J. 1987.** Experimental evidence that the active principle of the poisonous plant *Thesium lineatum* L.f. (Santalaceae) is a bufadienolide. *Onderstepoort J. Vet. Res.* 54: 645-650.
4. **Van Heerden, F.R., Vleggaar, R. & Anderson, L.A.P. 1988.** Structure elucidation of thesiuside, a bufadienolide glycoside from *Thesium lineatum. S. Afr. J. Chem.* 41: 39-41.

Thesium lineatum

Flowers and fruits of *Thesium lineatum*

Thesium namaquense

TRIBULUS TERRESTRIS

Zygophyllaceae

---

devil's thorn (English); dubbeltjie, duwweltjie (Afrikaans); inkunzane (Zulu)

DESCRIPTION Devil's thorn is an indigenous weed that spreads horizontally along the ground. The plant has compound leaves, each with several pairs of small leaflets and the attractive yellow flowers, followed by the characteristic thorny fruits. *T. zeyheri*, a closely related species, can easily be distinguished from *T. terrestris* by the much larger flowers[1,2]. This species often forms a spectacular display of colour along the roadsides in the dry Kalahari region.

TYPE OF TOXIN Triterpenoid (saponin).

IMPORTANCE *T. terrestris* is a troublesome weed that causes injury to people and animals through the vicious spikes on the fruit. In large parts of the dry interior of South Africa, however, it is considered to be a valuable fodder plant. *Tribulus* causes a serious disease in livestock known as *geeldikkop* (literally 'yellow thick head') [3,4]. In the 1926–27 season, more than 600 000 sheep were killed[3]. Outbreaks occur only sporadically, usually when the plants become wilted in summer. *Geeldikkop* appears to be exactly the same as *dikoor* (literally 'thick ear') caused by wilted *Panicum* pastures[4]. The two main

species involved are *P. maximum* (common buffalo grass) and *P. coloratum* (small buffalo grass)[4].

POISONOUS INGREDIENTS *Geeldikkop* is a complex disease that is not yet fully understood. It is thought that fungi growing on the plants play a contributing role[4]. However, it has been shown that saponins are responsible for the characteristic symptoms[5]. Diosgenin is an example of a sapogenin that has been found in *T. terrestris* (others include ruscogenin and gitogenin)[6]. Also present are the indole alkaloids harman and norharman[7].

PHARMACOLOGICAL EFFECTS *Geeldikkop* results in photosensitivity, with distinctive swelling of the head, lips, cheeks and ears of affected animals[3,4]. The liver shows extensive damage and an accumulation of crystalloid material[4,5]. The indole alkaloids are said to cause locomotor effects, unrelated to *geeldikkop*, in sheep grazing on *Tribulus*[7].

DISTRIBUTION *T. terrestris* is an exceptionally common weed in practically all parts of southern Africa[1,2]. The related *T. zeyheri* occurs mainly in the Kalahari region[2].

Saponin C

---

1. **Henderson, M. & Anderson, J.G. 1966.** *Common Weeds in South Africa. Memoirs of the Botanical Survey of South Africa* 37.
2. **Schweikerdt, H.G. 1937.** An account of the South African species of *Tribulus*. *Bothalia* 3: 157-178.
3. **Watt, J.M. & Breyer-Brandwijk, M.G. 1962.** *The Medicinal and Poisonous Plants of Southern and Eastern Africa*, 2nd edition. Livingstone, London.
4. **Kellerman, T.S., Coetzer, J.A.W. & Naudé, T.W. 1988.** *Plant Poisonings and Mycotoxicoses of Livestock in Southern Africa*. Oxford University Press, Cape Town.
5. **Kellerman, T.S., Erasmus, G.L., Coetzer, J.A.W., Brown, J.M.M. & Maartens, B.P. 1991.** Photosensitivity in South Africa. VI. The experimental induction of geeldikkop in sheep with crude steroidal saponins from *Tribulus terrestris*. *Onderstepoort J. Vet. Sci.* 58: 47-53.
6. **Wilkens, A.L., Miles, C.O., de Kock, W.T., Erasmus, G.L., Basson, A.T. & Kellerman, T.S. 1996.** Photosensitivity in South Africa. IX. Structure elucidation of a β-glucosidase-treated saponin chemotypes of South African *T. terrestris*. *Onderstepoort J. Vet. Res.* 63: 327-334.
7. **Harborne, J.B., Baxter, H. & Moss, G.P. (eds) 1997.** *Dictionary of Plant Toxins*. John Wiley & Sons, Chichester.

Tribulus terrestris

Tribulus zeyheri

TYLECODON WALLICHII

Crassulaceae

---

nenta, kandelaarsbos, krimpsiektebos (Afrikaans)

DESCRIPTION *T. wallichii* is a shrub with a thick, tuberculate stem and succulent leaves crowded at the branch tips. It is closely related to *T. cacalioides* and the two species cannot be distinguished in the vegetative state[1]. The flowers of the latter are sulphur yellow and 17–25 mm long, while those of *T. wallichii* are usually lemon yellow and only 7–12 mm long[1]. *T. grandiflorus* is easily recognised by the large orange flowers that are bilaterally symmetrical (zygomorphic) and not radially symmetrical as in all other *plakkies*[1]. *Tylecodon* is closely related to *Cotyledon* but can easily be distinguished by the deciduous leaves of all the species.

TYPE OF TOXIN Cardiac glycoside (bufadienolide).

IMPORTANCE *Tylecodon* species are extremely poisonous and cause *krimpsiekte* ('shrinking disease'), one of the major causes of stock losses in South Africa[2,3]. The meat of poisoned animals may cause secondary poisoning of dogs and even humans. Two types of *krimpsiekte* can be distinguished, an acute (*opblaas*) *krimpsiekte* resulting

in sudden death, or chronic (*dun*) *krimpsiekte* that may develop gradually (see *Cotyledon orbiculata*, p. 76)[3].

POISONOUS INGREDIENTS The active compound of *T. wallichii* is a bufadienolide known as cotyledoside[4]. Seven bufadienolides have been isolated from *T. grandiflorus*[5].

PHARMACOLOGICAL EFFECTS *Krimpsiekte* is an intoxication of livestock that affects the nervous and muscular systems (see *Cotyledon orbiculata*), usually with fatal results[6-7]. The subcutaneous LD_{50} of cotyledoside in guinea pigs was determined as 0,116 mg/kg body-weight and the oral LD_{50} 0,173 mg/kg[6].

DISTRIBUTION *T. wallichii* occurs in the dry western parts of South Africa (see map), while *T. cacalioides* is confined to the eastern parts of the Little Karoo. *T. grandiflorus* is found from the Cape Peninsula northwards along the coast to Clanwilliam.

Cotyledoside

1. **Tölken, H.R. 1985.** Crassulaceae. *Flora of Southern Africa* 14. Botanical Research Institute, Pretoria.
2. **Vahrmeijer, J. 1981.** *Poisonous Plants of Southern Africa That Cause Stock Losses.* Tafelberg Publishers, Cape Town.
3. **Kellerman, T.S., Coetzer, J.A.W. & Naudé, T.W. 1988.** *Plant Poisonings and Mycotoxicoses of Livestock in Southern Africa.* Oxford University Press, Cape Town.
4. **Steyn, P.S., Van Heerden, F.R. & Van Wyk, A.J. 1984.** The structure of cotyledoside, a novel toxic bufadienolide glycoside from *Tylecodon wallichii* (Harv.) Toelken. *J. Chem. Soc., Perkin Trans. I,* 1984: 965-967.
5. **Steyn, P.S., Van Heerden, F.R., Vleggaar, R. & Anderson, L.A.P. 1986.** Structure elucidation and absolute configuration of the tyledosides, bufadienolide glycosides from *Tylecodon grandiflorus*. *J. Chem. Soc., Perkin Trans. I,* 1986: 429-435.
6. **Naude, T.W. & Schultz, R.A. 1982.** Studies on South African cardiac glycosides. II. Observations on the clinical and haemodynamic effects of cotyledoside. *Onderstepoort J. Vet. Res.* 49: 247-254.
7. **Botha, C.J., Van der Lugt, J.J., Erasmus, G.L., Kellerman, T.S., Schultz, R.A. & Vleggaar, R. 1997.** Krimpsiekte, associated with thalamic lesions, induced by the neurotoxic cardiac glycoside, cotyledoside, isolated from *Tylecodon wallichii* (Harv.) Toelken subsp. *wallichii*. *Onderstepoort J. Vet. Res.* 64: 189-194.

Tylecodon wallichii

Leaves of *Tylecodon wallichii*

Tylecodon grandiflorus

Flowers of *Tylecodon wallichii*

Flowers of *Tylecodon cacalioides*

URGINEA SANGUINEA

Hyacinthaceae

---

sekanama (Sotho, Tswana); slangkop (Afrikaans)

DESCRIPTION *Sekanama* is a geophyte with reddish-purple bulbs resembling meat (*sekanama* literally means 'false meat'). Leaves and flowers appear at different times of the year. When emerging, the young flowering stalk is densely packed with small buds, resembling the scales on a snake's head. The flowers are white, with spreading lobes and stamens[1,2] (for the distinction with *Drimia*[1,2], see p. 96). Smooth, strap-shaped leaves emerge from the bulb in summer, after flowering.

TYPE OF TOXIN Cardiac glycoside (bufadienolide).

IMPORTANCE *Sekanama* is a very important traditional medicine in South Africa, and is commonly used as expectorant, emetic, diuretic, heart tonic and for wound healing. It is a major cause of accidental deaths by people using traditional medicine[3-4]. *Urginea* species also cause serious stock losses as a result of so-called *slangkop* poisoning[5-6].

POISONOUS INGREDIENTS Cardiac glycosides are responsible for both human and animal fatalities. These include scillaren A (*U. sanguinea*[7]), urginin (*U. altissima*)[8] and physodine A (*U. physodes*)[9]. European squill, *U. maritima*, has scillaren A and scilliroside[10].

PHARMACOLOGICAL EFFECTS *U. sanguinea* produces gastrointestinal symptoms, followed by nausea and vomiting. As a result, cardiac glycosides are sometimes overlooked in deaths from traditional medicine[3]. In 41 fatal cases in South Africa over a one-year period, 44% showed clear signs of cardiac glycosides during autopsy[3]. Livestock poisoning is well documented, especially for *U. sanguinea*[5,6]. Milled, dried bulbs fed to sheep at a dose of 2,5 g/kg body-weight killed them all in two or three days[6].

DISTRIBUTION *U. sanguinea* occurs in the northern region of South Africa.

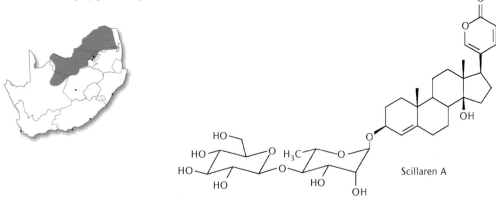

Scillaren A

1. **Jessop, J.P. 1977.** Studies in the bulbous Liliaceae in South Africa: 7. The taxonomy of *Drimia* and certain allied genera. *Jl S. Afr. Bot.* 43: 265-319.
2. **Deb, D.B. & Dasgupta, S. 1982.** Generic status of *Urginea* Steinheil (Liliaceae). *Journal of Economic and Taxonomic Botany* 3: 819-825.
3. **McVann, A., Havlik, I., Joubert, P.H. & Monteagudo, F.S.E. 1992.** Cardiac glycoside poisoning involved in deaths from traditional medicine. *S. Afr. Med. J.* 81: 139-141.
4. **Foukarides, G.N., Osuch, E., Mathibe, L. & Tsipa, P. 1995.** The ethopharmacology and toxicology of *Urginea sanguinea* in the Pretoria area. *J. Ethnopharmacol.* 49: 77-79.
5. **Kellerman, T.S., Coetzer, J.A.W. & Naudé, T.W. 1988.** *Plant Poisonings and Mycotoxicoses of Livestock in Southern Africa*. Oxford University Press, Cape Town.
7. **Majinda, R.R., Waigh, R.D. & Waterman, P.G. 1997.** Bufadienolides and other constituents of *Urginea sanguinea*. *Planta Med.* 63: 188-190.
8. **Pohl, T., Koorbanally, C., Crouch, N.R., & Mulholland, D.A. 2001.** Bufadienolides from *Drimia robusta* and *Urginea altissima* (Hyacinthaceae). *Phytochemistry* 58: 557-561.
9. **Van Heerden, F.R., Vleggaar, R. & Anderson L.A.P. 1988.** Bufadienolide glycosides from *Urginea physodes*. First report of natural 14-deoxybufadienolides. *S. Afr. J. Chem.* 41: 145-151.
10. **Harborne, J.B., Baxter, H. & Moss, G.P. (eds) 1997.** *Dictionary of Plant Toxins*. John Wiley & Sons, Chichester.

Urginea sanguinea

Urginea altissima

Flowers of *Urginea sanguinea*

Urginea physodes

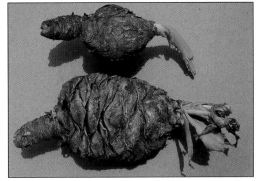

Bulbs of *Urginea epigea*

XANTHIUM STRUMARIUM

Asteraceae

---

large cocklebur (English); kankerroos (Afrikaans)

DESCRIPTION This troublesome weed is an erect annual with large, rounded, roughly hairy leaves. Inconspicuous flowers are borne at the branch tips, followed by oblong, bristly fruits (burs) that are covered with hooked spines. Another common weed, *X. spinosum* (spiny burweed, spiny cocklebur or *boetebossie*) has narrowly triangular, usually three-lobed, dark green leaves that are white-woolly below. Three sharp spines are present on the stem at each node, and the fruits (burs) are much smaller than those of *X. strumarium*[1].

TYPE OF TOXIN Diterpenoid.

IMPORTANCE In many parts of the world, *Xanthium* species cause fatalities in cattle, sheep and pigs after ingestion of new shoots, seeds or especially the seedling leaves (cotyledons)[2,3]. It seems that no animal deaths have yet been reported in South Africa[4]. In China, human fatalities occurred when people consumed young buds of *Xanthium sibiricum* (mistaken for those of soy or sesame)[2].

POISONOUS INGREDIENTS *Xanthium* species are rich in sesquiterpenoid lactones (such as xanthinin) but the toxicity is ascribed to carboxyatractyloside[1].

PHARMACOLOGICAL EFFECTS Carboxytractyloside causes damage to the liver, gall bladder and kidneys[2]. The lethal dose of seedlings in pigs is between 0,75 and 2% of body-weight[3].

DISTRIBUTION *X. strumarium* and *X. spinosum* are thought to have originated in South America but are now cosmopolitan weeds that are found over most parts of South Africa[1]. The distibution of *X. strumarium* is shown on the map.

Carboxyatractyloside

1. **Henderson, L. 2001.** *Alien Weeds and Invasive Plants.* Plant Protection Research Institute Handbook no. 12, Agricultural Research Council, Pretoria.
2. **Bruneton, J. 1999.** *Toxic Plants Dangerous to Humans and Animals.* Intercept, Hampshire.
3. **Harborne, J.B., Baxter, H. & Moss, G.P. (eds) 1997.** *Dictionary of Plant Toxins.* John Wiley & Sons, Chichester.
4. **Kellerman, T.S., Coetzer, J.A.W. & Naudé, T.W. 1988.** *Plant Poisonings and Mycotoxicoses of Livestock in Southern Africa.* Oxford University Press, Cape Town.

Xanthium strumarium

Leaves and burs of *Xanthium strumarium*

Xanthium spinosum

Hydrangea macrophylla – contains a skin allergin, hydrangenol

Mirabilis jalapa – contains the purgative trigenollin

Aquilegia vulgaris – contains a cyanogenic glycoside

Exotic Garden Plants

The majority of ornamental plants that are grown in gardens around South Africa have been imported from other parts of the world. It is important to know which ones are poisonous, so that infants and children can be kept away from danger. In a case of emergency, it may be useful to flip through these pages to see if the leaves, flowers or fruits can be identified. Those garden plants that have become weeds (e.g. *Nerium oleander*) are included in the previous section.

ACALYPHA HISPIDA

Euphorbiaceae

red-hot cat's tail (English)

Acalypha hispida

DESCRIPTION This plant is an herbaceous perennial of up to 2 m in height with large, simple leaves and attractive, drooping clusters of inconspicuous flowers. Another poisonous species, *A. indica* (Indian acalypha) is a smaller herb with round leaves and tiny yellow flowers[1].

TYPE OF TOXIN Unknown (*A. hispida*); cyanogenic glycoside (*A. indica*).

IMPORTANCE *A. hispida* is sometimes grown as a houseplant. Accidental ingestion results in severe gastrointestinal discomfort and skin contact may cause dermatitis in sensitive people. *A. indica* is known to be a cause of livestock losses.

POISONOUS INGREDIENTS Leaves and stems of *A. hispida* contain an irritant milky sap but the toxic components are poorly known. *A. indica* contains acalyphin, a cyanogenic glycoside[2].

PHARMACOLOGICAL EFFECTS The milky latex of *Acalypha* has irritant effects on the skin and the gastrointestinal tract[1]. Acalyphin is very toxic[3].

ORIGIN *A. hispida* originates from West Africa, while *A. indica* is widely distributed in India, Sri Lanka, East Africa and South Africa[1].

Acalyphin

1. **Roth, L., Daunderer, M. & Kormann, K. 1994.** *Giftpflanzen Pflanzengifte,* 4th edition. Nikol, Hamburg.
2. **Nahrstedt, A., Kant, J-D. & Wray, V. 1982.** Acalyphin, a cyanogenic glucoside from *Acalypha indica*. *Phytochemistry* 21: 101-105.
3. **Harborne, J.B., Baxter, H. & Moss, G.P. (eds) 1997.** *Dictionary of Plant Toxins.* John Wiley & Sons, Chichester.

ALEURITES FORDII

Euphorbiaceae

tung oil tree (English); tung neut (Afrikaans)

Flowers of *Aleurites fordii*

Fruits of *Aleurites fordii*

DESCRIPTION The tung oil tree is an attractive specimen tree with large, long-stalked heart-shaped leaves and white and pink flowers[1]. It is the commercial source of tung oil and is sporadically found in gardens in South Africa.

TYPE OF TOXIN Diterpenoid.

IMPORTANCE Poisoning may occur if the fruits or nuts are eaten[2,3].

POISONOUS INGREDIENTS The toxic principle is a diterpene ester, 12-O-palmitoyl-13-O-acetyl-16-hydroxyphorbol[2,3].

PHARMACOLOGICAL EFFECTS If tung oil or tung meal is ingested, it may cause diarrhoea and irritation of the skin and internal organs[3]. Phorbol diesters are potent tumour promoting agents.

ORIGIN The tree originates from central Asia. The seed oil (tung oil) is used as an ingredient in paints and varnishes.

$OCO(CH_2)_{14}CH_3$
OAc
H
OH
CH_2OH
H
O HO
CH_2OH

12-O-Palmitoyl-13-O-acetyl-16-hydroxyphorbol

1. **Poynton, R.J. 1973.** Trees in South Africa. Chapter V in *Our Green Heritage*. Tafelberg Publishers, Cape Town.
2. **Harborne, J.B., Baxter, H. & Moss, G.P. (eds) 1997.** *Dictionary of Plant Toxins*. John Wiley & Sons, Chichester.
3. **Okuda, T., Yoshida, T., Koike, S. & Toh, N. 1975.** New diterpene esters from *Aleurites fordii* fruits. *Phytochemistry* 14: 509-515.

ALOCASIA MACRORRHIZA
Araceae

elephant's ear, giant elephant's ear, giant alocasia (English); olifantsoor (Afrikaans)

Alocasia macrorrhiza

Flower of *Alocasia macrorrhiza*

DESCRIPTION The plant is a robust perennial herb with enormous leaves of up to 2 m long[1]. The greenish flowers emit a powerful sweet scent at night.

TYPE OF TOXIN Oxalate.

IMPORTANCE Poisoning occurs quite frequently after the leaves or tubers have been eaten (raw or cooked)[2]. The plant may cause severe inflammation of the mouth and throat (see also *Dieffenbachia*, p. 233). Oxalate poisoning is very rarely fatal.

POISONOUS INGREDIENTS The main toxic component was shown to be calcium oxalate[2].

PHARMACOLOGICAL EFFECTS The most common symptoms are sore throat, numbness of the oral cavity, swollen lips, difficulty in swallowing, salivation, and abdominal pain[2].

ORIGIN Elephant's ear originates from tropical Asia.

Calcium oxalate

1. **Griffiths, M. (ed.). 1994.** *Index of Garden Plants.* (The new Royal Horticultural Society Dictionary). Macmillan Press, London.
2. **Lin, T.J., Hung, D.Z., Hu, W.J., Yang, D.Y., Wu, T.C. & Deng, J.F. 1998.** Calcium oxalate is the main toxic component in clinical presentations of *Alocasia macrorrhiza* (L.) Schott and Endl. poisonings. *Vet. Hum. Toxicol.* 40: 93-95.

ANAGALLIS ARVENSIS

Primulaceae

---

scarlet pimpernel (English); blouselblommetjie (Afrikaans)

Anagallis arvensis (red form)

Anagallis arvensis (blue form)

DESCRIPTION The scarlet pimpernel is a creeping weed with opposite leaves and characteristic red or blue flowers. It is related to *Primula* species (primroses) that are cultivated as bedding and pot plants.

TYPE OF TOXIN Triterpenoid (Cucurbitacin) and possibly oxalate.

IMPORTANCE The plant is responsible for sheep losses in the Western Cape Province[1]. It is thought to be poisonous to humans when ingested and is also the cause of skin allergies[2]. Some *Primula* species (notably *P. obconica*) cause serious allergic reactions in sensitive people (only about 1% of the population)[3].

POISONOUS INGREDIENTS *A. arvensis* contains cucurbitacin B and two glucosides thereof [4] known as arvenin I and arvenin II. The skin-irritant principle in *P. obconica* and other species (including *A. hirtella*) is primin, a benzoquinone[3].

PHARMACOLOGICAL EFFECTS Sheep show severe kidney damage (nephrosis) and it is not yet clear if oxalate is responsible. Cucurbitacin B is nevertheless known to be very poisonous (see *Cucumis*, p. 82). Quinones sensitise the skin by reacting with amine and thiol functions of macromolecules.

DISTRIBUTION Both the red and blue varieties of *A. arvensis* originate from Europe and are now common garden weeds in South Africa.

Cucurbitacin B

Primin

1. **Kellerman T.S., Coetzer, J.A.W. & Naudé, T.W. 1988.** *Plant Poisonings and Mycotoxicoses of Livestock in Southern Africa.* Oxford University Press, Cape Town.
2. **Roth, L., Daunderer, M. & Kormann, K. 1994.** *Giftpflanzen Pflanzengifte,* 4th edition. Nikol, Hamburg.
3. **Bruneton, J. 1999.** *Toxic Plants Dangerous to Humans and Animals.* Intercept, Hampshire.
4. **Yamada, Y., Hagiwara, K., Iguchi K., Takahasi, Y. & Hsu, H-Y. 1978.** Cucurbitacins from *Anagallis arvensis.* *Phytochemistry* 17: 1798.

BRUGMANSIA CANDIDA

Solanaceae

---

moonflower, angel's trumpet (English); maanblom (Afrikaans)

Brugmansia candida

Brugmansia suaveolens

DESCRIPTION The moonflower is a shrub or small tree with velvety leaves and large pendulous, trumpet-shaped flowers. The plant was previously known as *Datura arborea* or *D. cornigera*.

TYPE OF TOXIN Tropane alkaloid.

IMPORTANCE Cases of poisoning are rare, even though the leaves, flowers and especially the seeds are considered to be very poisonous[1].

POISONOUS INGREDIENTS The plant contains scopolamine and norhyoscine as major alkaloids[2].

PHARMACOLOGICAL EFFECTS Scopolamine (also known as hyoscine) is less toxic than

hyoscyamine[3]. It is anticholinergic, with both central and peripheral actions[3]. The compound has been used to treat motion sickness and as a pre-operative medication to sedate and induce anaethesia[3].

ORIGIN *Brugmansia* species occur naturally in South America but have become popular garden ornamentals in many parts of the world.

Scopolamine: R=CH$_3$
Norhyoscine: R=H

1. **Watt, J.M. & Breyer-Brandwijk, M.G. 1962.** *The Medicinal and Poisonous Plants of Southern and Eastern Africa*, 2nd edition. Livingstone, London.
2. **Roses, O.E., Gambaro, V.E. & Rofi, R. 1988.** Presence of nor-hyoscine and hyoscine in *Brugmansia candida* Pers. flowers as possible characteristic of its origin. *Acta. Farm. Bonaerense* 7: 85-90.
3. **Harborne, J.B., Baxter, H. & Moss, G.P. (eds) 1997.** *Dictionary of Plant Toxins*. John Wiley & Sons, Chichester.

BRUNFELSIA PAUCIFLORA

Solanaceae

yesterday, today and tomorrow (English); verbleikblom (Afrikaans)

Brunfelsia pauciflora

DESCRIPTION This attractive garden plant is a woody shrub of up to 2 m in height with simple leaves and dark blue flowers that first fade to pale blue and then to white (hence the common name).

TYPE OF TOXIN Amidine.

IMPORTANCE *Brunfelsia* species are known to be toxic and even fatal to animals. A dog was killed after ingesting *B. pauciflora*[1].

POISONOUS INGREDIENTS The toxic substance in *B. pauciflora* appears to be unknown. However, brunfelsamidine, a compound that induces convulsions in animals, is known from *B. grandiflora*[2]. The same lethal compound is present in *Nierembergia hippomanica*.

PHARMACOLOGICAL EFFECTS The symptoms of *B. pauciflora* poisoning in a dog include vomiting, disorientation and muscle tremors[1,3].

ORIGIN *Brunfelsia* species all occur naturally in tropical America[4].

Brunfelsamidine

1. **Banton, M.I., Jowett, P.L.H., Renegar, K.R. & Nicolson, S.S. 1989.** *Brunfelsia pauciflora* ('yesterday, today and tomorrow') poisoning in a dog. *Vet. Hum. Toxic.* 31: 496-497.
2. **Lloyd, H.A., Fales, H.M., Goldman, M.E., Jerina, D.M., Plowman, T. & Schultes, R.E. 1985.** Brunfelsamidine: a novel convulsant from the medicinal plant *Brunfelsia grandiflora*. *Tetrahedron Lett.* 26: 2623-2624.
3. **Bruneton, J. 1999.** *Toxic Plants Dangerous to Humans and Animals.* Intercept, Hampshire.
4. **Griffiths, M. (ed.). 1994.** *Index of Garden Plants.* (The new Royal Horticultural Society Dictionary). Macmillan Press, London.

CAESALPINIA GILLIESII

Fabaceae

bird of paradise (English); paradysblom (Afrikaans)

Caesalpinia gilliesii

DESCRIPTION The bird of paradise is an ornamental shrub or small tree with compound, feathery leaves, attractive yellow flowers and long, red, protruding stamens.

TYPE OF TOXIN Non-protein amino acids and peptides?

IMPORTANCE Children may accidentally eat the seeds, which are said to produce severe and prolonged vomiting in young children[1].

POISONOUS INGREDIENTS The actual toxic principle is unknown[1], but it may possibly be one or more of several peptides that have been found in the seeds[2].

PHARMACOLOGICAL EFFECTS Unknown.

ORIGIN The plant occurs naturally in tropical America and is grown in gardens all over the world.

1. **Bruneton, J. 1999.** *Toxic Plants Dangerous to Humans and Animals*. Intercept, Hampshire.
2. **Southon, I.W. 1994.** *Phytochemical Dictionary of the Leguminosae*. Chapman & Hall, London.

CAPSICUM ANNUUM

Solanaceae

---

chilli pepper (English); rissie (Afrikaans)

Capsicum annuum

DESCRIPTION Chilli peppers are commonly cultivated annuals with white flowers and variously shaped fruits that are green at first but usually become red at maturity. It is often confused with Jerusalem cherry (*Solanum pseudocapsicum*) but the latter has rounded, bright orange fruits and the pollen is released, like in all species of *Solanum*, from pores in the tips of the anthers.

TYPE OF TOXIN Phenolic amide.

IMPORTANCE Chilli peppers are not really poisonous but they may cause severe pain and distress[1] – rare cases of fatal poisoning in infants have been reported[2].

POISONOUS INGREDIENTS Capsaicin is the pungent principle in chilli peppers.

PHARMACOLOGICAL EFFECTS Capsaicin is a powerful irritant and topical analgesic that may cause long-lasting desensitisation of the mucous membranes[1].

ORIGIN *Capsicum* species originate from tropical America.

Capsaicin

1. **Merck 1989.** *The Merck Index*. 11th edition. Merck, Rahway.
2. **Bruneton, J. 1999.** *Toxic Plants Dangerous to Humans and Animals*. Intercept, Hampshire.

CHRYSANTHEMUM CINERARIIFOLIUM

Asteraceae

---

pyrethrum (English); piretrumkrisant (Afrikaans)

Chrysanthemum cinerariifolium

DESCRIPTION This plant has deeply lobed, grey leaves and attractive white flower heads borne on long stalks. It is related to tansy (*Chrysanthemum vulgare*, previously known as *Tanacetum vulgare*), but the latter has bright green, feathery leaves and small yellow flower heads without ray florets.

TYPE OF TOXIN Monoterpenoid.

IMPORTANCE *C. cinerariifolium* is famous as the source of pyrethrum, which is widely used as a natural insecticide. The flower heads are harvested and processed. Natural does not necessarily mean harmless – pyrethrum is not very toxic to mammals but may cause severe allergic dermatitis[1].

POISONOUS INGREDIENTS The main poisonous compounds in pyrethrum are two monoterpenoids[1,2], pyrethrin I and pyrethrin II. The compounds are unstable in air and are refrigerated

and stored in the dark[2]. The toxicity of tansy (*C. vulgare*) is ascribed to thujone, a known neurotoxin[3].

PHARMACOLOGICAL EFFECTS Pyrethrins are much more toxic to insects than to humans and have a rapid knockout action. Pyrethrins I and II have an oral LD_{50} in rats of 1,2 g/kg body-weight[1,2]. They can cause severe allergic reactions in sensitive people[3].

ORIGIN Pyrethrum originates from eastern Europe and is grown commercially in many parts of the world. It is a popular garden plant and is believed to protect surrounding plants from insects.

Pyrethrin I: R=CH₃
Pyrethrin II: R=CO₂CH₃

1. **Harborne, J.B., Baxter, H. & Moss, G.P. (eds) 1997.** *Dictionary of Plant Toxins.* John Wiley & Sons, Chichester.
2. **Merck 1989.** *The Merck Index.* 11th edition. Merck, Rahway.
3. **Roth, L., Daunderer, M. & Kormann, K. 1994.** *Giftpflanzen Pflanzengifte,* 4th edition. Nikol, Hamburg.

CHRYSANTHEMUM XMORIFOLIUM
(=Dendranthemum xgrandiflorum)

Asteraceae

chrysanthemum (English); bloemiste-aster (Afrikaans)

Chrysanthemum xmorifolium (various colour forms)

DESCRIPTION This popular cut flower is a strongly scented perennial herb with lobed and toothed leaves. The flower heads show a wide variety of sizes, shapes and colours.

TYPE OF TOXIN Sesquiterpenoid lactone.

IMPORTANCE Chrysanthemums may cause allergic reactions in some people. Workers who grow and handle cut flowers are mainly at risk.

POISONOUS INGREDIENTS The main active compound is a skin irritant guaianolide known as arteglasin A[1,2]. Irritant lactones also occur in other commercial Asteraceae, such as artichoke, endive, Roman chamomile and sunflower[3].

PHARMACOLOGICAL EFFECTS Arteglasin causes contact dermatitis and has cytotoxic and antitumour activities[1].

ORIGIN The plant originated in China as a garden form of *C. indicum* (=*Dendranthemum indicum*)[4]. Chrysanthemums have been hybridised for centuries.

Arteglasin A

1. **Harborne, J.B., Baxter, H. & Moss, G.P. (eds) 1997.** *Dictionary of Plant Toxins.* John Wiley & Sons, Chichester.
2. **Lee, K.H., Matsueda, S. & Geissman, T.A. 1971**. Sesquiterpene lactones of *Artemisia*: New guaianolides from fall growth of *A. douglasiana. Phytochemistry* 10: 405-410.
3. **Bruneton, J. 1999.** *Toxic Plants Dangerous to Humans and Animals.* Intercept, Hampshire.
4. **Griffiths, M. (ed.). 1994.** *Index of Garden Plants.* (The new Royal Horticultural Society Dictionary). Macmillan Press, London.

COLOCASIA ESCULENTA

Araceae

cocoyam, taro potato, elephant's ear, (English); amadoembie, olifantsoor (Afrikaans); idumbe (Zulu)

Colocasia esculenta

Colocasia esculenta rhizomes

DESCRIPTION The plant is a robust, perennial herb with thick, spongy leaf stalks and large, soft leaves arising from a fleshy, starchy, edible rhizome below the ground. A form with small tubers was previously known as *Colocasia antiquorum*.

TYPE OF TOXIN Oxalate.

IMPORTANCE The leaves are used in oriental cooking after carefully cutting away the veins to prevent injuries to the mouth. The rhizomes should be peeled, and cooked or boiled. Other members of the family Araceae that may cause problems in humans, pets[1,2] and livestock[3] are the indigenous *Zantedeschia* species and exotic ornamental plants such as *Caladium, Monstera, Philodendron* and *Dieffenbachia* (see p. 233). These are often grown indoors where infants and domestic pets are at risk[1].

POISONOUS INGREDIENTS Calcium oxalate (insoluble crystals).

PHARMACOLOGICAL EFFECTS Calcium oxalate raphide (needle-like) crystals causes irritation of the mouth and throat of humans and animals. The sharp crystals actually pierce the tissue, which then becomes swollen and painful, with a burning sensation that takes time to subside. Ingestion of small amounts will not cause serious problems, but in rare cases severe injury or death in children have been reported[1,2].

ORIGIN The taro potato originates from Southeast Asia and has been cultivated as a starch food since ancient times.

Calcium oxalate

1. **Bruneton, J. 1999.** *Toxic Plants Dangerous to Humans and Animals.* Intercept, Hampshire.
2. **Harborne, J.B., Baxter, H. & Moss, G.P. (eds) 1997.** *Dictionary of Plant Toxins.* John Wiley & Sons, Chichester.
3. **Kellerman T.S., Coetzer, J.A.W. & Naudé, T.W. 1988.** *Plant Poisonings and Mycotoxicoses of Livestock in Southern Africa.* Oxford University Press, Cape Town.

CYCLAMEN PERSICUM

Primulaceae

cyclamen (English); siklaam (Afrikaans)

Cyclamen persicum

DESCRIPTION This well-known pot plant has simple, heart-shaped leaves arising from a rounded, fleshy tuberous rhizome below the ground. The attractive flowers are gracefully curved downwards and are usually white, pink or purple.

TYPE OF TOXIN Triterpenoid saponin.

IMPORTANCE Children and family pets may be at risk, because cyclamens are popular houseplants. However, the rhizomes are bitter and hidden below the ground[1,2]. The plant is quite toxic but very few actual cases of poisoning have been recorded[2,3].

POISONOUS INGREDIENTS The toxic triterpenoid glycoside cyclamin has been isolated from the tuberous rhizomes of *C. persicum*[4].

PHARMACOLOGICAL EFFECTS Cyclamin has a high haemolytic index and is very toxic[4]. Even a small piece of the tuber may cause cramps, vomiting and diarrhoea. Large quantities may prove fatal[4].

ORIGIN *C. persicum* originates from the eastern Mediterranean region and has been developed into numerous cultivars.

Cyclamin

1. **Roth, L., Daunderer, M. & Kormann, K. 1994.** *Giftpflanzen Pflanzengifte,* 4th edition. Nikol, Hamburg.
2. **Bruneton, J. 1999.** *Toxic Plants Dangerous to Humans and Animals.* Intercept, Hampshire.
3. **Spoerke, D.G., Spoerke, S.E., Hall, A. & Rumack, B.H. 1987.** Toxicity of *Cyclamen persicum. Vet. Hum. Toxicol.* 29: 250-251.
4. **Harborne, J.B., Baxter, H. & Moss, G.P. (eds) 1997.** *Dictionary of Plant Toxins.* John Wiley & Sons, Chichester.

DELPHINIUM GRANDIFLORUM

Ranunculaceae

---

delphinium, butterfly delphinium (English)

Flowers of *Delphinium grandiflorum* (various colour forms)

DESCRIPTION *Delphinium* species and related plants are commonly cultivated for the intense blue colours of the flowers. *D. grandiflorum* has small, few-flowered spikes of relatively large flowers, while *D. elatum* (giant larkspur) is up to 2 m in height. *Consolida ambigua* (the true larkspur or *ridderspoor*) has slender spikes of flowers and finely dissected leaves. Also related is *Aconitum napellus* (see p. 22)[1].

TYPE OF TOXIN Diterpenoid alkaloid.

IMPORTANCE Flowers are commonly sold in florist shops. Young children or domestic animals may be accidentally poisoned[2]. In Europe and North America, poisoning of livestock by *Delphinium* species occurs regularly.

POISONOUS INGREDIENTS *Delphinium* species contain mixtures of diterpenoid alkaloids such as nudicauline[1,3]. The main toxin in *Aconitum* is aconitine[1,3].

PHARMACOLOGICAL EFFECTS The toxic dose of nudicauline in cattle is about 6 mg/kg body-weight[3]. Aconitine is one of the most violent plant poisons known – the lethal dose in humans is said to be 5 mg, while 2 mg is sufficient to produce serious cardiovascular symptoms[1].

ORIGIN *Delphinium* and related plants are widely distributed in the Northern Hemisphere.

Nudicauline

1. **Bruneton, J. 1999.** *Toxic Plants Dangerous to Humans and Animals.* Intercept, Hampshire.
2. **Pfister, J.A., Gardner, D.R., Panter, K.E., Manners, G.D., Ralphs, M.H., Stegelmeier, B.L. and Schoch, T.K. 1999.** Larkspur (*Delphinium* spp.) poisoning in livestock. *J. Nat. Toxins* 8: 81-94.
3. **Harborne, J.B., Baxter, H. & Moss, G.P. (eds) 1997.** *Dictionary of Plant Toxins.* John Wiley & Sons, Chichester.

DIEFFENBACHIA MACULATA

Araceae

spotted dumb cane (English); gevlekte stomriet (Afrikaans)

Dieffenbachia maculata

Dieffenbachia amoena

DESCRIPTION *Dieffenbachia* species and cultivars are popular foliage plants with sturdy stems and attractive shiny green or variously mottled leaves.

TYPE OF TOXIN Oxalate.

IMPORTANCE Dumb canes frequently cause serious accidents through skin contact with the stems, or if the juice is ingested[1]. Severe inflammation of the mouth and throat may be experienced, in some cases temporarily preventing speech (hence dumb cane). Some fatalities amongst house pets (cats, dogs and birds) have been recorded[2].

POISONOUS INGREDIENTS The poisonous ingredient is calcium oxalate[2,3]. The insoluble material forms needle-shaped crystals that cause irritation by penetrating the mucous membranes of the mouth, throat or eyes. Crystals alone do not account for the severity of the reaction, and it is speculated that some additional factor, perhaps a proteolytic enzyme, may be present[2].

PHARMACOLOGICAL EFFECTS Serious symptoms include swelling of the mouth, tongue and face, often accompanied by a burning sensation or extreme pain[1-3]. Healing is typically slow and may take several days.

ORIGIN *Dieffenbachia* species originate from tropical America.

Calcium oxalate

1. **Fochtman, F.W., Manno, J.E., Winek, C.L. & Cooper, J.A. 1969.** Toxicity of the genus *Dieffenbachia*. *Toxicol. Appl. Pharmacol.* 15: 38-45.
2. **Bruneton, J. 1999.** *Toxic Plants Dangerous to Humans and Animals.* Intercept, Hampshire.
3. **Harborne, J.B., Baxter, H. & Moss, G.P. (eds) 1997.** *Dictionary of Plant Toxins.* John Wiley & Sons, Chichester.

DIGITALIS PURPUREA

Scrophulariaceae

---

foxglove (English); vingerhoedjie (Afrikaans)

Plants of *Digitalis purpurea*

Flowers of *Digitalis purpurea*

DESCRIPTION Foxglove is a biennial herb that forms a rosette of hairy leaves in the first year, and an elegant stalk of purple, spotted flowers in the second year. Various cultivars have been developed[1].

TYPE OF TOXIN Cardiac glycoside (cardenolide).

IMPORTANCE Digitalis is highly toxic but cases of human and animal poisoning are quite rare[2,3]. The plant is well known as a source of heart glycosides used as heart tonics[3]. The leaves are similar to those of comfrey (*Symphytum officinale*) or borage (*Borago officinalis*) and accidental poisoning through herbal teas have been described[2].

POISONOUS INGREDIENTS Digitoxin is one of several cardiac glycosides isolated from foxglove and is considered the most toxic of the constituents of *D. purpurea*[3].

PHARMACOLOGICAL EFFECTS Symptoms of poisoning include vomiting, nausea, sleepiness, confusion and visual disturbances[2].

ORIGIN Foxglove is indigenous to Europe[1].

Digitoxin

1. **Griffiths, M. (ed.). 1994.** *Index of Garden Plants.* (The new Royal Horticultural Society Dictionary). Macmillan Press, London.
2. **Bruneton, J. 1999.** *Toxic Plants Dangerous to Humans and Animals.* Intercept, Hampshire.
3. **Rietbrock, N. & Woodcock, B.G. 1985.** Two hundred years of foxglove therapy. *Trends Pharm. Sci.* 6: 267-269.

DURANTA ERECTA
(=*D. repens*)   Verbenaceae

golden dewdrops (English)

Flowers and berries of *Duranta erecta*

DESCRIPTION The plant is a spiny shrub of up to 3 m in height. Drooping clusters of blue flowers (rarely white) are followed by attractive yellow berries.

TYPE OF TOXIN Unknown (said to be a saponin).

IMPORTANCE *Duranta* is commonly cultivated in South Africa and children may be attracted to the berries. There is conflicting information about the toxicity[1]. The plant is suspected of causing livestock poisoning and there are reports that children have died after eating the berries[1].

POISONOUS INGREDIENTS Unknown. A series of iridoids (terpenoids) named durantoside I, II and III have been isolated from *D. erecta*[2] but it is not clear if any of them are poisonous.

PHARMACOLOGICAL EFFECTS In the reported case of fatal poisoning, the symptoms were sleepiness, high temperature, dilated pupils, fast pulse, swelling of the lips and eyelids and convulsions[1].

ORIGIN *D. erecta* occurs naturally in Central America but has become naturalised in many parts of the world. It is a popular garden shrub.

Durantoside I

1. **Watt, J.M. & Breyer-Brandwijk, M.G. 1962.** *The Medicinal and Poisonous Plants of Southern and Eastern Africa*, 2nd edition. Livingstone, London.
2. **Rimpler, H. & Timm, H. 1974.** Iridoids and ecdysones from Verbenaceae. V. Iridoids from *Duranta repens*. *Z. Naturforsch.*, C29: 111-115.

ESCHSCHOLZIA CALIFORNICA

Papaveraceae

Californian poppy (English); Kaliforniese papawer (Afrikaans)

Eschscholzia californica

Fumaria officinalis

DESCRIPTION This popular garden plant is a soft herb with finely divided, somewhat succulent, hairless leaves and large, golden yellow, poppy-like flowers borne on long stalks. Another member of the poppy family, *Fumaria officinalis* (common fumitory), is also known to be poisonous.

TYPE OF TOXIN Isoquinoline alkaloid.

IMPORTANCE Californian poppy and common fumitory are toxic to humans and animals[1,2].

POISONOUS INGREDIENTS The plants contain several alkaloids, of which dihydrosanguinarine is one of the main compounds in Californian poppy, and sanguinarine in common fumitory[1,2].

PHARMACOLOGICAL EFFECTS Dihydrosan-guinarine has cytotoxic effects and inhibits the activity of various enzymes[2]. Used as a herbal medicine, it may cause glaucoma if taken at high doses over long periods[2]. Dihydrosanguinarine[2] and sanguinarine were once included in dental rinses and toothpaste on account of their antiplaque activity[3], but the Food and Drug Administration of the USA has banned their use.

ORIGIN As the common name implies, the plant is indigenous to California in the USA. The common fumitory occurs naturally in Europe, Asia and North Africa but has become a weed of cultivated lands, especially in the Western Cape Province.

Sanguinarine

Dihydrosanguinarine

1. **Roth, L., Daunderer, M. & Kormann, K. 1994.** *Giftpflanzen Pflanzengifte,* 4th edition. Nikol, Hamburg.
2. **Harborne, J.B., Baxter, H. & Moss, G.P. (eds) 1997.** *Dictionary of Plant Toxins.* John Wiley & Sons, Chichester.
3. **Merck 1989.** *The Merck Index.* 11th edition. Merck, Rahway.

EUCALYPTUS CLADOCALYX

Myrtaceae

---

sugar gum (English); suikerbloekom (Afrikaans)

Eucalyptus cladocalyx

Fruit capsules of *Eucalyptus cladocalyx*

DESCRIPTION This gum tree is easily recognised by the 'clumpy' appearance of the crown and especially by the urn-shaped fruit capsules that accumulate in large quantities below the trees. Young trees form massive, woody, underground lignotubers that allow them to survive bush fires. Another species of interest is blue gum (*E. globulus*) easily distinguished by the bluish grey leaves and very large flowers and capsules.

TYPE OF TOXIN Cyanogenic glycoside (*E. cladocalyx*); monoterpenoid (*E. globulus*).

IMPORTANCE The sugar gum contains lower concentrations of essential oils than other species and is therefore palatable to stock[1]. However, it contains cyanogenic glycosides and is considered to be one of the main causes of cyanide poisoning in livestock in the Western Cape Province[1].

POISONOUS INGREDIENTS *E. cladocalyx* contains prunasin as the main cyanogenic glycoside[2,3]. The essential oil of blue gum (*E. globulus*) and other species contains high levels of 1,8-cineole (eucalyptol) that is known to be toxic when taken orally[3].

PHARMACOLOGICAL EFFECTS The symptoms are typical of prussic acid poisoning in livestock. 1,8-Cineole is toxic to man but is tolerated by other mammals such as the koala bear[3]. Even in small doses (5 to 30 ml) it may cause respiratory problems, coma and death[3].

ORIGIN All eucalypts are indigenous to Australia and Tasmania.

Prunasin   1,8-Cineole

1. **Kellerman T.S., Coetzer, J.A.W. & Naudé, T.W. 1988.** *Plant Poisonings and Mycotoxicoses of Livestock in Southern Africa.* Oxford University Press, Cape Town.
2. **Gleadow, R.M., Roslyn, M., Woodrow, I.E. & Ian, E. 2000.** Polymorphism in cyanogenic glycoside content and cyanogenic β-glucosidase activity in natural populations of *Eucalyptus cladocalyx. Aust. J. Plant Physiol.* 27: 693-699.
3. **Harborne, J.B., Baxter, H. & Moss, G.P. (eds) 1997.** *Dictionary of Plant Toxins.* John Wiley & Sons, Chichester.

FICUS CARICA

Moraceae

---

common fig tree (English); gewone vyeboom (Afrikaans)

Ficus carica

Ficus benjamina

DESCRIPTION The common fig is a deciduous shrub or tree of up to 9 m in height. All parts exude milky latex. Large leaves on long stalks are borne near the branch ends. They are three- to five-lobed, rough in texture above and somewhat hairy below. The figs are solitary, green, purplish or brown and pear-shaped or globose.

TYPE OF TOXIN Furanocoumarin.

IMPORTANCE The latex of the leaves and stems (but not the fruits) of *F. carica* contain furanocoumarins that cause photodermatitis[1]. *F. benjamina*, a popular house plant, does not trigger photodermatitis but causes severe asthma-like allergic reactions in sensitive people[2]. Some wild figs cause neurotoxicity in cattle (see *F. salicifolia*, p. 112).

POISONOUS INGREDIENTS Fig tree latex contains psoralen and bergapten[3], two well-known phototoxic furanocoumarins[1].

PHARMACOLOGICAL EFFECTS In the presence of sunlight, furanocoumarins cause dermatitis. Latex from the common fig tree has been used since the time of Dioscorides to treat the signs of vitiligo.

DISTRIBUTION The common fig occurs naturally in the Mediterranean region and Middle East, from southern Europe to Afghanistan.

Psoralen

Bergapten

1. **Lembo G., Lo Presti, M. & Balato, N. 1985.** Photodermatitis due to *Ficus carica*. *Photodermatology* 2: 119-120.
2. **Schmid, P., Stoger, P & Wuthrich, B. 1993.** Severe isolated allergy to *Ficus benjamina* after bedroom exposure. *Allergy* 48: 466-467.
3. **Zaynoun, S.T., Aftimos, B.G., Abi Abi, L., Tenekjian, K.K., Khalidi, U. & Kurban, A.K. 1984.** *Ficus carica*: isolation and quantification of the photoactive components. *Contact Dermatitis* 11: 21-25.

GELSEMIUM SEMPERVIRENS

Loganiaceae

yellow jasmine (English); geeljasmyn (Afrikaans)

Gelsemium sempervirens

DESCRIPTION The plant is an attractive creeper (vine) with twirling stems, bright green, hairless leaves and attractive, yellow, tubular flowers.

TYPE OF TOXIN Indole alkaloid.

IMPORTANCE *Gelsemium* is used as herbal medicine and an overdose may result in poisoning, sometimes with fatal consequences[1,2]. Children and domestic animals may accidentally be exposed to it in the garden.

POISONOUS INGREDIENTS The roots and rhizomes contain several alkaloids, of which gelsemicine is the most toxic[2].

PHARMACOLOGICAL EFFECTS Gelsemicine is a nervous system stimulant that causes respiratory paralysis in large doses[2].

ORIGIN Yellow jasmine originates from the southern parts of North America[1,2] but it is grown as a garden ornamental in many parts of the world, including South Africa.

Gelsemicine

1. **Roth, L., Daunderer, M. & Kormann, K. 1994.** *Giftpflanzen Pflanzengifte,* 4th edition. Nikol, Hamburg.
2. **Harborne, J.B., Baxter, H. & Moss, G.P. (eds) 1997.** *Dictionary of Plant Toxins.* John Wiley & Sons, Chichester.

GREVILLEA ROBUSTA

Proteaceae

---

silky oak (English); Australiese silwereik (Afrikaans)

Leaves and flowers of *Grevillea robusta*

DESCRIPTION The silky oak is a medium-sized tree with deeply dissected, silvery leaves and clusters of yellow flowers resembling bottlebrushes.

TYPE OF TOXIN Alkylphenol.

IMPORTANCE Silky oak is a popular ornamental tree and may cause contact allergies on the legs, arms and face[1-3] similar to those of 'poison ivy' – see *Smodingium argutum*, p. 194.

POISONOUS INGREDIENTS The skin irritant compound in silky oak is grevillol[1-3]. It is known to cause contact allergies in sensitive people.

PHARMACOLOGICAL EFFECTS Grevillol can cause severe dermatitis, with erythema and blistering[1-3].

ORIGIN *Grevillea* species are indigenous to Australia.

Grevillol

1. **Roth, L., Daunderer, M. & Kormann, K. 1994.** *Giftpflanzen Pflanzengifte,* 4th edition. Nikol, Hamburg.
2. **Harborne, J.B., Baxter, H. & Moss, G.P. (eds) 1997.** *Dictionary of Plant Toxins.* John Wiley & Sons, Chichester.
3. **Bruneton, J. 1999.** *Toxic Plants Dangerous to Humans and Animals.* Intercept, Hampshire.

HEDERA HELIX

Araliaceae

---

ivy, common ivy, Algerian ivy, Canary ivy, Madeira ivy (English)

Flowers of *Hedera helix*

Berries of *Hedera helix*

DESCRIPTION Ivy is a very popular creeper with decorative foliage that grows on walls or into trees to a height of up to 30 m. Small, greenish-white flowers are borne in rounded clusters (umbels), followed by dark purple, fleshy berries.

TYPE OF TOXIN Polyacetylene (polyalkyne).

IMPORTANCE Ivy causes dermatitis in people who handle the plants[1-3]. Children and domestic animals are often poisoned but severe symptoms are highly unlikely[2,3]. Some animal deaths have been ascribed to ivy but the cases were not well documented[3].

POISONOUS INGREDIENTS Ivy contains large amounts of saponins, such as glycosides of hederagenin, which may be partly responsible for reported toxic effects[1-3]. The skin-irritant activity is due to falcarinol, which also occurs in the common carrot (*Daucus carota*) and in *Schefflera arboricola*[1-3].

PHARMACOLOGICAL EFFECTS Ingestion of berries often causes no symptoms at all, or perhaps vomiting and stomach cramps[3]. Reports of convulsions and hallucinations are rare and need to be confirmed[4]. Skin reactions are well documented and include rashes, red, swollen skin, blisters, oedema and pain[1-3].

ORIGIN The ivy occurs naturally in Europe, Asia and North America[4]. Numerous cultivars are found in South African gardens.

Falcarinol

Hederagenin

1. **Harborne, J.B., Baxter, H. & Moss, G.P. (eds) 1997.** *Dictionary of Plant Toxins.* John Wiley & Sons, Chichester.
2. **Roth, L., Daunderer, M. & Kormann, K. 1994.** *Giftpflanzen Pflanzengifte,* 4th edition. Nikol, Hamburg.
3. **Bruneton, J. 1999.** *Toxic Plants Dangerous to Humans and Animals.* Intercept, Hampshire.
4. **Griffiths, M. (ed.). 1994.** *Index of Garden Plants.* (The new Royal Horticultural Society Dictionary). Macmillan Press, London.

ILEX AQUIFOLIUM
Aquifoliaceae

holly, English holly (English); Europese huls (Afrikaans)

Leaves and berries of *Ilex aquifolium*

DESCRIPTION This well-known plant is a shrub or small tree with dark green, sharply toothed leaves and bright red berries. The berries are often depicted on Christmas cards.

TYPE OF TOXIN Unknown (possibly triterpenoid saponins).

IMPORTANCE Holly shrubs commonly occur in gardens, and children or domestic animals may be attracted to the bright red berries.

POISONOUS INGREDIENTS The active compounds of *I. aquifolia* appear to be unknown but a triterpenoid saponin of the ursane type, known as ilexolide A, has been isolated from *I. pubescens* and *I. chinensis*[1].

PHARMACOLOGICAL EFFECTS In adults 20 to 30 berries of *I. aquifolia* are considered to be lethal; even two or more berries can cause distress in a small child[2]. Symptoms include gastroenteritis, diarrhoea and irregular heartbeat[1].

ORIGIN *I. aquifolium* is indigenous to Europe, West Asia and North Africa[3]. Several cultivars are grown in South Africa.

Ilexolide A

1. **Harborne, J.B., Baxter, H. & Moss, G.P. (eds) 1997.** *Dictionary of Plant Toxins.* John Wiley & Sons, Chichester.
2. **Roth, L., Daunderer, M. & Kormann, K. 1994.** *Giftpflanzen Pflanzengifte,* 4th edition. Nikol, Hamburg.
3. **Griffiths, M. (ed.). 1994.** *Index of Garden Plants.* (The new Royal Horticultural Society Dictionary). Macmillan Press, London.

IPOMOEA PURPUREA

Convolvulaceae

common morning glory (English); gewone purperwinde (Afrikaans)

Ipomoea purpurea

Ipomoea tricolor

DESCRIPTION *Ipomoea* species are common herbaceous, twining creepers with attractive purple, pink or white flowers. One of the most common species is *I. purpurea*, which may be recognised by the large flowers (usually dark blue or purple) and somewhat hairy leaves. Another distinctive species is *I. tricolor*, easily recognised by the attractive blue, white and yellow colour pattern of the flowers.

TYPE OF TOXIN Indole alkaloid.

IMPORTANCE *Ipomoea* species are not particularly poisonous but their seeds contain toxic alkaloids and cases of fatal poisoning have been recorded[1-3].

POISONOUS INGREDIENTS Several indole alkaloids are known from *Ipomoea* species. An example is ergine, which is present in many species, including *I. tricolor*[1].

PHARMACOLOGICAL EFFECTS Like other indole alkaloids of the Convolvulaceae, ergine is a powerful hallucinogen[1,2]. Large amounts can be fatal.

ORIGIN Both *I. purpurea* and *I. tricolor* are thought to have originated in Mexico and Central America, but they are now commonly cultivated in most parts of the world[4].

Ergine

1. **Harborne, J.B., Baxter, H. & Moss, G.P. (eds) 1997.** *Dictionary of Plant Toxins.* John Wiley & Sons, Chichester.
2. **Roth, L., Daunderer, M. & Kormann, K. 1994.** *Giftpflanzen Pflanzengifte,* 4th edition. Nikol, Hamburg.
3. **Bruneton, J. 1999.** *Toxic Plants Dangerous to Humans and Animals.* Intercept, Hampshire.
4. **Griffiths, M. (ed.). 1994.** *Index of Garden Plants.* (The new Royal Horticultural Society Dictionary). Macmillan Press, London.

LIGUSTRUM LUCIDUM

Oleaceae

---

privet, Chinese privet (English); Chinese liguster (Afrikaans)

Ligustrum lucidum

Ligustrum ovalifolium

DESCRIPTION Privets are large shrubs or small trees with white-dotted stems and opposite, glossy leaves. Small, fragrant, white flowers are followed by small, round, dark purple to black berries. *L. lucidum* is a small tree with large, leathery leaves, while *L. ovalifolium* (Californian privet) is a shrub with much smaller, pale green leaves[1]. Variegated forms of both species are grown in gardens.

TYPE OF TOXIN Monoterpenoid (secoiridoid).

IMPORTANCE The berries of *Ligustrum* species are attractive to children and are poisonous when large numbers are eaten[2].

POISONOUS INGREDIENTS The berries of *L. vulgare* (common privet) are known to contain large amounts of secoiridoid glucosides, mainly ligustroside and oleuropein[3]. It is likely that the same or similar compounds are present in other privets as well.

PHARMACOLOGICAL EFFECTS Ingestion of a few berries may lead to nausea, vomiting and stomach pain but usually there are no symptoms at all. Large quantities however, are dangerous, and can lead to convulsions, irregular heartbeat and respiratory problems[2].

DISTRIBUTION Chinese privet (*L. lucidum*) originates from China and Korea, while Californian privet (*L. ovalifolium*) is found in Japan. Both are popular garden and hedge plants in South Africa that have started to invade natural veld[1].

Ligustroside: R=H
Oleuropein: R=OH

1. **Henderson, L. 2001.** *Alien Weeds and Invasive Plants.* Plant Protection Research Institute Handbook no. 12, Agricultural Research Council, Pretoria.
2. **Bruneton, J. 1999.** *Toxic Plants Dangerous to Humans and Animals.* Intercept, Hampshire.
3. **Willems, M. 1988.** Quantitative determination of secoiridoid glucosides from the fruits of *Ligustrum vulgare* by HPLC. *Planta Med.* 54: 66-68.

LUPINUS ANGUSTIFOLIUS

Fabaceae

---

blue lupin (English); bloulupien (Afrikaans)

Lupinus angustifolius

Lupinus luteus

DESCRIPTION Lupins are erect annuals with digitately compound leaves and attractive clusters of blue, white or yellow flowers. Two species are commonly found in South Africa, namely blue lupin (*L. angustifolius*) and yellow lupin (*L. luteus*) but species such as *L. digitatus*, *L. sericeus* and *L. polyphyllus* are sometimes cultivated[1,2].

TYPE OF TOXIN Quinolizidine alkaloid.

IMPORTANCE Lupins are grown as green manure and are responsible for three different diseases in South Africa[1,2]. Lupinosis is a poisoning caused by a fungus (*Phomopsis leptostromiformis*) that grows on lupins, while crooked calf disease occurs when cows graze on *L. sericeus* during gestation. Lupine poisoning occurs when mature, dried plant material or seeds of bitter lupins (mainly *L. angustifolia*) are fed to animals[2].

POISONOUS INGREDIENTS Bitter lupins contain large quantities of quinolizidine alkaloids such as sparteine and lupanine.

PHARMACOLOGICAL EFFECTS Lupine (alkaloidal) poisoning may result in tremors, convulsions, paralysis and death, usually within three hours[2]. Acetic acid is sometimes used as emergency treatment[2].

DISTRIBUTION The lupins most commonly cultivated in South Africa (*L. angustifolia* and *L. luteus*) are of Mediterranean origin.

Lupanine: R=O
Sparteine: R=H$_2$

1. **Vahrmeijer, J. 1981.** *Poisonous Plants of Southern Africa That Cause Stock Losses.* Tafelberg Publishers, Cape Town.
2. **Kellerman, T.S., Coetzer, J.A.W. & Naudé, T.W. 1988.** *Plant Poisonings and Mycotoxicoses of Livestock in Southern Africa.* Oxford University Press, Cape Town.

MANIHOT ESCULENTA

Euphorbiaceae

---

cassava (English); kassava (Afrikaans)

Manihot esculenta

Flowers and fruits of *Manihot esculenta*

DESCRIPTION Cassava is a woody shrub with attractive digitately lobed leaves, inconspicuous yellow flowers and ribbed fruits. Large, fleshy tubers are formed below the ground. It may be confused with *Jatropha multifida* but the latter has a distinctive, bright orange nectar disc visible in the flower and fruit (see photograph on p. 131).

TYPE OF TOXIN Cyanogenic glycoside.

IMPORTANCE Cassava tubers are widely used as a staple diet in Africa and South America, but it is not really popular in South Africa[1]. Two forms are found, namely a sweet type (selected for its low glycoside content, so that the tubers can be directly cooked and eaten) and the bitter type, which is only edible after a lengthy leaching process. Animals fed on the remains of the plants are sometimes poisoned[2].

POISONOUS INGREDIENTS Cassava leaves and roots contain a cyanogenic glycoside, linamarin (also known as manihotoxin)[3]. This bitter-tasting substance releases hydrocyanic acid when plant tissue is damaged. Linamarin co-occurs with lotaustralin in white clover (*Trifolium repens*) birdsfoot trefoil (*Lotus corniculatus*), flax (*Linum usitatissimum*) and passion fruit (*Passiflora* species).

PHARMACOLOGICAL EFFECTS Acute poisoning is rare but may occur in stock animals[2]. In humans, regular ingestion of bitter cassava may have a cumulative effect due to the thiocyanate that is formed in the body during detoxification[3].

DISTRIBUTION Cassava originated in central America but is now widely cultivated in the tropics.

Linamarin

1. **Van Wyk, B-E. & Gericke, N. 2000.** *People's Plants. A Guide to Useful Plants of Southern Africa.* Briza Publications, Pretoria.
2. **Kellerman, T.S., Coetzer, J.A.W. & Naudé, T.W. 1988.** *Plant Poisonings and Mycotoxicoses of Livestock in Southern Africa.* Oxford University Press, Cape Town.
3. **Harborne, J.B., Baxter, H. & Moss, G.P. (eds) 1997.** *Dictionary of Plant Toxins.* John Wiley & Sons, Chichester.

NIEREMBERGIA HIPPOMANICA

Solanaceae

---

nierembergia (English)

Nierembergia hippomanica

DESCRIPTION *N. hippomanica* is a much-branched perennial herb with narrow leaves and cup-shaped, blue or purplish flowers. Various flower colour forms have been described as different varieties[1].

TYPE OF TOXIN Amidine.

IMPORTANCE *N. hippomanica* has been responsible for a recent outbreak of neurotoxicity in calves in the Free State Province[2].

POISONOUS INGREDIENTS The toxin in *Nierembergia*[3] is the same compound that was found in *Brunfelsia grandiflora*, namely brunfelsamidine[4].

PHARMACOLOGICAL EFFECTS Plant material of *Nierembergia* causes nervous and other signs in cattle, including chewing motions, partial paralysis, ataxia, salivation and irregular heartbeat[2].

ORIGIN *N. hippomanica* occurs naturally in South America (Argentina)[1] and has become a popular garden plant in South Africa.

Brunfelsamidine

1. **Griffiths, M. (ed.). 1994.** *Index of Garden Plants*. (The new Royal Horticultural Society Dictionary). Macmillan Press, London.
2. **Botha, C.J., Schultz, R.A., Van der Lugt, J.J., Retief, E. & Labuschagne, L. 1999.** Neurotoxicity in calves induced by the plant, *Nierembergia hippomanica* Miers var. *violacea* Millán in South Africa. *Onderstepoort J. Vet. Res.* 66: 237-244.
3. **Buschi, C.A. & Pomiluo, A.B. 1987.** Pyrrole-3-carbamidine: a lethal principle from *Nierembergia hippomanica*. *Phytochemistry* 26: 863-865.
4. **Lloyd, H.A., Fales, H.M., Goldman, M.E., Jerina, D.M., Plowman, T. & Schultes, R.E. 1985.** Brunfelsamidine: a novel convulsant from the medicinal plant *Brunfelsia grandiflora*. *Tetrahedron Lett.* 26: 2623-2624.

PERSEA AMERICANA

Lauraceae

---

avocado pear (English); avokadopeer (Afrikaans)

Flowers of *Persea americana*

Fruit of *Persea americana*

DESCRIPTION Avocado pear is a large tree with large, oblong leaves that are characteristically dark green above and paler bluish green below. Inconspicuous yellow flowers are followed by the large, green or blackish, pear-shaped fruits. The fruit flesh is yellow and oily and contains a very large, single seed.

TYPE OF TOXIN Long chain alcohol.

IMPORTANCE Large quantities of avocado pear may be poisonous to people who are treated with MAO inhibitors (monoamine oxidase inhibitors)[1]. The toxicity of the fruit in this case is ascribed to tyramine, an amine that would normally be degraded by the MAO[1]. The leaves and fruits are poisonous to a wide range of animals but not all cultivars are poisonous. The Guatemala variety and cultivars derived thereof (such as 'Fuerte') are known to be poisonous[1].

POISONOUS INGREDIENTS The leaves contain a long chain alcohol known as persin[2].

PHARMACOLOGICAL EFFECTS Animals poisoned by avocado pear leaves show breathing difficulties and cardiotoxic effects that may lead to death[1]. In goats, poisoning leads to a decrease in milk production and necrosis of the secretory epithelium of the milk glands (mammitis)[1,2].

DISTRIBUTION Avocado pear trees occur naturally in Central America.

Tyramine   Persin

1. **Bruneton, J. 1999.** *Toxic Plants Dangerous to Humans and Animals.* Intercept, Hampshire.
2. **Oelrichs, P.B., Ng, J.C., Seawright, A.A., Ward, A., Schäffeler, L. & MacLeod, J.K. 1995.** Isolation and identification of a compound from avocado (*Persea americana*) leaves which causes necrosis of the acinar epithelium of the lactating mammary gland and the myocardium. *Natural Toxins* 3: 344-349.

PRUNUS LAUROCERASUS

Rosaceae

---

cherry laurel (English); kersielourier (Afrikaans)

Fruits of *Prunus laurocerasus*

Fruits of *Cotoneaster* species

DESCRIPTION Cherry laurel is a common ornamental shrub of up to 4 m in height, with pale green, simple leaves and oblong clusters of white flowers, followed by small black berries[1].

TYPE OF TOXIN Cyanogenic glycoside.

IMPORTANCE Cherry laurel is one of several members of the rose family with attractive berries resembling miniature apples that may be tempting to children. These include hawthorn (*Crataegus* species), show-berry bushes (*Cotoneaster* species) and fire-thorn bushes (*Pyracantha* species). Eating a few fruits is unlikely to cause any severe symptoms, because the fruit flesh is harmless and the seeds are usually spat out or pass through the stomach undamaged[1].

POISONOUS INGREDIENTS The leaves of cherry laurel contain prunasin, while the seeds contain amygdalin[1]. Human poisoning is rare and the symptoms are usually not serious. Animals may be fatally poisoned (1 kg leaves is sufficient to kill a cow)[1] but they rarely have access to the plants.

PHARMACOLOGICAL EFFECTS Poisoning symptoms are typical for cyanogenic glycosides in general (irritation, flushing face, heavy breathing, scratchy throat, headache, and in severe cases, respiratory and cardiac arrest)[2].

DISTRIBUTION Cherry laurel is indigenous to south-eastern Europe and Asia Minor[3].

Prunasin

1. **Bruneton, J. 1999.** *Toxic Plants Dangerous to Humans and Animals.* Intercept, Hampshire.
2. **Roth, L., Daunderer, M. & Kormann, K. 1994.** *Giftpflanzen Pflanzengifte,* 4th edition. Nikol, Hamburg.
3. **Griffiths, M. (ed.). 1994.** *Index of Garden Plants.* (The new Royal Horticultural Society Dictionary). Macmillan Press, London.

QUERCUS ROBUR

Fagaceae

common oak, English oak (English); gewone akkerboom, steeleik (Afrikaans)

Quercus robur

DESCRIPTION *Q. robur* is a large, deciduous tree with lobed leaves, inconspicuous flowers borne in catkins and characteristic, oblong acorns. More than 20 different species of oak trees are found in gardens and parks in South Africa.

TYPE OF TOXIN Tannins and polyphenols.

IMPORTANCE Animals may be chronically or fatally poisoned after ingestion of leaves, buds or acorns[1]. Cattle (especially young animals), sheep and horses are known to be susceptible, while pigs and birds seem to be resistant to poisoning[1].

POISONOUS INGREDIENTS Oak tannins contain digallic acid, which may be converted by bacterial fermentation to gallic acid and pyrogallol[1,2]. These compounds are thought to be responsible for the toxic effects[3] but ellagitannins such as castalagin is known to be toxic and has also been implicated in cattle poisoning[4].

PHARMACOLOGICAL EFFECTS Oak poisoning results in gastroenteritis and severe kidney damage[1].

ORIGIN *Q. robur* was one of the first ornamental trees to be introduced from western Europe.

Digallic acid

Gallic acid

Pyrogallol

1. **Kellerman, T.S., Coetzer, J.A.W. & Naudé, T.W. 1988.** *Plant Poisonings and Mycotoxicoses of Livestock in Southern Africa.* Oxford University Press, Cape Town.
2. **Anderson, G.A., Mount, M.E., Vrins, A.A. & Ziemer, E.L. 1983.** Fatal acorn poisoning in a horse: Pathological findings and diagnostic considerations. *J. Am. Vet. Med. Assoc.* 182: 1105-1110.
3. **Dollahite, J.W., Pigeon, R.F. & Camp, B.J. 1962.** The toxicity of gallic acid, pyrogallol, tannic acid and *Quercus havardi* in the rabbit. *Am. J. Vet. Res.* 23: 1264-1267.
4. **Harborne, J.B., Baxter, H. & Moss, G.P. (eds) 1997.** *Dictionary of Plant Toxins.* John Wiley & Sons, Chichester.

RHODODENDRON INDICUM

Ericaceae

azalea (English)

Rhododendron indicum

DESCRIPTION Azaleas are garden shrubs with deciduous leaves and colourful red, pink or white flowers. As in all members of the family, the pollen is released from a round pore in the anther (and not from a slit as in most other plants).

TYPE OF TOXIN Diterpenoid.

IMPORTANCE Azaleas are mainly a threat to livestock and domestic animals[1]. Human fatalities are rare, and mainly result from the ingestion of honey contaminated by azalea nectar[1]. Young children are sometimes poisoned after eating the flowers or leaves.

POISONOUS INGREDIENTS *Rhododendron* species contain toxic diterpenes, of which grayanotoxin I (also known as andromedotoxin) is a major compound[2,3].

PHARMACOLOGICAL EFFECTS In humans, poisoning may result in vomiting, sleepiness, respiratory depression, blue coloration of the skin (cyanosis), hypotension and irregular heartbeat[1]. Animals, including cats and dogs, show similar symptoms. When injected in mice, the LD_{50} of grayanotoxin I is 1,31 mg/kg body-weight[3].

DISTRIBUTION Azaleas are indigenous to Europe and Asia – *R. indicum* originated from Japan[4]. It is only one of a very large number of species and hybrids, many of which are not suited to the climatic conditions in South Africa.

Grayanotoxin I

1. **Bruneton, J. 1999.** *Toxic Plants Dangerous to Humans and Animals*. Intercept, Hampshire.
2. **Kakisawa, H., Kozima, T., Yanai, M. & Nakanishi, K. 1965.** Stereochemistry of grayatoxins. *Tetrahedron* 21: 3091-3104.
3. **Harborne, J.B., Baxter, H. & Moss, G.P. (eds) 1997.** *Dictionary of Plant Toxins*. John Wiley & Sons, Chichester.
4. **Griffiths, M. (ed.). 1994.** *Index of Garden Plants*. (The new Royal Horticultural Society Dictionary). Macmillan Press, London.

ROBINIA PSEUDOACACIA

Fabaceae

---

false acacia, black locust (English); witakasia (Afrikaans)

Robinia pseudoacacia

Flowers and fruits of *Robinia pseudoacacia*

DESCRIPTION The black locust is an erect tree with a furrowed bark, thorny stems and compound leaves. Clusters of attractive, white, pea-like flowers (noticeably blotched with yellowish green) are followed by small, oblong, flat pods.

TYPE OF TOXIN Lectin.

IMPORTANCE The bark and seeds are poisonous and numerous cases of human and animal poisoning have been reported[1].

POISONOUS INGREDIENTS The main toxic substance in *R. pseudoacacia* is robin, a lectin[1,2].

PHARMACOLOGICAL EFFECTS Robin is a haemagglutinating and mitogenic substance[1,2] that is responsible for the gastrointestinal problems, weakness and headache observed in children poisoned with black locust bark[1]. Robin is known to be less toxic that abrin (see *Abrus*, p. 30) and the symptoms are usually temporary[1].

ORIGIN Black locust originates from the eastern and central parts of the United States of America. It is a popular garden tree but has become an invader of riverbanks and roadsides[3].

1. **Bruneton, J. 1999.** *Toxic Plants Dangerous to Humans and Animals.* Intercept, Hampshire.
2. **Harborne, J.B., Baxter, H. & Moss, G.P. (eds) 1997.** *Dictionary of Plant Toxins.* John Wiley & Sons, Chichester.
3. **Henderson, L. 2001.** *Alien Weeds and Invasive Plants.* Plant Protection Research Institute Handbook no. 12, Agricultural Research Council, Pretoria.

SCHINUS TEREBINTHIFOLIUS

Anacardiaceae

Brazilian pepper tree (English); Brasiliaanse peperboom (Afrikaans)

Schinus terebinthifolius

Schinus molle

DESCRIPTION This is an evergreen shrub or small tree of up to 15 m in height, with a flat crown and horizontal branches. The compound leaves have broad leaflets with conspicuous veins arising from a distinctly winged main leaf axis (rachis). Inconspicuous white flowers are followed by pinkish red berries that emit a resinous, peppery smell when crushed. The common pepper tree or Peruvian pepper tree (*Schinus molle*) is similar but has a rounded crown, graceful, drooping branches and narrow leaflets giving the leaves a feathery appearance. It also lacks the prominent wing on the rachis[1].

TYPE OF TOXIN Alkylphenol.

IMPORTANCE The berries are sometimes used as a pepper substitute (known as pink pepper)[2,3]. They are poisonous and potentially harmful if ingested in large quantities. The resins from the leaves and fruit may cause severe skin reactions and also irritate the respiratory tract[2,3].

POISONOUS INGREDIENTS The irritant effect of the berries of *S. terebinthifolius* is due to (15:1)-cardanol, a compound that is also found in the fruit of *Ginkgo biloba* and the seed oil of cashew nut (*Anacardium occidentale*)[4,5].

PHARMACOLOGICAL EFFECTS (15:1)-cardanol is a skin irritant that inhibits cyclo-oxygenase and 5-lipoxygenase[4,5]. Terpenoids in the berries inhibit pancreatic phospholipase and may cause digestive problems in large doses[6].

DISTRIBUTION *S. terebinthifolius* is indigenous to Brazil, while *S. molle* has a much wider natural distribution in South America. The former has become naturalised along the KwaZulu-Natal coast, while *S. molle* is common in the interior of South Africa[1].

(15:1)-Cardanol

1. **Henderson, L. 2001.** *Alien Weeds and Invasive Plants.* Plant Protection Research Institute Handbook no. 12, Agricultural Research Council, Pretoria.
2. **Bruneton, J. 1999.** *Toxic Plants Dangerous to Humans and Animals.* Intercept, Hampshire.
3. **Roth, L., Daunderer, M. & Kormann, K. 1994.** *Giftpflanzen Pflanzengifte*, 4th edition. Nikol, Hamburg.
4. **Harborne, J.B., Baxter, H. & Moss, G.P. (eds) 1997.** *Dictionary of Plant Toxins.* John Wiley & Sons, Chichester.
5. **Stahl, E., Keller, K., Blinn, C. 1983.** Cardanol, a skin irritant in pink pepper. *Planta Med.* 48: 5-9.
6. **Jain, M.K., Yu, B.-Z., Rogers, J.M., Smith, A.E., Boger, A.T.A., Ostrander, R.L. & Rheingold, A.L. 1995.** Specific competitor inhibitor of secreted phopholipase A$_2$ from berries of *Schinus terebinthifolius*. *Phytochemistry* 39: 537-547.

SOLANUM PSEUDOCAPSICUM

Solanaceae

Jerusalem cherry (English); Jerusalemkersie (Afrikaans)

Solanum pseudocapsicum

DESCRIPTION This plant is an evergreen shrub of up to 2 m in height, with small, white, solitary flowers. Various cultivars of Jerusalem cherry are popular for growing in pots indoors or in flowerbeds because the attractive berries stay on the plant for a considerable period.

TYPE OF TOXIN Steroid alkaloid.

IMPORTANCE The brightly coloured berries are attractive to young children and to domestic animals and cases of poisoning are reported every year[1]. Fortunately they are only mildly poisonous when taken by mouth and the symptoms are rarely serious[1,2].

POISONOUS INGREDIENTS The toxicity is ascribed to the main alkaloid, solanocapsine, which occurs with solacapine and other alkaloids[1-3].

PHARMACOLOGICAL EFFECTS When one to five of the berries are eaten, symptoms such as nausea, stomach pain, dilation of the pupils and drowsiness may occur[3] or more often no symptoms at all[1]. Large numbers of the berries may also cause convulsions. Solanocapsine may cause abnormally slow heart action but it is not readily absorbed when taken by mouth[1].

ORIGIN *S. pseudocapsicum* originates from Madeira[4]. As the name implies, it is sometimes mistaken for chilli peppers (*Capsicum annuum*).

Solanocapsine

1. **Bruneton, J. 1999.** *Toxic Plants Dangerous to Humans and Animals.* Intercept, Hampshire.
2. **Harborne, J.B., Baxter, H. & Moss, G.P. (eds) 1997.** *Dictionary of Plant Toxins.* John Wiley & Sons, Chichester.
3. **Roth, L., Daunderer, M. & Kormann, K. 1994.** *Giftpflanzen Pflanzengifte,* 4th edition. Nikol, Hamburg.
4. **Griffiths, M. (ed.). 1994.** *Index of Garden Plants.* (The new Royal Horticultural Society Dictionary). Macmillan Press, London.

SOLANUM TUBEROSUM

Solanaceae

---

potato (English); aartappel (Afrikaans)

Solanum tuberosum

DESCRIPTION The common potato is a perennial with annual herbaceous stems arising from a fleshy tuber. Attractive white or purple flowers (depending on the cultivar) are borne on the branch ends.

TYPE OF TOXIN Steroid alkaloid.

IMPORTANCE Potato plants are very poisonous and have been responsible for numerous human or animal fatalities[1,2]. Poisoning occurs when green potatoes or potato sprouts are eaten[1] or fed to farm animals.

POISONOUS INGREDIENTS The domestic potato contains α-solanine as the main toxic component, in concentrations of up to 5% of dry weight in sprouts[3]. It also occurs in black nightshade (*S. nigrum*) and in the tomato (*Lycopersicon esculentum*)[3]. Potato tubers fortunately contain only low levels of solanine (less than 10 mg per 100 g in most cultivars)[1]. Peeling and cooking reduce the

alkaloid level, so that healthy, non-diseased potatoes rarely cause problems.

PHARMACOLOGICAL EFFECTS Symptoms of potato poisoning include stomach pain, prolonged vomiting, non-bloody diarrhoea, fever, confusion, weak and rapid pulse, hallucinations, headache and coma[1]. The minimum toxic dose in humans is 2–5 mg solanine per kg of body-weight[1]. Teratogenic effects are also known[2].

ORIGIN *S. tuberosum* is indigenous to South America but has become a cultivated crop in most parts of the world.

α-Solanine

1. **Bruneton, J. 1999.** *Toxic Plants Dangerous to Humans and Animals.* Intercept, Hampshire.
2. **Morris, S.C. & Lee, T.H. 1984.** The toxicity and teratogenicity of Solanaceae glycoalkaloids, particularly those of the potato (*Solanum tuberosum*). *Food Technol. Aust.* 36: 118-124.
3. **Harborne, J.B., Baxter, H. & Moss, G.P. (eds) 1997.** *Dictionary of Plant Toxins.* John Wiley & Sons, Chichester.

SPARTIUM JUNCEUM

Fabaceae

Spanish broom, rush broom (English); Spaanse besem (Afrikaans)

Spartium junceum – Spanish broom

Cytisus scoparius – Scotch broom

DESCRIPTION This is a shrub of up to 4 m in height with erect, cylindrical, seemingly leafless stems and large, yellow, pea-like flowers. The leaves are simple (undivided), small, oblong and short-lived. Clusters of erect pods, each containing several seeds, are borne on the branch ends. Spanish broom may be confused with Scotch broom (*Cytisus scoparius*), but the latter has fluted (ridged) stems, trifoliate leaves and short, curved, hanging pods[1].

TYPE OF TOXIN Quinolizidine alkaloid.

IMPORTANCE Both Spanish and Scotch broom are poisonous to livestock as they contain high levels of alkaloids. Human poisoning is rare but young children may be poisoned after ingesting the seeds[2].

POISONOUS INGREDIENTS The leaves, flowers, pods and seeds contain high concentrations of cytisine and other quinolizidine alkaloids[3]. The same types of compound are found in indigenous members of the family, such as *Lebeckia*, *Argyrolobium* and *Melolobium* (see also *Lupinus angustifolius*, p. 245).

PHARMACOLOGICAL EFFECTS Cytisine is highly toxic, with an LD_{50} in mice of 18 mg/kg body-weight when injected[4]. It is a respiratory stimulant with a nicotine-like action and is known to have teratogenic effects in some animals[4].

ORIGIN Spanish broom and Scotch broom are both indigenous to Europe, but have become troublesome weeds – the former mainly in the Western Cape Province, the latter in the high-lying parts of southern KwaZulu-Natal[1].

Cytisine

1. **Henderson, L. 2001.** *Alien Weeds and Invasive Plants.* Plant Protection Research Institute Handbook no. 12, Agricultural Research Council, Pretoria.
2. **Roth, L., Daunderer, M. & Kormann, K. 1994.** *Giftpflanzen Pflanzengifte*, 4th edition. Nikol, Hamburg.
3. **Greinwald, R., Lurz, G., Witte, L. & Czygan, F.C. 1990.** A survey of alkaloids in *Spartium junceum* L. (Genisteae-Fabaceae). *Z. Naturforsch.* 45C: 1085-1089.
4. **Harborne, J.B., Baxter, H. & Moss, G.P. (eds) 1997.** *Dictionary of Plant Toxins.* John Wiley & Sons, Chichester.

STYPHNOLOBIUM JAPONICUM

(= Sophora japonica)

Fabaceae

Japanese pagoda tree (English); Japanse pagodeboom (Afrikaans)

Flowers and green pods of *Styphnolobium japonicum*

DESCRIPTION This is an ornamental tree with a rounded crown, compound leaves, loose clusters of white, pea-like flowers and distinctive, fleshy pods. The tree is easily recognised by the bright green stems, dotted with white spots (lenticels).

TYPE OF TOXIN Isoflavonoid, pyrazine alkaloid, lectin.

IMPORTANCE Large numbers of fleshy pods are produced each year, and there is a danger that children and domestic animals may be poisoned[1]. The seeds are thought to be very poisonous but they have an impermeable seed coat and it is unlikely that the toxins will be released if intact seeds are swallowed.

POISONOUS INGREDIENTS The leaves, flowers, pods and seeds contain isoflavonoids, of which sophoricoside (genistein 4'-glucoside) is one of the main ingredients (up to 2% of the fruit wall)[1,2]. Seeds contain stizolamine, a pyrazine alkaloid[3]. The toxicity may also be due to lectins.

PHARMACOLOGICAL EFFECTS Isoflavonoids are found only in members of the Fabaceae and are well known for their oestrogenic effects, causing reproductive disturbances in livestock that feed on clovers (*Trifolium repens*, *T. pratense* and *T. subterraneum*) and lucerne (*Medicago sativa*).

ORIGIN *S. japonicum* was introduced as a garden tree from China and Korea[2].

Stizolamine

Sophoricoside

1. **Roth, L., Daunderer, M. & Kormann, K. 1994.** *Giftpflanzen Pflanzengifte*, 4th edition. Nikol, Hamburg.
2. **Balbaa, S.I., Zaki, A.Y., El Shami, A.M. 1974.** Qualitative and quantitative study of the flavonoid content of the different organs of *Sophora japonica* at different stages of development. *Planta Med.* 25: 325-330.
3. **Yoshida, T. & Hasegawa, M. 1977.** Distribution of stizolamine in some leguminous plants. *Phytochemistry* 16: 131-132.
4. **Griffiths, M. (ed.). 1994.** *Index of Garden Plants*. (The new Royal Horticultural Society Dictionary). Macmillan Press, London.

TAXUS BACCATA

Taxaceae

common yew (English); gewone taksisboom (Afrikaans)

Taxus baccata

DESCRIPTION The yew is a slow-growing shrub or small tree with dark green, linear leaves arranged in two rows on either side of the stems. Each cone is surrounded by a bright red, fleshy aril.

TYPE OF TOXIN Diterpenoid.

IMPORTANCE Yew trees are relatively rare in South Africa so that they do not really pose a threat to humans and animals. All parts of the plant, with the exception of the fleshy seed aril, are very poisonous and fatal human and animal poisonings have been recorded[1]. The red seed arils are known to be edible and harmless as long as the poisonous seeds inside them are discarded[1].

POISONOUS INGREDIENTS The common yew contains taxine A as the main poisonous substance[2]. Only trace amounts of taxol, a well-known anticancer compound, are found in this species[2].

PHARMACOLOGICAL EFFECTS Taxine A is very poisonous and has been used for suicide, because there is no known antidote[1]. The symptoms of poisoning are nausea, dizziness, stomach pain, and shallow breathing[1]. As little as 50–100 g of leaves can be fatal to humans[2], causing respiratory paralysis and diastolic arrest of the heart muscle[1].

ORIGIN The common yew tree is indigenous to Europe and Asia Minor. Numerous cultivars have been developed.

Taxine A

1. **Roth, L., Daunderer, M. & Kormann, K. 1994.** *Giftpflanzen Pflanzengifte,* 4th edition. Nikol, Hamburg.
2. **Harborne, J.B., Baxter, H. & Moss, G.P. (eds) 1997.** *Dictionary of Plant Toxins.* John Wiley & Sons, Chichester.

THEVETIA PERUVIANA

Apocynaceae

yellow oleander (English); geel-oleander (Afrikaans)

Thevetia peruviana

DESCRIPTION Yellow oleander is a leafy shrub of up to 10 m in height, with glossy leaves and attractive, trumpet-shaped, yellow flowers. The triangular fruit are slightly fleshy and green at first, but turn black when they ripen. Each contains two to four flat seeds. The plant was previously known as *T. neriifolia*.

TYPE OF TOXIN Cardiac glycoside (cardenolide).

IMPORTANCE The leaves, flowers, milky latex and especially the seeds are all extremely poisonous. About four seeds can be fatal to a child[1] (eight to ten in adults)[2] and it is claimed that two leaves are sufficient to kill an infant[1]. Leaves and seeds are often used in suicide attempts[1] and the ground seeds have been used as rat poison[3].

POISONOUS INGREDIENTS Numerous cardiac glycosides are known from yellow oleander, of which thevetin A and B are the main compounds[1]. A mixture of the two was formerly available as a commercial heart stimulant under the name thevetin[1].

PHARMACOLOGICAL EFFECTS The symptoms are typical for heart glycosides (vomiting, diarrhoea, stomach pain, slow and irregular heartbeat and atrio-ventricular block)[1]. The bitter taste is fortunately a deterrent and vomiting usually prevents serious consequences[2]. However, rapid death may occur if large quantities of the plant have been ingested.

DISTRIBUTION The plant occurs naturally in Mexico and the northern parts of South America. It is a popular garden shrub in South Africa and has become naturalised in the north-eastern parts[4].

Thevetin A: R=CHO
Thevetin B: R=CH$_3$

1. **Bruneton, J. 1999.** *Toxic Plants Dangerous to Humans and Animals.* Intercept, Hampshire.
2. **Roth, L., Daunderer, M. & Kormann, K. 1994.** *Giftpflanzen Pflanzengifte,* 4th edition. Nikol, Hamburg.
3. **Harborne, J.B., Baxter, H. & Moss, G.P. (eds) 1997.** *Dictionary of Plant Toxins.* John Wiley & Sons, Chichester.
4. **Henderson, L. 2001.** *Alien Weeds and Invasive Plants.* Plant Protection Research Institute Handbook no. 12, Agricultural Research Council, Pretoria.

VINCA MINOR
Apocynaceae

---

common periwinkle (English)

Vinca minor

DESCRIPTION The periwinkle is a spreading perennial herb of about 50 cm in height, with dark green, opposite leaves and attractive blue flowers of about 20 mm in diameter. A variegated form of the species is commonly found in gardens in South Africa. The closely related *Vinca major* (greater periwinkle) is very similar but the flowers are larger, about 50 mm in diameter.

TYPE OF TOXIN Indole alkaloid.

IMPORTANCE All parts of the plant are poisonous but cases of human poisoning are rare. Animals may be at risk if large quantities are ingested[1].

POISONOUS INGREDIENTS The main alkaloid in *V. minor* is the (–)-form of eburnamonine[2]. The greater periwinkle, *V. major*, contains vincamine as one of the major alkaloids[2].

PHARMACOLOGICAL EFFECTS Eburnamonine and vincamine both have vasodilatory activity and are used medically to stimulate blood circulation and muscle activity[2].

DISTRIBUTION *Vinca minor* (and *V. major*) are indigenous to central and southern Europe[1].

(-)-Eburnamonine   Vincamine

1. **Roth, L., Daunderer, M. & Kormann, K. 1994.** *Giftpflanzen Pflanzengifte,* 4th edition. Nikol, Hamburg.
2. **Harborne, J.B., Baxter, H. & Moss, G.P. (eds) 1997.** *Dictionary of Plant Toxins.* John Wiley & Sons, Chichester.

Plants listed according to class of toxin

TOBACCO ALKALOIDS (piperidine & pyridine types)
Piperidine alkaloid:
Conium maculatum (Umbelliferae)
Dioscorea dregeana (Dioscoreaceae)
Ricinus communis (Euphorbiaceae)
Sesbania punicea (Fabaceae)
Pyridine alkaloid:
Albizia tanganyicensis (Fabaceae)
Nicotiana glauca (Solanaceae)

TROPANE ALKALOIDS (atropine type)
Brugmansia candida (Solanaceae)
Datura stramonium (Solanaceae)

ISOQUINOLINE ALKALOIDS
Erythrina caffra (Fabaceae)
Eschscholzia californica (Papaveraceae)
Amaryllidaceae alkaloid:
Amaryllis belladonna (Amaryllidaceae)
Boophane disticha (Amaryllidaceae)
Clivia miniata (Amaryllidaceae)
Crinum bulbispermum (Amaryllidaceae)
Scadoxus puniceus (Amaryllidaceae)
Benzylisoquinoline alkaloid:
Argemone ochroleuca (Papaveraceae)
Cissampelos capensis (Menispermaceae)

INDOLE ALKALOIDS
Catharanthus roseus (Apocynaceae)
Gelsemium sempervirens (Loganiaceae)
Ipomoea purpurea (Convolvulaceae)
Rauvolfia caffra (Apocynaceae)
Strychnos spinosa (Strychnaceae)
Vinca minor (Apocynaceae)

PYRROLIZIDINE ALKALOIDS (*Senecio* alkaloids)
Crotalaria spartioides (Fabaceae)
Echium vulgare (Boraginaceae)
Senecio latifolius (Asteraceae)

QUINOLIZIDINE ALKALOIDS (lupin alkaloids)
Cystisus scoparius (Fabaceae)
Lupinus angustifolius (Fabaceae)
Spartium junceum (Fabaceae)

STEROID ALKALOIDS & TERPENOID ALKALOIDS
Steroid alkaloid:
Solanum incanum (Solanaceae)
Solanum pseudocapsicum (Solanaceae)

Solanum tuberosum (Solanaceae)
Diterpenoid alkaloid:
Delphinium grandiflorum (Ranunculaceae)
Erythrophleum lasianthum (Fabaceae)

OTHER ALKALOIDS & NITROGEN-CONTAINING COMPOUNDS
Brunfelsia pauciflora (Solanaceae) – amidine
Capsicum annuum (Solanaceae) – phenolic amide
Chenopodium mucronatum (Chenopodiaceae) – amine
Encephalartos longifolius (Zamiaceae) – azoxy compound
Equisetum ramosissimum (Equisetaceae) – macrocyclic alkaloid
Fadogia homblei (Rubiaceae) – amine
Gloriosa superba (Cholchinaceae) – amide
Leucaena leucocephala (Leguminosae) – amino acid
Nierembergia hippomanica (Solanaceae) – amidine
Pachystigma pygmaeum (Rubiaceae) – amine
Salsola tuberculatiformis (Chenopodiaceae) – aziridine
Taxus baccata (Taxaceae) – amine

COUMARINS
Melilotus alba (Fabaceae)
Furocoumarins:
Ficus salicifolia (Moraceae)
Ficus carica (Moraceae)
Peucedanum galbanum (Apiaceae)

CYANOGENIC GLYCOSIDES
Acacia sieberiana (Fabaceae)
Acalypha indica (Euphorbiaceae)
Adenia digitata (Passifloraceae)
Brabejum stellatifolium (Proteaceae)
Dimorphotheca cuneata (Asteraceae)
Eucalyptus cladocalyx (Myrtaceae)
Lotononis laxa (Fabaceae)
Manihot esculenta (Euphorbiaceae)
Prunus laurocerasus (Rosaceae)
Sorghum bicolor (Poaceae)

TERPENOIDS
Monoterpenoid:
Chrysanthemum cinerariifolium (Asteraceae)
Eucalyptus globulus (Myrtaceae)
Ligustrum lucidum (Oleaceae) (Secoiridoid)
Sesquiterpenoid:
Chrysanthemum xmoriflorum (Asteraceae)
Geigeria ornativa (Asteraceae)

Hyananche globosa (Euphorbiaceae)
Lasiospermum bipinnatum (Asteraceae)
Pteridium aquilinum (Dennstaedtiaceae)
Diterpenoid:
Aleurites fordii (Euphorbiaceae)
Callilepis laureola (Asteraceae)
Cestrum laevigatum (Solanaceae)
Euphorbia ingens (Euphorbiaceae)
Gnidia kraussiana (Thymelaeaceae)
Jatropha curcas (Euphorbiaceae)
Peddiea africana (Thymelaeaceae)
Rhododendron indicum (Ericaceae)
Spirostachys africana (Euphorbiaceae)
Synadenium capulare (Euphorbiaceae)
Taxus baccata (Taxaceae)
Xanthium strumarium (Asteraceae)
Triterpenoid / Saponin:
Anagallis arvensis (Primulaceae)
Cucumis africanus (Cucurbitaceae*)*
Cyclamen persicum (Primulaceae) – saponin
Hedera helix (Araliaceae) – saponin
Lantana camara (Verbenaceae)
Lippia rehmannii (Verbenaceae)
Melia azedarach (Meliaceae) – limonoid
Phytolacca dioica (Phytolaccaceae) – saponin
Tribulus terrestris (Zygophyllaceae) – saponin
Steroid glycoside:
Cynanchum africanum (Asclepiadaceae)
Dioscorea dregeana (Dioscoreaceae)
Ornithogalum thyrsoides (Hyacinthaceae)
Sarcostemma viminale (Asclepiadaceae)

CARDIAC (HEART) GLYCOSIDES
Cardenolides:
Acokanthera oppositifolia (Apocynaceae)
Adenium multiflorum (Apocynaceae)
Asclepias fruticosa (Asclepiadaceae)
Digitalis purpurea (Scrophulariaceae)
Nerium oleander (Apocynaceae)
Strophanthus speciosus (Apocynaceae)
Thevetia peruviana (Apocynaceae)
Bufadienolides:
Bowiea volubilis (Hyacinthaceae)
Cotyledon orbiculata (Crassulaceae)
Drimia robusta (Hyacinthaceae)
Homeria pallida (Iridaceae)
Kalanchoe rotundifolia (Crassulaceae)
Melianthus comosus (Melianthaceae)
Moraea polystachya (Iridaceae)
Scilla natalensis (Hyacinthaceae)
Thesium lineatum (Santalaceae)
Tylecodon wallichii (Crassulaceae)
Urginea sanguinea (Hyacinthaceae)

PHYTOTOXINS (LECTINS)
Abrus precatorius (Fabaceae)
Adenia digitata (Passifloraceae)
Erythrina caffra (Fabaceae)
Jatropha curcas (Euphorbiaceae)
Ricinus communis (Euphorbiaceae)
Robinia pseudoacacia (Fabaceae)

OXALIC ACID / OXALATE
Alocasia macrorrhiza (Araceae)
Colocasia esculenta (Araceae)
Dieffenbachia maculata (Araceae)
Oxalis pes-caprae (Oxalidaceae)

MISCELLANEOUS COMPOUNDS
Alkylphenol:
Grevillea robusta (Proteaceae)
Smodingium argutum (Anacardiaceae)
Schinus terebinthifolius (Anacardiaceae)
Bianthraquinone:
Hypericum aethiopicus (Clusiaceae)
Fatty alcohol:
Persea americana (Lauraceae)
Lactone:
Ranunculus multifidus
Monofluoroacetate:
Dichapetalum cymosum (Dichapetalaceae)
Nitrate:
Amaranthus hybridus (Amaranthaceae)
Chenopodium mucronatum (Chenopodiaceae)
Phenol:
Salsola tuberculatiformis (Chenopodiaceae)
Polyacetylene:
Hedera helix (Araliaceae)
Polyphenol / tannin:
Quercus robur (Fagaceae)
Rotenoid:
Mundulea sericea (Fabaceae)

NO INFORMATION (SOUTH AFRICAN PLANTS ONLY)
Athanasia minuta (Asteraceae)
Chrysocoma ciliata (Asteraceae)
Cotula nigellifolia (Asteraceae)
Dipcadia glaucum (Hyacinthaceae)
Galenia africana (Aizoaceae)
Helichrysum argyrosphaerum (*Asteraceae*)
Melica decumbens (Poaceae)
Ornithoglossum viride (Liliaceae)
Pteronia pallens (Asteraceae)

Plants listed according to type of livestock poisoning

The best way to diagnose the type of poisoning is to inspect the actual locality, so that the poisonous plants present on the site can be studied for indications that they had been grazed. A link can then be made between the clinical signs and any poisonous plants that were available to the animals. Characteristic plant parts can also be identified from the rumen content or the faeces of affected animals.

CARDIAC GLYCOSIDE POISONING

The cardiac glycosides of plants can either be cardenolides or bufadienolide (see overview of the chemical structures of toxic compounds on p. 28). Plants with cardenolides are seldom available to animals and they rarely cause problems. Bufadienolide-containing plants are therefore the main culprits in causing stock losses. Acute poisoning is also known as *tulp* poisoning (caused by *Moraea* and *Homeria* species), *slangkop* poisoning (caused by *Drimia* and *Urginea* species) and *witstorm* poisoning (caused by *Thesium lineatum*). Chronic poisoning is known as *krimpsiekte*, and results from members of the family Crassulaceae (mainly *Tylecodon wallichii*, *T. grandiflorus* and *Cotyledon orbiculata*). It is interesting that secondary poisoning may occur, when domestic animals or humans eat the meat from an animal that died of *krimpsiekte*. The main symptoms are briefly described under the main entries for the plants listed above. Note that in acute poisoning, the cardiovascular, gastro-intestinal and nervous systems are affected, while in chronic poisoning nervous disorders are more prominent.

Acute poisoning
Acokanthera oblongifolia
Acokanthera oppositifolia
Asclepias fruticosa
Asclepias physocarpa
Bowiea volubilis
Homeria flaccida
Homeria miniata
Homeria pallida
Melianthus comosus
Melianthus major
Moraea graminifolia
Moraea huttonii
Moraea polyanthos
Moraea polystachya
Moraea spathulacea
Moraea stricta
Moraea unguiculata
Moraea venenata
Nerium oleander
Ornithoglossum viride

Scilla natalensis
Scilla rigidifolia
Thesium lineatum
Thesium namaquense
Thevesia peruviana
Urginea altissima
Urginea physodes
Urginea sanguinea

Chronic poisoning (*krimpsiekte*)
Cotyledon orbiculata
Kalanchoe lanceolata
Kalanchoe paniculata
Kalanchoe rotundifolia
Kalanchoe thyrsiflora
Tylecodon grandiflorus
Tylecodon ventricosus
Tylecodon wallichii

LIVER POISONING WITHOUT PHOTOSENSITIVITY

Seneciosis is the most serious type of poisoning, caused by *Senecio* species (mainly *S. latifolius* and *S. retrorsus* (see p. 190). *Crotalaria* species contain the same toxic substances (pyrrolizidine alkaloids) and have also caused stock losses in the past (see p. 80). The latter causes diseases known as *jaagsiekte* and *stywesiekte*.
Cestrum aurantiacum
Cestrum laevigatum
Cestrum parqui
Crotalaria burkeana
Crotalaria dura
Crotalaria globifera
Crotalaria juncea
Crotalaria spartioides
Galenia africana
Hertia cluytiifolia
Hertia pallens
Pteronia pallens
Senecio retrorsus
Senecio burchellii
Senecio harveyanus
Senecio isatideus
Senecio latifolius

Xanthium spinosum
Xanthium strumarium

LIVER POISONING WITH PHOTOSENSITIVITY (hepatogenous photosensitivity)

Lantana poisoning causes the most severe stock losses but the following plants are also of importance:

Athanasia minuta
Athanasia trifurcata
Lantana camara
Lasiospermum bipinnatum

GIFBLAAR POISONING

This condition is caused by *gifblaar* (*Dichapetalum cymosum*), which contains monofluoroacetate as the toxic principle (see p. 88).

GOUSIEKTE

This intoxication causes sudden heart failure about six to eight weeks after ingestion of plants from the family Rubiaceae. The animals simply drop dead without warning (hence the name *gousiekte*, literally 'quick disease'). For more information see *Pachystigma pygmaeum* (p. 164). The plants are listed below in order of importance.

Pachystigma pygmaeum
Fadogia homblei
Pavetta harborii
Pachystigma thamnus
Pavetta schumanniana
Pachystigma latifolium

GEELDIKKOP AND *DIKOOR*

Geeldikkop is a disease of sheep and goats resulting from poisoning by *Tribulus terrestris*, while *dikoor* is a closely related condition caused by *Panicum coloratum*. Details are given under *Tribulus terrestris* (p. 210).

VERMEERSIEKTE

This intoxication is caused by *Geigeria* species (mainly *G. ornativa* and *G. aspera* – see p. 116). It has been reported that more than a million sheep were killed by *vermeersiekte* in Griqualand West in a single season.

DIPLODIOSIS

Although poisoning by fungi and mushrooms (mycotoxicosis) is not included in this book, it is important to note the occurrence of neuromycotoxicosis that may be confused with plant poisoning. Diplodiosis is a disease caused by a common fungus, *Diplodia maydis*, which is found in decaying maize cobs on harvested maize lands. The symptoms are ataxia, paresis and paralysis.

NERVOUS DISORDERS

Many different plants cause nervous conditions as the main symptom of poisoning, or at least as one of the symptoms. These plants are listed below, with the type of poisoning (if it has been given a distinct name) given in brackets.

Albizia tanganyicensis (albiziosis)
Albizia versicolor (albiziosis)
Chrysocoma tenuifolia (valsiekte; also kaalsiekte, lakseersiekte)
Cotula nigellifolia (stootsiekte, pushing disease)
Cynanchum africanum (cynanchosis)
Cynanchum capense (cynanchosis)
Cynanchum obtusifolium (cynanchosis)
Cynodon dactylon
Datura ferox
Datura innoxia
Datura stramonium
Dipcadi glaucum
Equisetum ramosissimum (equisetosis, shivers, dronksiekte)
Euphorbia mauritanica
Helichrysum argyrosphaerum
Lupinus angustifolius (lupine alkaloid poisoning)
Lupinus luteus (lupine alkaloid poisoning)
Melia azedarach
Melica decumbens
Nicotiana glauca
Nicotiana tabacum
Nierembergia hippomanica
Phalaris minor (*Phalaris* staggers)
Pteridium aquilinum
Sarcostemma viminale
Solanum kwebense (maldronksiekte)
Trachyandra divaricata
Trachyandra laxa

GASTROINTESTINAL DISORDERS

In additional to *vermeersiekte* (see above), a diversity of other types of poisoning results in gastrointestinal symptoms.

Abrus precatorius
Cucumis africanus
Cucumis myriocarpus
Gnidia burchelii
Gnidia polycephala
Jatropha curcas
Jatropha multifida
Ornithogalum conicum
Ornithogalum ornithogaloides
Ornithogalum prasinum
Ornithogalum saundersiae
Ornithogalum thyrsoides
Ornithogalum toxicarum

Pennisetum clandestinum (kikuyu poisoning)
Phytolacca dioica
Ricinus communis
Sesbania punicea
Solanum aculeastrum
Solanum incanum
Solanum nigrum
Solanum panduriforme

KIDNEY, BLADDER AND REPRODUCTIVE SYSTEM

Poisonous plants cause a diversity of problems relating to the urogenital system.

Miscellaneous

Anagallis arvensis
Nolletia gariepina
Pteridium aquilinum
Quercus robur
Salsola tuberculatiformis
Trifolium pratense
Trifolium repens
Trifolium subterraneum

Oxalate poisoning

Beta vulgaris
Opuntia species
Oxalis latifolia
Oxalis pes-caprae
Psilocaulon species
Rheum rhabarbarum
Rumex acetosa
Rumex angiocarpus
Spinacia oleracea

HYDROGEN CYANIDE POISONING

Hydrogen cyanide (HCN, prussic acid) is released when animals ingest plant material containing cyanogenic glycosides. When plant cells are damaged (through chewing, wilting, hail storms or some other mechanism) the glycosides in the cells are mixed with enzymes. As a result, the glucosides are broken down and hydrogen cyanide is released (see p. 24). This important type of poisoning is known as prussic acid poisoning (*geilsiekte* or *blousuurvergiftiging*). Ruminants are more at risk than non-ruminants because in the latter the release of prussic acid is stopped by the low stomach pH. The main symptoms of acute poisoning result from respiratory distress and include dyspnoea (breathing difficulty) polypnoea (rapid breathing) and cyanosis (blue discoloration of skin due to the presence of de-oxygenated blood).

Acacia caffra
Acacia erioloba
Acacia sieberiana var. *woodii*
Arctotheca calendula
Cynodon dactylon
Dimorphotheca cuneata
Dimorphotheca nudicaulis
Dimorphotheca spectabilis
Dimorphotheca zeyheri
Epaltes gariepina
Eucalyptus cladocalyx
Jatropha multifida
Manihot esculenta
Osteospermum ecklonis
Sorghum bicolor
Sorghum halepense

Checklist of poisonous plants

In the following list, some indication is given about the potential toxicity of each plant, and their importance in human or livestock poisoning. Actual poisoning depends on many circumstances (how much material was actually ingested, how much of it was expelled through vomiting, what plant parts were eaten – fruits may be perfectly safe, while the leaves may be dangerous; sometimes different plants of the same species may differ in their toxicity, as is the case with syringa berries). The following symbols are used:

- ● not really poisonous
- ☣ poisonous
- ☣ very poisonous
- ☠ deadly
- ↯ causes skin allergies or contact dermatitis
- 🐎 poisonous to animals (usually not important in human toxicology)

Abrus precatorius ☠
Acacia caffra 🐎
Acacia erioloba 🐎
Acacia nilotica 🐎
Acacia sieberiana var. woodii 🐎
Acalypha hispida ☣
Acalypha indica ☣
Acokanthera oblongifolia ☠
Acokanthera oppositifolia ☠
Acokanthera schimperi ☠
Aconitum napellus ☠
Acorus calamus ☣
Adenia digitata ☠
Adenia glauca ☠
Adenia gummifera ☠
Adenium boehmianum ☠
Adenium multiflorum ☠
Agapanthus africanus ☣
Ailanthus altissima ☣
Albizia tanganyicensis 🐎
Albizia versicolor 🐎
Aleurites fordii ☣
Alocasia macrorrhiza ☣
Aloe ferox ☣
Amaranthus hybridus 🐎
Amaranthus reflexus 🐎
Amaryllis belladonna ☣
Ammi majus ↯
Ammocharis coranica ☠
Anacardium occidentale ↯
Anagallis arvensis ☣
Aquilegia vulgaris ☣
Araujia sericifera 🐎
Arctotheca calendula 🐎
Argemone mexicana ☣
Argemone ochroleuca subsp. ochroleuca ☣
Argyrolobium species ☣
Artemisia absinthium ☣
Asclepias fruticosa ☠
Asclepias physocarpa ☣
Athanasia minuta 🐎
Athanasia trifurcata 🐎
Atropa belladonna ☠
Beta vulgaris ●

Boophane disticha ☣
Bowiea gariepensis ☣
Bowiea volubilis ☣
Brabejum stellatifolium ☣
Brassica species ●
Brugmansia candida ☣
Brunfelsia grandiflora ☣
Brunfelsia pauciflora ☣
Caesalpinia gilliesii ☣
Caladium species ☣
Callilepis laureola ☣
Capsicum annuum ●
Catharanthus roseus ☠
Cestrum aurantiacum ☠
Cestrum laevigatum ☠
Cestrum parqui ☠
Chenopodium album ●
Chenopodium ambrosioides ☣
Chenopodium mucronatum 🐎
Chenopodium multifidum ☠
Chloris gayana 🐎
Chrysanthemum cinerariifolium ☣
Chrysanthemum vulgare ☣
Chrysanthemum xmoriflorum ↯
Chrysocoma ciliata 🐎
Cinchona pubescens ☣
Cissampelos capensis ☣ 🐎
Clivia miniata ☣
Colchicum autumnale ☠
Colocasia esculenta ☣
Conium maculatum ☠
Cotoneaster species ●
Cotula nigellifolia 🐎
Cotyledon orbiculata ☣ 🐎
Crinum bulbispermum ☠
Crinum macowanii ☣
Crotalaria burkeana 🐎
Crotalaria dura 🐎
Crotalaria globifera 🐎
Crotalaria juncea 🐎
Crotalaria spartioides 🐎
Crotalaria virgultalis 🐎
Croton tiglium ☣
Cucumis africanus ☣

Cucumis myriocarpus subsp. *leptodermis*
Cucumis myriocarpus subsp. *myriocarpus*
Cyclamen persicum
Cynanchum africanum
Cynanchum capense
Cynanchum obtusifolium
Cynodon dactylon
Cytisus scoparius
Datura ferox
Datura innoxia
Datura stramonium
Delphinium elatum
Delphinium grandiflorum
Derris elliptica
Dichapetalum cymosum
Dieffenbachia amoena
Dieffenbachia maculata
Digitalis purpurea
Dimorphotheca spectabilis
Dimorphotheca cuneata
Dimorphotheca nudicaulis
Dimorphotheca zeyheri
Dioscorea dregeana
Dioscorea elephantipes
Dipcadi glaucum
Drimia robusta
Duranta erecta
Echium plantagineum
Echium vulgare
Encephalartos longifolius
Epaltes gariepina
Equisetum ramosissimum
Erythrina caffra
Erythrina crista-galli
Erythrina lysistemon
Erythrophleum africanum
Erythrophleum lasianthum
Erythrophleum suaveolens
Erythroxylum coca
Eschscholzia californica
Eucalyptus cladocalyx
Eucalyptus globulus
Euphorbia ingens
Euphorbia mauritanica
Euphorbia pulcherrima
Euphorbia tirucalli
Fadogia homblei
Fadogia monticola
Ficus carica
Ficus cordata
Ficus ingens
Ficus salicifolia
Fumaria officinalis
Galenia africana
Geigeria aspera
Geigeria burkei
Geigeria ornativa
Gelsemium sempervirens
Gerbera jamesonii
Ginko biloba
Gloriosa superba

Gnidia burchellii
Gnidia kraussiana
Gnidia polycephala
Gossypium species
Grevillea robusta
Haemanthus coccineus
Hedera helix
Helichrysum argyrosphaerum
Helichrysum cephaloideum
Hertia cluytiifolia
Hertia pallens
Homeria glauca
Homeria miniata
Homeria pallida
Hyaenanche globosa
Hypericum aethiopicum
Hypericum perforatum
Ilex aquifolium
Ipomoea purpurea
Ipomoea tricolor
Jatropha curcas
Kalanchoe lanceolata
Kalanchoe rotundifolia
Knowltonia bracteata
Lantana camara
Lasiospermum bipinnatum
Lebeckia cytisoides
Ledebouria ovatifolia
Leucaena leucocephala
Ligustrum lucidum
Ligustrum ovalifolium
Ligustrum vulgare
Lippia javanica
Lippia rehmannii
Lippia scaberrima
Lolium species
Lotononis carnosa
Lotononis fruticoides
Lotononis involucrata
Lotononis laxa
Lupinus angustifolius
Lupinus digitatus
Lupinus luteus
Lupinus polyphyllus
Lupinus sericeus
Manihot esculenta
Medicago sativa
Melia azedarach
Melianthus comosus
Melianthus major
Melica decumbens
Melilotus alba
Melilotus indica
Melilotus officinalis
Melolobium species
Mesembryanthemum species
Monadenium lugardii
Monstera deliciosa
Moraea graminicola
Moraea huttonii
Moraea polystachya

Moraea spathulata
Moraea stricta
Moraea unguiculata
Mundulea sericea
Neorautanenia species
Nerium oleander
Nicotiana glauca
Nicotiana tabacum
Nierembergia hippomanica
Nolletia gariepina
Ornithogalum conicum
Ornithogalum ornithogaloides
Ornithogalum prasinum
Ornithogalum saundersiae
Ornithogalum tenellum
Ornithogalum thyrsoides
Ornithogalum toxicarium
Ornithoglossum viride
Osteospermum ecklonis
Oxalis latifolia
Oxalis pes-caprae
Pachystigma pygmaeum
Pachystigma thamnus
Papaver somniferum
Paspalum dilatatum
Passiflora species
Pavetta harborii
Pavetta schumanniana
Peddiea africana
Peganum harmala
Pegolettia retrofracta
Persea americana
Peucedanum galbanum
Phalaris minor
Philodendron selloum
Phytolacca americana
Phytolacca dioica
Phytolacca dodecandra
Plumeria rubra ?
Primula obconica
Prunus dulcis var. amara
Prunus laurocerasus
Psilocaulon species
Pteridium aquilinum
Pteronia pallens
Quercus robur
Ranunculus multifidus
Rauvolfia caffra
Rheum species
Rhododendron indicum
Rhus (Toxicodendron) diversilobum
Rhus (Toxicodendron) radicans
Rhus (Toxicodendron) vernix
Ricinus communis
Robinia pseudoacacia
Rumex species
Ruta graveolens
Salsola tuberculatiformis
Sarcostemma viminale
Scadoxus puniceus
Schefflera arboricola

Schinus molle
Schinus terebinthifolius
Scilla natalensis
Scilla rigidifolia
Senecio burchellii
Senecio isatideus
Senecio latifolius
Senecio retrorsus
Sesbania punicea
Smodingium argutum
Solanum elaeagnifolium
Solanum incanum
Solanum kwebense
Solanum mauritianum
Solanum nigrum
Solanum panduriforme
Solanum pseudocapsicum
Solanum sisymbriifolium
Solanum tuberosum
Sorghum bicolor
Spartium junceum
Spirostachys africana
Stangeria eriopus
Stipagrostis uniplumis
Strophanthus gratus
Strophanthus kombe
Strophanthus speciosus
Strychnos henningsii
Strychnos madagascariensis
Strychnos nux-vomica
Strychnos spinosa
Styphnolobium japonicum
Symphytum officinale
Synadenium cupulare
Synadenium grantii
Taxus baccata
Tephrosia species
Themeda triandra
Thesium lineatum
Thesium namaquense
Thevesia peruviana
Tribulus terrestris
Tribulus zeyheri
Trifolium pratense
Trifolium repens
Trifolium subterraneum
Tulipa hybrids
Tylecodon grandiflorus
Tylecodon ventricosus
Tylecodon wallichii
Urginea altissima
Urginea physodes
Urginea sanguinea
Veratrum album
Vinca major
Vinca minor
Viscum album
Wisteria sinensis
Xanthium spinosum
Xanthium strumarium
Zantedeschia aethiopica

Glossary of medical terms

alimentary tract transmitting food from mouth to anus

alopecia abnormal loss of hair

anticoagulant prevents coagulation of blood

antileukaemic substance used against leukaemia

antineoplastic stops abnormal multiplication of cells

apathetic uninterested

apnoea cessation of breathing

ataxia imperfect control of voluntary bodily functions

bradycardia slowed heart rate with pulse rate below 60

bronchitis inflammation of the bronchial mucous membrane

cardiac pertaining to the heart

cardiotonic heart stimulant

congestive pertaining to accumulation of blood

congestive heart failure accumulation of blood in the heart chambers with impaired cardiac function with peripheral oedema

cirrhosis of the liver disease of the liver

convulsions violent irregular movement of limbs or body

cyanosis bluish discoloration of skin and mucous membranes due to excess levels of reduced haemoglobin

cytotoxic toxic to cells

delirium disordered state of mind

dermatitis inflammation of the skin

distension enlargement

fibrillation rapid involuntary abnormal contractions

gastric pertaining to the stomach

glaucoma pronounced pressure increase in the eyeball leading to blindness

goitre enlarged and protruding thyroid gland

haematuria presence of blood in urine

haemoglobin oxygen carrying substance in blood containing iron

haemolysis breaking up of red blood cells

haemorrhage bleeding

hallucinogen substance causing hallucinations

hepatotoxic substance toxic to the liver

hypoglycaemic abnormally low blood glucose

hypotensive abnormally low blood pressure

icterogenic causing jaundice

icterus jaundice

isoenzymes multiple forms of the same enzyme

LD$_{50}$ lethal dose for 50 % of test animals

leukaemia excess white cells in blood

lumbago pain in the lower back or lumbar region of the spine

lymphoma cancerous disorder of the lymphatic system

necrosis cell death and consecutive morphological changes

neuromuscular of nerves and muscles

neuropathological diseased state of nervous system

neurotoxin toxic to the nervous system

obesity excessive accumulation of body fat

ocular pertaining to the eye

oedema swollen state of tissue

palpitations rapid or irregular heartbeat

pruritis itching

psoriasis skin disease with red scaly patches

purging plants yielding purgatives

retching making motion of vomiting

rodentiside agent that destroys rodents

salivation unusual secretion of saliva

tachycardia excessive rapid heart rate

teratogenic substance that causes physical defects in developing embryos

thrombosis formation of blood clots causing vascular obstruction

tremor involuntary trembling

tumour abnormal growth of cells

urticaria vascular reaction of upper dermis marked by the development of wheals

vesiculation presence or formation of vesicles

vitiligo anomaly of pigmentation, white areas surrounded by very pigmented areas

References and further reading

Bruneton, J. 1999. *Toxic Plants Dangerous to Humans and Animals*. Intercept, Hampshire.

Coates Palgrave, K. 1977. *Trees of Southern Africa*. Struik, Cape Town.

Codd, L. E. W. 1951. Trees and shrubs of the Kruger National Park. *Memoirs of the Botanical Survey of South Africa* 26. Botanical Research Institute, Pretoria.

Dyer, R.A. 1956. Poisonous Plants. *Farming in South Africa*, Volume 32, No 1: 10-11, 38-39 (with two loose posters in full colour).

Gelfand, M., Mavi, S., Drummond, R.B. & Ndemera, B. 1985. *The Traditional Medical Practitioner in Zimbabwe*. Mambo Press, Gweru, Zimbabwe.

Harborne, J.B., Baxter, H. & Moss, G.P. (eds) 1997. *Dictionary of Plant Toxins*. John Wiley & Sons, Chichester.

Heinz, H. J. & Maguire, B. 1974. The ethnobiology of the !Ko Bushmen -- their botanical knowledge and plant lore. *Occasional Paper* No 1, Botswana Society, Gaborone.

Helly, K. 1906. Die wirkungsweise des Pachypodiins, eines Africanischen pfeilgifte. *Z. exp. Path. Ther.* 2: 247-251.

Henderson, L. 1995. *Plant Invaders of Southern Africa*. Agricultural Research Council, Pretoria.

Henderson, M. & Anderson, J.G. 1966. *Common weeds in South Africa. Memoirs of the Botanical Survey of South Africa* 37.

Juritz, C. F. 1915. South African plant poisons and their investigation *S. Afr. J. Sci.* 11: 109-145.

Kellerman T.S., Coetzer, J.A.W. & Naudé, T.W. 1988. *Plant Poisonings and Mycotoxicoses of Livestock in Southern Africa*. Oxford University Press, Cape Town.

Kellerman, T.S. & Coetzer, J.A.W. 1985. Hepatogenous photosensitivity diseases in South Africa. *Onderstepoort J. Vet. Res.* 52: 157-173.

Kellerman, T.S., Naudé, T.W. & Fourie, N. 1996. The distribution, diagnoses and estimated economic impact of plant poisonings and mycotoxicoses in South Africa. *Onderstepoort J. Vet. Res.* 63: 65-90.

Lewin, L. 1923. *Die pfeilgifte*. J. A. Barth, Leipzig.

Liengme, C.A. 1983. A survey of ethnobotanical research in southern Africa. *Bothalia* 14, 3&4: 621-629.

Malan, J.S. & Owen-Smith, G.L. 1974. The ethnobotany of Kaokoland. *Cimbebasia* Ser. B 2,5: 131-178.

Merck 1989. *The Merck Index*. 11th edition. Merck, Rahway.

Moll, E. & Moll, G. 1989. *Poisonous Plants*. Struik, Cape Town.

Munday, J. 1988. *Poisonous Plants in South African Gardens and Parks*. Delta Books, Johannesburg.

Neuwinger, H.D. 1996. *African Ethnobotany: Poisons and Drugs: Chemistry, Pharmacology, Toxicology*. Chapman & Hall, Germany.

Palmer, E. & Pitman, N. 1972. *Trees of Southern Africa*. (3 vols). Balkema, Cape Town.

Phillips, E.P. 1926. *A Preliminary List of Known Poisonous Plants Found in South Africa. Memoirs of the Botanical Survey of South Africa* 9.

Poisons Unit of Guy's & St. Thomas' Hospital Trust & The Royal Botanic Gardens, Kew 1995. Poisonous Plants in Britain and Ireland (CD-ROM).

Rodin, R.J. 1985. *The Ethnobotany of the Kwanyama Ovambos*. Monographs in Systematic Botany 9. Missouri Botanical Garden.

Roth, L., Daunderer, M. & Kormann, K. 1994. *Giftpflanzen Pflanzengifte*, 4th edition. Nikol, Hamburg.

Schapera, I. 1925. Bushmen arrow poisons. *Bantu Stud.* 2: 190-214.

Shaw, E. M., Woolley, P.L. & Rae, F.A. 1963. Bushmen arrow poisons. *Cimbebasia* 7: 2-41.

Smith, C.A. 1966. *Common Names of South African Plants. Memoirs of the Botanical Survey of South Africa* 35.

Steyn, D.G. 1934. *The Toxicology of Plants in South Africa*. Central News Agency, South Africa.

Steyn, D.G. 1949. *Die Vergiftiging van Mens en Dier*. Van Schaik, Pretoria.

Steyn, H. P. 1981. Nharo Plant Utilization. An Overview. *Khoisis* 1.

Vahrmeijer, J. 1981. *Poisonous Plants of Southern Africa That Cause Stock Losses*. Tafelberg Publishers, Cape Town.

Verdcourt, B. & Trump, E.C. 1969. *Common Poisonous Plants of East Africa*. Collins, London.

Von Koenen, E. 1996. *Heil-, Gift- u Essbare Pflanzen in Namibia*. Klaus Hess Verlag, Göttingen.

Von Koenen, E. 2001. *Medicinal, Poisonous, and Edible Plants in Namibia*. Klaus Hess Publishers, Windhoek & Göttingen.

Walsh, L.H. 1909. *South African Poisonous Plants*. Maskew Miller, Cape Town.

Watt, J.M. & Breyer-Brandwijk, M.G. 1962. *The Medicinal and Poisonous Plants of Southern and Eastern Africa*, 2nd edition. Livingstone, London.

INTERNET DATA BASES:

TOXLINE is an extensive collection of online bibliographic information covering the biochemical, pharmacological, physiological and toxicological effects of, amongst others, poisonous plants. (http://sis.nlm.nih.gov or http://igm.nlm.nih.gov).

MEDLINE covers, to some extent, medicinal and poisonous plants. (http://www.ncbi.nih.gov/entrez or Internet Grateful Med http://igm.nlm.nih.gov)

Index